PLAIN
and
PRECIOUS

PLAIN *and* PRECIOUS

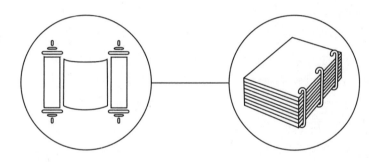

FINDING THE FULNESS OF THE GOSPEL THROUGH
THE BIBLE-BOOK OF MORMON CONNECTION

YONG-IN SPENCER SHIN, PHD

Covenant Communications, Inc.

Cover Painting: *None Were With Him* © Rose Datoc Dall. For more information visit www.rosedatocdall.com.
Cover Design by Michelle Fryer

Cover design copyright © 2019 by Covenant Communications, Inc.

Published by Covenant Communications, Inc.
American Fork, Utah

Printed in the United States of America
First Printing: September 2019

25 24 23 22 21 20 19 · 10 9 8 7 6 5 4 3 2 1

ISBN 978-1-52441-065-0

To my son Samuel

Contents

Acknowledgments

HAVING BEEN GUIDED BY THE Spirit during the course of research for this book, I should first acknowledge divine help from the Lord. Whenever I felt difficulties while going forward, inspirations and new ideas from the Spirit led me to progressive and productive solutions.

I acknowledge many who have helped me with this book. My wife supported me as a sounding board the entire time I was writing this book, and has offered many supplications to the Lord in my behalf. My children helped as needed at different times, providing constructive criticism. Michael Paskett painstakingly reviewed and checked the whole manuscript twice and has provided much invaluable input throughout the entire process. My daughter-in-law, Heidi, proofread every word over a period of months.

Whenever I requested help, Alicia Francom, Sunny Washington, Matt Oehler, Derek Driggs, and Janet Eyring Thompson rendered their time and effort without hesitation. Patricia Hernandez helped design a cover with her graphic design expertise. James Faulconer, John McCuin, Michael Ringwood, and Julie Beck also reviewed the manuscript and provided counsel and encouragement.

Preface

I CONSIDER THIS BOOK THE result of major events in my life, beginning with my childhood in Korea. My religious views were influenced by my grandmother and mother, both of whom practiced a form of shamanistic belief of gods from the surrounding nature, a derivative form of Buddhism in Korea. I was also influenced by my grandfather and father, who practiced the Korean version of neo-Confucianism mixed with some practices of Taoism. They observed the five moral principles[1] and the ritual ceremonies honoring their ancestors. These two practices observed by my parents and grandparents were common religious traditions among rural peasant communities of Korea in my childhood. Looking back now, they seem reminiscent of superstitious tendencies of European Christians during the middle ages and of the strict law-abiding Jewish traditions.

During my high school and college days, I attended a few Christian churches in urban areas with some of my Christian friends, but their manner of worship was so foreign to me that I had little interest in Christianity. However, in my early twenties I joined The Church of Jesus Christ of Latter-day Saints in Seoul through the efforts of missionaries who taught me. I did not understand much about Jesus Christ or His doctrines at the time, but I felt good about what I had been taught.

When I came to the United States to start my post-secondary education at Brigham Young University in 1974, I had an opportunity to

---

[1] The five principles are (1) Loyalty between a king and his officers, (2) Special relationship between husband and wife, (3) Closeness between parents and children, (4) Trust between friends, and (5) Social order between the old and the young.

reside with the Trotter family in Provo, Utah, for two years. As a new convert, I observed and learned how their Christian beliefs played a role in their home and ward community, and it was both educational and inspiring to me.

After I married the former Hyo-Sun Chi in 1977, her strong and uncompromising faith in Jesus Christ influenced me to study the scriptures more seriously. She was brought up by a Catholic family in Korea, and she converted to The Church of Jesus Christ of Latter-day Saints in her early twenties. Following her conversion, she served a full-time mission for the Church for approximately two years. We were blessed with six wonderful children, and the holy scriptures became a foundation of my personal and family life. Through many different callings and assignments in the Church over the decades, I have had sacred experiences with inspiration and revelation, and my faith in Jesus Christ and His restored gospel has continued to grow stronger.

While my wife and I were serving a full-time mission for the Church, presiding over hundreds of young and dedicated missionaries in the Korea Daejeon Mission for three years, I met many new people with diverse religious backgrounds whom I would never have met had I not served the mission. Having spent my career life as a business executive and a professor in the USA, Europe, and Asia, I developed an affinity for meeting many new people, and visiting with new people was one of my favorite mission activities. I have visited with many people from different Christian backgrounds and have learned about the various theological differences among Christian churches. To understand the Judeo-Christians, I have studied the theological points of different denominations and their interpretations of many specific passages of the Bible.

A month after returning home from our mission, my second son, Samuel, had an accident while rock climbing and passed to the other side of the veil at the age of twenty-eight.[2] He lived a very righteous life and was a serious student of the scriptures, having keen spiritual insights from his early boyhood. Amid this sudden and devastating situation, my family and I experienced multiple spiritual encounters and tender mercies. In retrospect, during many sleepless nights since my son's

---

[2] Some details can be found at https://www.lds.org/church/news/what-my-son-taught-me-after-his-death?lang=eng

passing, my in-depth research of the scriptures while writing this book has therapeutically helped me. As I have had the privilege of experiencing divine help while writing this book, I cannot help but think that my son Samuel may have been the angelic instigator for the divine help I have received. I am honored to dedicate this book to my precious Samuel.

During the course of writing this book, I have been guided by the Spirit many times. As an example, I realized at one point that the two greatest commandments of love taught by Jesus Christ (see Matthew 22:35–40, Mark 12:28–34, and Luke 10:25–37) can be combined with the Apostle Paul's teaching on faith, hope, and charity (see 1 Corinthians 13), and they can be connected to the Atonement of Jesus Christ through the prophet Mormon's discourse on charity (see Moroni 7:38–48).[3] I labored on this with much deliberation and many prayers for weeks.

One early morning while dreaming or half-awake (I could not tell which), I found myself continuously uttering the words "Moroni 7, Mormon 7, Alma 7" over and over for what seemed to be an hour. As soon as I woke up, I reviewed those three chapters very carefully. I was well aware that Mormon's discourse in Moroni 7 was the bridge or enabler to connect Jesus Christ and the Apostle Paul's teachings on charity to the Atonement of Christ and the power of His Resurrection, but I did not know what Mormon 7 and Alma 7 had to do with this. After careful review, I discovered that Alma taught that faith, hope, and charity should abound in good works (see Alma 7:24) and that works are an essential part of charity. Later, I found out that Moroni also taught that faith, hope, and charity bring us to the fountain of all righteousness, which is the Lord (see Ether 12:28). I now realize that these findings are good examples of the unfolding of the fullness of the gospel of Jesus Christ jointly by the Bible and the Book of Mormon as Mormon prophesied (see Mormon 7:9). This is a lesson from the Holy Ghost I will never forget.

I have also had multiple "Aha!" moments with new realizations of God's messages in the scriptures, and these have increased the joy I have found in studying the scriptures. As an example, I have wondered for years if the prophet Abinadi taught the doctrine of consubstantiality of the Father and the Son in Mosiah 15:1–5. His teachings seem very similar to Trinitarian doctrine that many Judeo-Christian churches teach. After studying these five verses for about four months, sometimes

---

[3] Mormon defined charity as "the pure love of Christ" (Moroni 7:47).

studying these five verses for two hours a day during my mission, I started to realize that Abinadi did not teach the doctrine of the consubstantial Deity. I discussed my findings with four expert language and religion professors, and they confirmed my discoveries. Through this process, I am convinced that Abinadi confirmed the angel Gabriel's message to Mary recorded in Luke 1:35 that Jesus is the son of the Highest (the Father).

As another example, until recently I thought the Book of Mormon did not teach the baptismal ordinance for the dead. I contemplated this topic in 1 Corinthians 15:29–30 for weeks in conjunction with vicarious works for the dead performed in Latter-day Saint temples. While I was studying 3 Nephi 26, the Spirit enlightened me on this topic; I realized that the resurrected Jesus indirectly taught vicarious works for the dead when He explained the reason why He quoted Malachi 3–4 to the Nephites, saying it was for a future generation (see 3 Nephi 26:2). The Lord preserved priesthood ordinances for the dead specifically for a future generation—our generation—after Elijah's visit on April 3, 1836. Most of my realizations through "Aha!" moments are discussed in the question-and-answer section of the appendix.

Since religious views on theological subjects are generally subjective matters, it is easy to dispute one's views using others with contradictory or different views. In an effort to make my research and findings more objective in this book, I have mostly limited my sources to the canonized King James Bible, the Book of Mormon, and some official creeds or announcements from different Christian denominations. With my background in science and engineering, I wrote this book the way I would approach any scientific process: collecting information (mostly from scriptures), analyzing it, and deriving conclusions from the results of the analysis. I have put many quotes of relevant scriptures in tables so they can be easily compared. Overall, my approach has been to find fact, and I have strived to adhere to the Apostle Peter's admonition: "Knowing this first, that no prophecy of the scripture is of any private interpretation. For the prophecy came not in old time by the will of man: but holy men of God spake as they were moved by the Holy Ghost" (2 Peter 1:20–21).

I am happy to share with readers my discoveries about the plain and precious parts mentioned by Nephi (see 1 Nephi 13), sharing my research on the doctrinal correlation between the Bible (the stick or record from the tribe of Judah) and the Book of Mormon (the stick or record from the tribe of Joseph). This book will validate and confirm that the prophecies of ancient prophets have been and are being fulfilled: the Bible came forth from the Jews, and the Book of Mormon came forth from the other sheep, the Josephites (see John 10:16, 3 Nephi 15:21–24). They jointly expound the fulfillment of the prophecies from Joseph in Egypt (see 2 Nephi 3:12),[4] Ezekiel (see Ezekiel 37:15–19), Zechariah (see Zechariah 10:6–7), Nephi (see 1 Nephi 13:40–41, 2 Nephi 30:3–5), and Mormon (see Mormon 7:9).

Writing this book has significantly enhanced my unwavering conviction, intellectually as well as spiritually, that the Bible and the Book of Mormon are the predestined scriptures of Israel; that they jointly teach the correct doctrine of Christ; and that they testify of the divinity of the Father, of the Son, and of the Holy Ghost. In tumultuous environments of today's society as a whole (including some religious societies), moral corruption and apostasy have been quite prevalent because of negativism based on not-well-verified historical reports, the perceived misconducts of leadership, intellectual sophistications laced with skepticism, and the availability of so much information (both correct and incorrect). Having had spiritual experiences multiple times during the course of my research for this book, I feel that I have written this book with help from both sides of veil. I hope this book will help readers enhance their correct understanding of the Bible and the Book of Mormon and will strengthen their faith in and testimony of Jesus Christ.

Yong-In Spencer Shin
Highland, Utah
May 2019

---

[4] Similar prophecies are recorded in Genesis 50 of the Joseph Smith Translation.

Foreword

I FIRST MET YONG-IN AND his wife, Hyo-Sun, prior to the marriage of our daughter Heidi to their son Daniel. The Shins had just arrived from Korea, and we immediately felt the power of their strong spirits. They were impressive in their demeanor and clear-eyed and confident in their appearance. We greeted them with gladness, and we knew this was going to be the beginning of a wonderful association. As our children were sealed in the temple, our love for one another was sealed also, and we became, in essence, members of an extended family, linked by faith, by children, and by grandchildren.

The study that forms the foundation of this book came out of Yong-In's love, reverence, and devotion to Jesus Christ and His restored gospel. As a young man, Yong-In was reared in the Buddhist tradition. Discovering Christianity and the Restoration enriched his life beyond imagination. As his faith and knowledge of the restored gospel increased, it grew on him, and he drew upon the strength of the Atonement again and again through his life experience. It is important to note that his wife, Hyo-Sun, is not one whit less in the strength of her conversion and faith. They met and married under the power of heaven, and they took their union as a matter of revelation and covenant. In their combined faith, they have been united in purpose. As Yong-In and Hyo-Sun have explored the restored gospel together, they have always noted the blessing of the Book of Mormon in their lives. They have never missed the central messenger of that book—Jesus Christ—and they have looked for Him on every page. The Book of Mormon was then and still is their primary teacher of Him and His power to save.

When Yong-In was called to preside over the Korea Taejon Mission in 2013, he began to study the Book of Mormon in a new way. He needed to help his missionaries and those whom they were teaching learn about Jesus Christ and His restored gospel. Yong-In's study also addressed the unique culture and beliefs held by the majority of Koreans. Soon after their return from the mission in 2016, when their son Samuel suddenly passed away in a climbing accident, his doctrinal research and writing of this book became the healing pursuit that filled his wakeful nights. This book cemented his faith in the Lord Jesus Christ and His promises for our salvation and eternal life. The study Yong-In had started for his missionaries then became essential, therapeutic, and curative; a walk with the Lord in the lonely and difficult hours of missing a beloved son, an exercise that has been life-giving, helped heal a soul in mourning. In the study of the scriptures, especially The Book of Mormon: Another Testament of Jesus Christ, was found the actual evidence, the promises of the Lord that His Atoning sacrifice had the power to heal and bless.

Yong-In seems to approach his analytical research in unique ways, using qualitative and quantitative data-based comparisons from both the Bible and the Book of Mormon. Multiple times in this book, Yong-In shares many newly discovered doctrinal insights revealed to him through inspiration. He personally feels that his son, Samuel, has been helping him from the other side of the veil, and he commented that he felt he got help from the both sides of veil in researching and writing this book.

Yong-In details these teachings for us in a beautiful way and helps us realize how blessed we are by the completeness of the restored gospel. In this book, we learn about the Lord's interaction with His "other sheep," a remnant of the tribe of Joseph who was sold into Egypt. We learn about the prophecies concerning Christ in both the Old Testament, from the tribe of Judah, and the Book of Mormon, from the tribe of Joseph. He focuses on the Lord's ministry on two continents. He shows how the Book of Mormon completes our understanding of the Deity of Jesus Christ and our Heavenly Father. He highlights how important the Book of Mormon is to our understanding of the teachings of the Bible regarding doctrines taught by Jesus Christ and His prophets.

Yong-In reviews the history of Christianity and the canonization process of the Bible as a record (he calls this a "stick," as Ezekiel called it) from the tribe of Judah, and he compares them to the beginning of The

Church of Jesus Christ of Latter-day Saints and the Book of Mormon, a "stick" or record of the tribe of Joseph. He also reviews the Christology in his unique approach.

Through his in-depth research in connecting the Bible and the Book of Mormon, he connects these two records of Israel in a way that clarifies some doctrine, confirms details not taught in the Bible through the Book of Mormon, identifies contradicting teachings in the Bible, and provides the correct understanding of them through the Book of Mormon. He shows that the Book of Mormon reveals new teachings not found in the Bible and demonstrates how the Book of Mormon validates the truthfulness of some teachings or passages in the Bible that some Bible scholars dispute.

Some of his important research centers on the importance of priesthood ordinances, patriarchal blessings, and the birthright of Israel. He emphasizes that the Book of Mormon as another witness of Jesus Christ will help readers understand the fullness of doctrines and covenants by including the plain and precious parts missing in the Bible. Yong-In summarizes his findings in the following six categories:

- Twenty-four plain and precious elements found in the Book of Mormon that are missing from the Bible.
- Five priesthood ordinances with the associated covenants and the exact manner of performing them as shown in the Book of Mormon, but not in the Bible.
- Twenty-five subjects relating to the infinite Atonement of Jesus Christ specifically taught in the Book of Mormon.
- Thirteen unique prophecies found only in the Book of Mormon.
- Nine inferences by quantitative word count comparisons between the Bible and the Book of Mormon.
- Twelve incorrect beliefs and practices of mainstream Christianity pointed out in the Book of Mormon.

As you study this book, you will learn new aspects of the relationship between the Bible and the Book of Mormon, and you will have your mind enlightened by truths you will learn in your own study. You will be blessed by seeing how profoundly blessed we are to have the Book of Mormon as a record from the tribe of Joseph and the Bible as a record from the tribe of Judah, both serving as witnesses of the life and mission of Jesus Christ. Prophets of the latter days have encouraged us to read, study, even immerse ourselves in a study of the scriptures, and we have been urged with great intensity to make the Book of Mormon an integral part of our learning and testimony. It is my hope that your study of this book by Yong-In will increase your love and appreciation of the fullness of the restored gospel of Jesus Christ through the Book of Mormon and its teachings of the central figure of that record, Jesus Christ, our Savior.

Julie B. Beck

Introduction

ISRAEL, OR JACOB, GAVE HIS patriarchal blessings to his twelve sons before his death; those blessings showed that the tribes of Judah and Joseph would be leaders over the others. These blessings show that the tribe of Judah will be doing well; that Shiloh (in other words, the Messiah) will be born from the tribe of Judah; that the Jews will have the scepter (emblem of authority) until Shiloh's coming; and that people will gather to Shiloh. The blessings also show that the tribe of Joseph will be fruitful; that some will run over the wall (in other words, be carried to a different place); that the Lord will protect them from their enemies; and that they will be blessed by ancestors to have the crown of the head (the birthright or priesthood) that separates them from other tribes. Thus, as confirmed in 1 Chronicles 5:1–2, the tribe of Joseph is the legal heir of Israel.

Consider the blessings from the patriarch Jacob to these two tribes:

Patriarchal Blessing upon Judah (Genesis 49:8–12)	Patriarchal Blessing upon Joseph (Genesis 49:22–26)
Judah, thou *art he* whom thy brethren shall praise: thy hand *shall be* in the neck of thine enemies; thy father's children shall bow down before thee. Judah *is* a lion's whelp: from the prey, my son, thou art gone up: he stooped down, he couched as a lion, and as an old lion; who shall rouse him up? The sceptre shall not depart from Judah, nor a lawgiver from between his feet, until Shiloh come; and unto him *shall* the gathering of the people *be*. Binding his foal unto the vine, and his ass's colt unto the choice vine; he washed his garments in wine, and his clothes in the blood of grapes: His eyes *shall be* red with wine, and his teeth white with milk.	Joseph *is* a fruitful bough, *even* a fruitful bough by a well; *whose* branches run over the wall: The archers have sorely grieved him, and shot *at him*, and hated him: But his bow abode in strength, and the arms of his hands were made strong by the hands of the mighty *God* of Jacob; (from thence is the shepherd, the stone of Israel:) *Even* by the God of thy father, who shall help thee; and by the Almighty, who shall bless thee with blessings of heaven above, blessings of the deep that lieth under, blessings of the breasts, and of the womb: The blessings of thy father have prevailed above the blessings of my progenitors unto the utmost bound of the everlasting hills: they shall be on the head of Joseph, and on the crown of the head of him that was separate from his brethren.

Jacob adopted Joseph's two sons, Manasseh and Ephraim, and gave them patriarchal blessings announcing that Ephraim should have the birthright (see Genesis 48).[5] The prophet Zechariah was also told by the Lord that the house of Judah and Joseph would gather together, and that the Ephraimites would be mighty in the latter days (see Zechariah 10:6–9). Thus, it seems

---

[5] See also 1 Chronicles 5:1–2: "Now the sons of Reuben the firstborn of Israel, (for he was the firstborn; but, forasmuch as he defiled his father's bed, his birthright was given unto the sons of Joseph the son of Israel: and the genealogy is not to be reckoned after the birthright. For Judah prevailed above his brethren, and of him *came* the chief ruler; but the birthright *was* Joseph's:)."

that both tribes of Judah and Joseph (the Ephraimites) are predestined to be the leading tribes of Israel again in the latter days as they were before they were scattered, starting in the eighth century BC.

Jesus Christ taught the Jews about the other sheep: "And other sheep I have, which are not of this fold: them also I must bring, and they shall hear my voice; and there shall be one fold, and one shepherd" (John 10:16). He confirmed that the remnant of Joseph (the Nephites) are the "other sheep" by teaching the Nephites: "And verily I say unto you, that ye are they of whom I said: Other sheep I have which are not of this fold; them also I must bring, and they shall hear my voice; and there shall be one fold, and one shepherd" (3 Nephi 15:21).

Thus, Israel's patriarchal blessings to Judah, Joseph, and Ephraim have been fulfilled, and the resurrected Jesus Christ confirmed that the Nephites are the branch of the Josephites carried away to a different place.

Whereabouts of the Tribes of Judah and Joseph

When the kingdom of Israel was divided into two kingdoms in 975 BC, the Northern Kingdom was comprised of the ten tribes, led by the tribe of Ephraim; the Southern Kingdom, comprised of the two remaining tribes, was led by the tribe of Judah. After the Northern Kingdom was conquered by the Assyrians in 721 BC, these ten tribes lost their traces and identities over time and are now referred to as the ten lost tribes. The Southern Kingdom was later conquered by the Babylonians in 587 BC, but they were able to return to Jerusalem after seventy years of exile and reestablish a Jewish nation. This Jewish nation existed until AD 70, when the Romans destroyed Jerusalem. The Jewish people were exiled until AD 1948, when the United Nations reestablished an Israeli nation. The stick or record from the tribe of Judah is the Bible (the Judeo-Christian scripture).

In 600 BC, about a decade or so before the kingdom of Judah was conquered by the Babylonians, two families from the tribe of Joseph—Lehi's family from the tribe of Manasseh and Ishmael's family from the tribe of Ephraim—were led by the Lord to leave Jerusalem. They migrated to a promised land provided by God. Not long after they arrived in the promised land, these people split into two groups, the Nephites and the Lamanites. They called themselves the remnant of the tribe of

Joseph (or Jacob). The Nephites kept a thousand-year record of their history spanning the period from when they left Jerusalem until they were annihilated by the Lamanites around AD 400. Their record was buried in the ground, where it was protected by the Lord until it was discovered in AD 1827. That stick or record of the remnant of the tribe of Joseph is the Book of Mormon (the Josephite scripture).

Two Sticks to Join Together: The Bible and the Book of Mormon
The Bible begins with the creation of the world and ends with apocalyptic prophecies of the end of the world. The Book of Mormon begins with the prophet Lehi's family departing from Jerusalem in 600 BC, around the time of the dispersion of the Israelites (587 BC), and ends with the annihilation of the Nephites by the Lamanites around AD 400, around the time of the last stage of the canonization of the Bible (AD 419). Thus, the Book of Mormon covers a specific period of one thousand years from the dispersion of the covenanted Israelites to the formation of the Bible and Christianity by the Gentiles.

The Lord told the prophet Ezekiel that He will combine these two sticks or records into one in Him:

> The word of the Lord came again unto me, saying,
> Moreover, thou son of man, take thee one stick, and write upon it, For Judah, and for the children of Israel his companions: then take another stick, and write upon it, For Joseph, the stick of Ephraim, and *for* all the house of Israel his companions:
> And join them one to another into one stick; and they shall become one in thine hand.
> And when the children of thy people shall speak unto thee, saying, Wilt thou not shew us what thou *meanest* by these?
> Say unto them, Thus saith the Lord God; *Behold, I will take the stick of Joseph, which is in the hand of Ephraim, and the tribes of Israel his fellows, and will put them with him, even with the stick of Judah, and make them one stick, and they shall be one in mine hand.* (Ezekiel 37:15–19; emphasis added)

The Book of Mormon provides more information about what the prophet Ezekiel was told about putting two sticks together. Quoting Joseph in Egypt, Lehi taught the joint roles of the Bible and the Book of Mormon. This prophecy is not included in the canonized Bible, but it is presumably quoted from the plates of brass:

> Wherefore, the fruit of thy [Joseph's] loins shall write; and the fruit of the loins of Judah shall write; and *that which shall be written by the fruit of thy loins, and also that which shall be written by the fruit of the loins of Judah, shall grow together, unto the confounding of false doctrines and laying down of contentions, and establishing peace among the fruit of thy loins, and bringing them to the knowledge of their fathers in the latter days, and also to the knowledge of my covenants, saith the Lord.* (2 Nephi 3:12; emphasis added)

Thus, both the Bible and the Book of Mormon are predestined to come forward together, representing two major tribes of Israel.

The Stick of Judah: The Bible

The Bible is a compilation of the Old Testament and the New Testament. It consists of sixty-six books excluding the Apocrypha: thirty-nine books in the Old Testament and twenty-seven books in the New Testament. It starts out with the creation of the world in Genesis and ends with the apocalyptic prophecies of the end of the world in Revelation. The development of the Old Testament is closely connected with Jewish history, and the development of the New Testament is connected closely with the initial days of Christianity.

Canonization of the Bible

The Old Testament is mostly a record written by prophets and scribes from Moses to Malachi. A set of thirty-nine books in the Old Testament is a derivation of the twenty-four books of the Jewish scripture Tanakh, which was known to be canonized by Ezra around the fifth century BC. It starts with the five books of Moses (the Torah or Pentateuch) and ends with the book of Malachi.

The New Testament is a record of Jesus Christ written by some of His Apostles and other disciples in the first century AD. The set of twenty-seven books in the New Testament is a compilation of Christian documents that were selected in the councils of the Catholic Church. The Christian Bible was originally canonized in the Councils of Carthage led by St. Augustine and others of the Catholic Church (AD 397 and AD 419). In AD 419, the book of Revelation was added as the last book in the canonization process, and it was put at the end of the New Testament. However, some orthodox churches have not accepted the book of Revelation.

Beginning in the sixteenth century, some reformation leaders and scholars have translated the Bible into multiple languages. As a result, most Christians have been able to study the Bible in their own languages.

Most Influential Book in the World

The Bible has touched billions of people throughout the history of the Hebrew/Jewish nations and of Christianity. As a vast library, it has been a tremendous source for the laws from Jehovah and the gospel of Jesus Christ: the law of Moses for Jews and the life and teachings of Jesus Christ for Christians. Hundreds of thousands, if not millions, of scholarly scribes and clergies dedicated and even sacrificed their lives to write, translate, protect, canonize, and preserve this sacred record over many thousands of years. Its invaluable influence on the entire human society has been enormous.

However, there is a large chasm between the Judeo and Christian perspectives that is yet to be resolved: an opposite view about Jesus of Nazareth being the Savior, the Son of God. Because it is a compiled library written, copied, and translated by so many people throughout many dispensations over thousands of years, it is understandable that the Bible contains some errors, discrepancies, and/or inconsistencies. Additionally, different Christian denominations have different interpretations of some Bible teachings. Nonetheless, the Bible has been the most influential book in the world, especially after being translated into many languages since the sixteenth-century reformation movements. Along with the spread of the Bible throughout the world, Christianity has become the largest worldwide religion.

The Jews versus the Christians

Even though both the Jews and the Christians believe in the Tanakh (the Old Testament), the Jews do not believe in the New Testament, nor have they recognized Jesus of Nazareth as the Messiah, the Son of God. The Christians, however, believe in the New Testament and worship Jesus as their Savior, the Son of God.

There are many prophecies of the forthcoming Messiah in the Old Testament, but these prophecies do not lead the Jews to accept Jesus as their Messiah. In the New Testament, Jesus taught that He was the Messiah, and His Apostles testified of Jesus's messiahship and that He is the Son of God. This difference existed during the ministry of Jesus Christ and His Apostles in the first century AD, and it still exists in the present time, more than two thousand years later. This difference has created a large chasm in beliefs between Jews and Christians. The New Testament writers would not have known that their personal writings would be a part of the canonized Bible a few centuries later and would play significantly important roles for billions of Christians.

Historicity of Christian Churches

In his blessing, Jacob pronounced that people would gather unto Shiloh, and the fulfillment of that blessing is demonstrated in the billions of people professing Christian faith. While Judaism is a monolithic religious organization for the Jewish people (the tribe of Judah), Christian churches have been diversified over many centuries. The following diagram depicts diversifications of Christian churches and their development since the ascension of Jesus Christ in the millennial time.

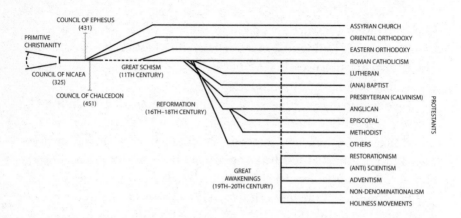

Viewing from left to right, during the days before the Council of Nicaea, there were many small local Christian groups scattered throughout the area surrounding the Mediterranean Sea. The two main centers of these groups were the Hebrew (or Jewish) Christians in Jerusalem and the Hellenic Christians in Rome.

Roman Catholic and Orthodox Churches

The Christians before the Council of Nicaea (AD 325) had suffered severely under the rule of the Roman Empire's anti-Christian leaders. They had to hide underground to survive. Despite severe persecutions and being separated in a wide area along the Mediterranean Sea, many small congregations of Christians began to be established locally, and the number of Christians continued to grow rapidly. However, no strong, central leadership for the whole Christian church was established. By operating independently with very limited communication between the groups for the first couple of centuries, it was natural that different dogmas developed locally. Despite all good intentions, an apostasy from the teachings of Jesus Christ slowly began to creep in during this period.

Under direction from the Roman Emperor Constantine, the Catholic Church started officially in Rome at the Council of Nicaea (AD 325). At the Council of Ephesus (AD 431), the Assyrian Church branched out from the Roman Catholic Church. Twenty years later at the Council of Chalcedon (AD 451), the Oriental Orthodox Church branched out.

When the Eastern Orthodox Church, mostly on the Greek side, broke off from the Roman Catholic Church in AD 1054, there was a separation between the Roman and the Greek Catholic churches. At the time, feuds and contentions in the church were so great that they were referred to as "the Great Schism" or "the East-West Schism." From then on, the Roman Catholic Church was called the *Western Rites*, and the Greek Orthodox churches were called the *Eastern Rites*. Later, a small fraction of the orthodox churches rejoined the Roman Catholic Church.

Reformation and Protestant Churches

Around the sixteenth to seventeenth centuries, some Catholic clergies, Bible scholars, and political leaders revolted against the Roman Catholic Church and the Pope. Challenging the authority of the Pope, they started their own churches. The main protestant churches were Lutheran (established in AD 1526), the Anglican Church of England (AD 1534), Calvinist (AD 1536), Presbyterian (AD 1560), Baptist (AD 1609), Methodist (AD 1739), etc.

Initially, these protestant churches went through much persecution from the Catholic Church in Europe, but they found religious freedom in the new land of America. Within a few centuries, they were spread throughout the world, and collectively they became a significant part of Christianity. Since no authority figure like the Pope presided over the groups of protestant churches, most of them basically regard the canonized Bible as the sole source of all of their doctrines and inspirations.

Great Awakenings and More Diversification

After the Bible became available to all laymen in the mid centuries, there were movements, largely occurring in the United States, to correct the traditional interpretations or understanding of the doctrines and principles. Some protestant church leaders wanted to unify many different denominations among the protestant churches. Some others started to predict the Second Coming of Jesus Christ based on their calculation from the apocalyptic messages in the Bible.[6]

Some focused on proving the teachings in the Bible and avoided influences of newly developed medical science. Others attempted to restore

---

[6] This seemed to be a kind of Christian fad in the nineteenth and twentieth centuries.

religious practices back to the ones taught in the New Testament. The churches in these groups include the Seventh-day Adventists (established in AD 1863), Jehovah's Witnesses (AD 1870s), Christian Science (AD 1879), the Assembly of God (AD 1914), and other evangelical movements. All these new Christian movements over time are referred to as "the Great Awakening(s)."

One Root of Christianity

All the churches in the above diagram have the same root. In the early days of Christianity, the Roman Catholic Church was dominant religiously and politically in Western Europe. Around the time of the reformation movements in Europe, the Bible was translated into many European languages and became available to all people. Most of their doctrines were heavily influenced by the ones developed by the Roman Catholic Church, but with some variations based on different interpretations of the Bible.[7]

As the level of literacy increased among common people in recent centuries, many have established new denominations by offering different interpretations of the Bible passages and have differentiated their doctrines from other denominations. Since the reformation, the Bible became most important for Protestants, while Catholics continue to revere the authority of their Pope and their traditions. This diversification is quite an opposite phenomenon from what the Apostle Paul taught: "One Lord, one faith, one baptism" (Ephesians 4:5). Nonetheless, it may be reasonable to say that Christianity (some call them the "creedal Christianity") as we know it was basically rooted in the Council of Nicaea and the canonized Bible by the Roman Catholic Church in the fourth and fifth centuries.

Christian Traditions

Christian churches have rich traditions that have been developed for many millennia, and it seems that some traditions are as important for them as what their scriptures teach. For example, rich traditions of Christians have brought strong beliefs or practices such as the Trinity, infant baptism, salaried clergy systems, priestly celibacy, localized ritual ceremonies, (vicarious) indulgence, cross usage, prayer through Mary, faith versus

---

[7] The Apocrypha was taken out of the Bible.

work arguments, the exact timing of the Second Coming of Jesus Christ, and so on. Interestingly, none of these are taught directly in the Bible.

The Stick of Joseph: The Book of Mormon

This is the book that God commanded Nephi, the first writer, to write (see 1 Nephi 19:2–3; 2 Nephi 5:30–31). It consists of fifteen books written by more than twenty authors (588 pages in the first edition). As a historical record, the writing style in the Book of Mormon is a metanarrative with commentaries from both Mormon and Moroni. For example, narrative phrases like "It came to pass" are used often (appearing 1,359 times in all fifteen books except the last, the book of Moroni). In general, the writing styles are somewhat elaborate, with detailed descriptions and oft-repeated messages. Chiasmus is even included in many parts of the book.

History of the Book

The Book of Mormon is a thousand-year historical record by a couple of families from the tribe of Joseph who migrated from Jerusalem to the promised land (the present land of America) under the direction of the Lord. It begins with a record of a father-and-son team, Lehi and Nephi, and ends with a record by another father-and-son team, Mormon and Moroni.

The first writer, Nephi, discovered much gold in the area where his group settled in the promised land (the land of Nephi), and he made gold plates[8] on which he engraved his writings in a language that he called reformed Egyptian. The first nine writers, from Nephi to Amaleki, followed the blood lineage of Nephi and his brother Jacob in writing on the gold plates (their combined record covers more than four hundred years).

After King Benjamin took over the plates from Amaleki around 130 BC, he and his son King Mosiah managed the plates for about forty years, until around 90 BC. King Mosiah recorded his writings and delivered the plates to the prophet Alma the Younger. Alma's descendants continued to engrave their records, preserving the plates for about four hundred years until Ammaron hid them in the ground at Shim around AD 321.

When Mormon (a pure descendant of Lehi) was ten years old, Ammaron instructed him to dig up the records when he was twenty-four. Mormon followed the instruction and obtained the plates. He edited the plates starting from King Benjamin's record, added his own writing,

---

[8] He was well trained in making ore when he built a ship to cross over an ocean.

and named the compiled records the Book of Mormon after his name. He buried most of the plates at the Hill Cumorah; he gave a few of the plates to his son Moroni, instructing him to record the remaining story of their history. After Mormon was killed in a war, Moroni added the last part of their history and the book of Ether, which he edited. Translated by King Mosiah,[9] the book of Ether is the history of another group who migrated to the same land. Moroni also added his own writing with his final remarks and buried all the records together at the Hill Cumorah in AD 421.

Joseph Smith was taught about the buried golden plates by the angel Moroni—the same Moroni who buried them about 1,400 years earlier—in AD 1823; he was allowed to retrieve them from Hill Cumorah on September 22, 1827. Even though he had only about a third-grade education, it took less than three months (April–June AD 1829)[10] for Joseph Smith to translate the Book of Mormon from a dead ancient language to English under divine guidance, with help from Oliver Cowdery and others, who acted as scribes. It was published as the Book of Mormon in AD 1830.

While the Old Testament has been known and available from Moses's day (sometime around 1500 BC), the Book of Mormon has been known and available to the world only since AD 1830—only in this dispensation. When it was first published, it was new knowledge to the world.

Record from the Josephites

The Nephites in the Book of Mormon were the remnants of the Joseph (Josephites) who held the birthright of Israel; the prophet Lehi from

---

[9] The Book of Mormon also introduces two other groups who migrated to the present American continents under guidance from the Lord: the Jaredites and the Mulekites. The former group migrated to the land of America around the time of the Tower of Babel; they ended up destroying themselves through wickedness and conspiracy among the royal families as well as internal wars for many generations (see Ether 15). The latter group migrated to the land of America from Jerusalem when the kingdom of Judah was destroyed by Babylon in 587 BC. They ended up merging with the Nephites in a place called Zarahemla (see Omni 1:13–19).

[10] Joseph Smith did not know how to write well. Oliver Cowdery and a few others served as scribes and wrote Joseph's translation as he dictated it. Soon after the translation was completed, Joseph Smith returned the plates to the angel Moroni.

the tribe of Manasseh was the patriarch of the first family that started to write their own records. Lehi was not known in the Bible, but presumably was one of the minor prophets of his day in Jerusalem. His name is the same as a city of Lehi[11] where Samson resided (see Judges 15). At the time, the prophet Jeremiah was the major prophet. Lehi's family was able to persuade the family of Ishmael from the tribe of Ephraim to join them, and these two families left Jerusalem in 600 BC, the first year of the reign of King Zedekiah over the kingdom of Judah. This group was led by divine guidance to a promised land, the present American continent.

Beginning with Lehi and Nephi, numerous prophets in the promised land wrote their history, consisting of sociopolitical stories, wars, teachings, prophecies, and testimonies of their God (mostly called Jesus or Jesus Christ, but also called Jehovah in a single case). Their teachings and prophecies are comparable with the Bible in many aspects, but also clarify or even correct some histories and teachings in the Bible. Unlike the writers in the New Testament, the writers in the Book of Mormon were aware that their writings would be a part of scripture for their descendants and others and that they would play a role in the Restoration of the gospel of Jesus Christ in the latter days.

The Book of Mormon reveals Jesus Christ's three-day visit to the Nephites on the American continent after His resurrection (Jesus identified them as the "other sheep"; see John 10:16). Being scripture from the tribe of Joseph, it contains many prophecies about the future of the descendants of Joseph in the latter days, such as the Restoration of the gospel of Jesus Christ through the Josephites, the land of their inheritance, the New Jerusalem, and so forth. Thus, while the Bible is the Judeo-Christian scripture from the tribe of Judah, the Book of Mormon is the Christian scripture from the tribe of Joseph.

Another Testament of Jesus Christ with the Plain and Precious Parts and Covenants

The Book of Mormon is another scriptural record of the gospel and doctrine of Jesus Christ. The writers of the Book of Mormon were Christians who believed in Jesus Christ, and they were basically taught His

---

[11] In Hebrew, the word *lehi* means a jawbone, which is reminiscent of Samson. Excavation work is going on in the city of Lehi in Israel at the time of this writing. See beitlehi.org for more details.

doctrine and the reality of the infinite Atonement from the start of the record around 600 BC. As did the Jews, the Nephite people also kept the law of Moses for six hundred years until the resurrected Jesus came to visit them around AD 33–34.

In general, the Book of Mormon elaborates on and/or complements with more detail and plainness the doctrines taught in the Bible. It is remarkably consistent with the gospel and historical messages throughout the book. It also restores plain and precious truths that have been removed from the Bible, especially the prophecies of the tribe of Joseph and their roles in the latter days. It also contains revelations on priesthood ordinances and covenants. It teaches that Gentiles converted to Jesus Christ through baptism become part of the covenant Israelites, the same as the Israelites who received the covenant through the blood lineage of Abraham. It repeatedly teaches that it is critical to have faith in Jesus Christ, be baptized by water and the Holy Ghost (the Holy Spirit), and endure to the end by keeping His commandments, exercising agency righteously and applying the Atonement of Jesus Christ to daily life.

One of the unique teachings in the Book of Mormon related to the Bible is what an angel taught Nephi. According to the Book of Mormon, after the pure record of Judah containing the fullness of the gospel of the Lord (the original Bible) will go forth from the twelve Apostles to the Gentiles, a great and abominable church will take away many plain and precious parts and covenants from the book of the Lamb of God. As a result, a great many will stumble under the influence of Satan because of the lost parts (see 1 Nephi 13:24–28). But the lost plain and precious parts and covenants will be restored through the records of Nephi's people—in other words, the Book of Mormon.

Christian Record Both Before and After Christ

Contrary to the Jewish people who have not accepted Jesus as their Christ even to the present day, Lehi's descendants worshipped Jesus as their Christ throughout their entire thousand-year history.

The first writer of their history, Nephi, testified that Jesus was the Christ, the Savior, as early as 559–545 BC (see 2 Nephi 10:3, 7; 2 Nephi 25:19, 20). They called themselves Christians (see Alma 46:15–16; 48:10). As his parting words around AD 421, the last writer, Moroni, pleaded with readers of the Book of Mormon to come unto Christ and be perfected and sanctified by the grace of God in Christ (see Moroni 10:32).

The main message of the book is that Jesus is the Christ, the Son of God, and that one can be saved only through His graceful and infinite Atonement. The Book of Mormon testifies of Jesus Christ in our present day as a record of the birthright holders (the Ephraimites) in a similar way that Abraham, Isaac, and Jacob testified of Jehovah in the ancient days. Through the Book of Mormon, tens of millions of people have found that Jesus of Nazareth is the Son of God, the Savior, and that one can obtain eternal salvation only through His graceful and infinite Atonement.

The Church of Jesus Christ of Latter-day Saints

Contrary to many diversified Christian churches in the Judeo-Christian group, the church of the tribe of Joseph is near monolithic in representing the tribe of Joseph like the Jewish religion represents the tribe of Judah.[12] The Church of Jesus Christ of Latter-day Saints was organized by Joseph Smith and half a dozen others in upper New York state in AD 1830 under specific instructions from heaven (see D&C 20).

The organization of the Church was the fulfillment of the promise that Heavenly Father and Jesus Christ made to Joseph Smith in the First Vision in AD 1820. In the vision, Joseph Smith was told not to join any other churches, but to wait until he was given further instructions. Ten years after the vision, Joseph Smith was instructed to start the true Church of Jesus Christ. The Church believes that both the Bible and the Book of Mormon are the word of God, and the Book of Mormon is the keystone of its religion. The Church has two more canonized scriptures: the Doctrine and Covenants and the Pearl of Great Price. The former is a collection of continuous revelations received by modern-day prophets, and the latter is a collection of various records of the Church and contains additional revelations on some sections of the Bible.

---

[12] There are some other churches that accept the Book of Mormon as their scripture, including the Community of Christ and multiple fundamentalist groups. However, some of them have been converging to some of the Judeo-Christian churches, and most fundamentalist groups are very small in size, generally made up of only a few families, and have very little doctrinal influence. In this book, The Church of Jesus Christ of Latter-day Saints will be treated monolithically, just as the Jews in the Judeo side were treated monolithically.

The governing body of the Church is the First Presidency and the Quorum of the Twelve Apostles headed by a living prophet who holds the priesthood authority to exercise all the priesthood keys (the Aaronic or Levitical Priesthood and the Melchizedek Priesthood). There is no paid clergy system, and all local leaderships are called (in other words, invited) from among the faithful members in volunteer assignments for limited periods. The members of the Church are commonly known for their faithful discipleship of Jesus Christ, personal integrity and honesty, family-centered life, charity, self-reliance, missionary work, faithfulness in performing vicarious works for the dead in their temples, and so forth.

In This Book

This book is comprised of ten chapters and an appendix. In an effort to identify those plain and precious parts and covenants missing from the Bible that were mentioned by Nephi, nine different topics are selected (one topic per chapter). While not necessarily connected, these topics fall into the categories of Christology (Chapters 1–3), doctrines and teachings (Chapters 4–8), and prophecies (Chapter 9). In each chapter, most of the related teachings and messages that are related to topics from both the Bible and the Book of Mormon are put together, compared, and analyzed to show their commonalities and differences. In the last chapter (Chapter 10), all the discoveries are combined and categorized, and the representative topics are extracted. A list of these topics approximates some of the plain and precious parts and covenants that Nephi mentioned.

Here are brief introductions of each chapter:

Prophecies of Jesus Christ from the Jews and the Nephites

In Chapter 1, prophecies of the birth, ministry, death, and resurrection of Jesus Christ from both scriptures are analyzed. When Jesus was born, fewer than a dozen people recognized Him as the Son of God, the Messiah. During His three-year ministry, He performed countless miracles and taught the divine gospel. Many Jews recognized Him as a great teacher from God, but not as their Messiah; this was especially true of Christ's contemporaries like the Pharisees and Sadducees in the Sanhedrin. These leaders were very pious experts of the scriptures, and they should have had vast knowledge on the prophecies about the Messiah. Whatever their reasons and motivations were, they arranged for the execution of Jesus Christ with the conclusion that their nation would be better off without Him. Analyzing the prophecies of Jesus from both the Old Testament and the period of the Book of Mormon before Jesus's birth, this chapter addresses the root causes for the chasm about Jesus's messiahship between the Jews and Christians.

Ministry of Jesus Christ with Deity and People

In Chapters 2 and 3, the ministry of Jesus Christ is analyzed. During His ministry to the Jews for three years and to the Nephites (the remnant of Joseph) for three days, Jesus Christ worked with the Father and the Holy Ghost in ministering to the people.

In Chapter 2, Jesus's work with Deity is categorized in two areas: a fulfillment of the law of Moses through His Atonement for the eternal life of man, and His working relationship as a member of the Godhead. Under the law of Moses, sacrificial animal offerings for atoning from sins were strictly observed. The Jews also observed Yom Kippur, a special day of fasting on the Sabbath for the Atonement. Jesus Christ was crucified and resurrected to replace the atoning sacrifice of the law of Moses with the infinitely reconciliatory Atonement between the Father and mankind.

In Chapter 3, Jesus's ministerial work to people is categorized into five areas: organizing His Church, ministering to the needy with many miracles, teaching the principles of the gospel, performing sacred priesthood ordinances, and prophesying of the short- and long-term future. Each category is discussed by comparing the related records from the Bible and the Book of Mormon. Many of Jesus's teachings among both the Jews and the Nephites overlap, but His prophecies did not. For example, while His prophecies in Matthew 24 are mostly about the destruction of Jerusalem in AD 70 and some about the end of the world, His prophecies in 3 Nephi 16, 20, and 21 are about the scattering and gathering of the Jews and of the Josephites in the latter days.

The True Nature of Deity

In Chapter 4, the true Deity between the Father and the Son are discussed. If one's view of Deity is not correct, the rest of theology should not matter too much. Since the Councils of Nicaea and Constantinople in the fourth century AD, the doctrine of Trinity has been the de facto orthodox doctrine of Christianity. Even if there has been some opposition, most Christians have believed that the Father, the Son, and the Holy Ghost are consubstantial.

In the Bible, the word *trinity* does not appear, but both those who are for and those who are against the Trinity can quote different passages in the Bible to justify their own views. In the Book of Mormon, the resurrected Jesus taught His relationship with the Father during His three-day visit to the Nephites. The prophet Abinadi taught this subject as well (see Mosiah 15:1–5), and its in-depth analyses help us understand the true nature of the Deity. This case may be an example of what the Apostle Paul described: "God hath revealed them unto us by his Spirit: for the Spirit searcheth all things, yea, the deep things of God" (1 Corinthians 2:10).

Connecting the Bible and the Book of Mormon

In Chapter 5, all the quotes from the Bible in the Book of Mormon are analyzed to connect these two great scriptures. The Book of Mormon has many quotes from the Bible: it quotes about 35 percent of the book of Isaiah (mostly from Isaiah 2–14, 29, 48–54), about 42 percent of the book of Malachi (Malachi 3 and 4), and a few verses from the book of Micah. During His three-day visit to the Nephites, the resurrected Jesus also retaught the Sermon on the Mount found in Matthew 5–7 with some variation. There are many additions, omissions, and corrections in the quoted passages in the Book of Mormon.

In addition to these quotes, there are also a dozen different messages about the Bible in the Book of Mormon. This shows that the Nephites had access to the ancient scripture from which to quote. In the Book of Mormon, Lehi, Nephi, and others quoted or referred to the plates of brass that they obtained around 600 BC. The plates of brass were a set of scripture and genealogy of the tribe of Joseph (in other words, a set of the Hebrew records of the seventh century BC). Thus, they might have had access to information somewhat different from that contained in the Old Testament (canonized by Ezra in the fifth century BC) and the Septuagint (translated into Greek in the fourth century BC).

In Chapter 5, a belief in the infallibility of the Bible is discussed as well. Some Bible scholars have pointed out inconsistencies in the Bible as well as differences between various versions of the Bible. Some liberal scholars have even insisted on rewriting the Bible, particularly after new findings from many newly discovered biblical texts, the Dead Sea Scrolls, the Nag Hammadi library, and others. Thus, opinions among Bible experts vary widely from its infallibility to the necessity of rewriting it.

Two Priesthoods of God

In Chapter 6, the priesthood of God and its practices are analyzed. Moses was commanded by Jehovah to assign the Levites to be in charge of temple affairs and ordinances, and they received the Levitical Priesthood (see Exodus 40). Both Paul and Alma described the Melchizedek Priesthood (see Hebrews 7 and Alma 13).

Jesus Christ and His Apostles practiced priesthood ordinances such as baptizing, conferring the Holy Ghost, administering sacramental bread and wine, and so on. John the Baptist also performed his baptisms in water with priesthood authority. However, the Bible does not explain how to ordain or perform these ordinances. Thus, there have been disagreements on how to perform the priesthood ordinances (for example, there have been multiple methods of baptism). On the other hand, the Book of Mormon contains specifics on how to baptize, how to confer the Holy Ghost, how to administer the sacramental bread and wine, and how to ordain priests and teachers.

Moreover, while translating the Book of Mormon, Joseph Smith and Oliver Cowdery received the Aaronic (Levite) and the Melchizedek priesthoods directly from angels in AD 1829 (see D&C 13, 27). In AD 1836, they also received the priesthood keys from three ancient prophets authorizing them to gather the Israelites, to receive a fullness of the gospel, and to turn the hearts of the children to the fathers and vice versa (see D&C 110). Thus, the priesthood of God and its keys were restored on the earth again in this dispensation.

Joint Teaching Examples between the Bible and the Book of Mormon

In Chapter 7, ten different examples of joint teaching between the Bible and the Book of Mormon are analyzed: the doctrine of Christ; faith, hope, and charity; justification by faith versus judgment according to works; the parable of the sower and the analogy of the seed; Adam's transgression and the Atonement of Jesus Christ; dramatic conversion cases; the prophecy of "the first being last, and the last being the first"; an example of hand-and-glove fit, point-by-point teaching; the discipleship of Jesus Christ; and a unique teaching example of the Book of Mormon. These examples demonstrate that the Book of Mormon supports the Bible in multiple aspects, such as a clear definition of the doctrine of Christ and of faith-hope-charity, avoiding wresting the teachings in the Bible, and a case of similar teaching with Oriental religions. These examples also show that the Book of Mormon complements many areas of teachings in the Bible and that both scriptures are very comparable companions. Above all, these examples demonstrate that both the Bible and the Book of Mormon teach together as one stick.

The Last Words of Patriarchs and Prophets

In Chapter 8, the last words of prophets and patriarchs are analyzed from the Bible and the Book of Mormon. The last words of a dying person are often the most sincere and precious. The Old Testament contains few successive prophetic records; Jacob and Moses gave their last blessings to all twelve tribes of Israel. The New Testament is a record of a single generation, but Jesus Christ gave His last charge or commandments to His disciples.

Since the Book of Mormon had clear succession from one prophet to the next throughout the Nephite history of one thousand years, there are many cases of last words. However, considering the length of the discussions, only a few of them are reviewed in this chapter. Those include the last words from Lehi, Nephi, King Benjamin, and Moroni. Through their last words, they taught significant gospel principles and doctrines that are not found in the Bible.

Unique Prophecies in the Book of Mormon

In Chapter 9, the unique prophecies in the Book of Mormon are analyzed. They are mostly from 1 Nephi 10–14, 22; 2 Nephi 3, 25–33; Jacob 5; 3 Nephi 16–29; Mormon 7–8; and Ether 4 and 13. Instead of apocalyptical prophecies about the end of the world like those found in the book of Revelation by John, most of the prophecies focus on the scattering and gathering of the Israelites, the Old and the New Jerusalem, the land of inheritance of the tribe of Joseph, the commencement of the Lord's work in the latter days in conjunction with a latter-day prophet and the coming forth of the Book of Mormon. The last writer in the book, Moroni, also left six prophecies for our day and eight exhortations for readers of the Book of Mormon (see Mormon 8, Moroni 10)

The Plain and Precious Parts and Covenants and Other Findings:

As mentioned earlier, Nephi was taught by an angel that many plain and precious parts and covenants of the Lord would be taken away from the Bible by a large Gentile church, but those parts would be restored through the Book of Mormon (see 1 Nephi 13:26, 34).

Chapter 10 discusses twenty-four different plain and precious parts, twenty-five subjects related to the Atonement of Jesus Christ, and five specific priesthood ordinances with their associated covenants. These are supplementary teachings missing in the Bible but provided by the Book of Mormon. Thirteen unique prophecies in the Book of Mormon that are not found in the Bible are also discussed. Comparing some of quantitative statistical data (word counts) from both the Bible and the Book of Mormon during this research, nine different inferences are extracted and discussed in this chapter. Moreover, twelve different traditional beliefs that have been developed throughout Judeo-Christian history but not specified in the Bible are discovered through the teachings in the Book of Mormon, and they are listed in this chapter. All of these should approximate some of what the angel showed to Nephi in the vision.

Many Pertinent Questions and Answers

Many questions have arisen as I wrote this book. Out of many, I have selected forty different questions and have provided their answers. These answers can be found throughout this book in most cases, but they are summarized in the appendix for convenience. These questions and answers reinforce the discussions stemming from this research and enhance understanding of the discussed subjects with more clarity.

In Summary

The sticks or records from the tribes of Judah and Joseph mentioned by Ezekiel and Lehi—the Bible and the Book of Mormon—are records that help fulfill the patriarchal blessings of Jacob and Joseph's prophecy (see Genesis 49; 2 Nephi 3). For the tribe of Judah, its fulfillments are manifest in the Bible and the historicity of the Judeo-Christian churches. For the tribe of Joseph, its fulfillments are manifest in the Restoration of the gospel of Jesus Christ in these latter days through the Book of Mormon and The Church of Jesus Christ of Latter-day Saints. Both of these scriptures have also fulfilled the prophecies by Ezekiel and Mormon regarding their teaching as one stick (see Ezekiel 37:19; Mormon 7:9).

The Jews delivered the Bible (stick of Judah) to the Gentiles after the days of the Apostles of Jesus Christ in the first century, and plain and precious parts and covenants were left out during this transfer. The Book of Mormon from the tribe of Joseph is a record that includes the plain and precious parts and covenants missing from the Bible. This book reveals many of those plain and precious parts and covenants along with some other findings and corrections that the Book of Mormon provides for the Bible.

Chapter 1

Prophecies of Jesus Christ

BUT BEHOLD, THE JEWS WERE a stiffnecked people; and they despised the words of plainness, and killed the prophets, and sought for things that they could not understand. Wherefore, because of their blindness, which blindness came by looking beyond the mark, they must needs fall; for God hath taken away his plainness from them, and delivered unto them many things which they cannot understand, because they desired it. And because they desired it God hath done it, that they may stumble.

And now I, Jacob, am led on by the Spirit unto prophesying; for I perceive by the workings of the Spirit which is in me, that by the stumbling of the Jews they will reject the stone upon which they might build and have safe foundation.

But behold, according to the scriptures, this stone shall become the great, and the last, and the only sure foundation, upon which the Jews can build. (Jacob 4:14–16)

The New Testament contains a host of quotes and comments about Old Testament teachings and prophecies, particularly by well-educated writers like the Apostle Paul and Luke. In the four Gospels, there are also many quotes and prophecies from the Old Testament. In this chapter, the prophecies in the Old Testament will be limited to those confirmed in the four Gospels—Matthew, Mark, Luke, and John. The Book of Mormon covers six hundred years before the birth of Jesus Christ, and it also contains many prophecies of Jesus Christ. In general, the prophecies in the Book of Mormon are plain[13] to understand, detailed, and specific.

Following are examples of the prophecies related to the birth, baptism, ministry, Crucifixion, and Resurrection of Jesus Christ that are found in the present Old Testament as confirmed in the present four Gospels of the New Testament and in the Book of Mormon in the period before Christ's birth.

Prophecies about the Birth of Jesus Christ

Prophecies in the Old Testament Confirmed in the Four Gospels

The Old Testament contains only four passages related to the birth of Jesus and His infancy. These prophecies are given by the prophets Isaiah, Micah, Jeremiah, and Hosea:

- A virgin shall conceive and bear a son, and his name will be Immanuel (see Isaiah 7:14; Matthew 1:23).
- There will be an everlasting ruler (or governor) of Israel (see Micah 5:2; Matthew 2:6).
- Rachel would weep and refuse to be comforted because there are no children (see Jeremiah 31:15; Matthew 2:16–18).
- The Lord called His son out of Egypt (see Hosea 11:1; Matthew 2:15).

Relying on these recorded prophecies alone, it would have been difficult for the Jews to recognize the baby Jesus as their long-awaited Messiah during His birth and infancy. The four Gospels recorded that only a select few recognized Jesus as the Messiah: Mary, Joseph, Elisabeth, Simeon, Anna, some shepherds in Bethlehem, and the Wise Men. This knowledge of the baby Jesus being the Messiah was given to them through the visitation of angels or the witness of the Spirit.

---

[13] It seems that Nephi, the first writer of the Book of Mormon, set a tone for being plain in his writing when he wrote, "my soul delighteth in plainness unto my people, that they may learn" (2 Nephi 25:4).

In the Book of Mormon

As shown in the following examples, the prophecies in the Book of Mormon about the birth of the Savior are specific, containing names and time. Moreover, there was a prophecy about a sign of no darkness (or night) and a new star in their region when Jesus was born.

Year of Birth

- Six hundred years after Lehi left Jerusalem, God would raise the Messiah (see 1 Nephi 10:4, 600–592 BC).
- The Messiah would come six hundred years after Lehi left Jerusalem (see 2 Nephi 25:19, 559–545 BC).
- In five years, the Redeemer will come to redeem those who believe Him (see Helaman 14:2, about 6 BC).

Specific Name (and/or Titles)

- "According to words of the prophets and also the word of the angel of God, his name shall be Jesus Christ, the Son of God" (2 Nephi 25:19, 559–545 BC).
- "He shall be called Jesus Christ, the Son of God, the Father of heaven and earth, the Creator of all things from the beginning; and his mother shall be called Mary" (Mosiah 3:8, about 124 BC).
- "He shall be born of Mary, at Jerusalem which is the land of our forefathers, she being a virgin, a precious and chosen vessel, who shall be overshadowed and conceive by the power of the Holy Ghost, and bring forth a son, yea, even the Son of God" (Alma 7:10,[14] 93 BC).

---

[14] Interestingly, the prophet Alma called the birthplace Jerusalem, not Bethlehem. This type of comment seems to be used in some cases in the ancient days, as shown in 2 Kings 14:20: "And they brought him on horses: and he was buried at Jerusalem with his fathers in the city of David." The city of David should be Bethlehem, not Jerusalem. This casual consideration may be because of a short distance between these two cities (approximately five miles).

While Luke said that an angel told Mary "The Holy Ghost shall come upon thee, and the power of the Highest shall overshadow thee" (Luke 1:35), Alma said a "virgin [Mary] shall be overshadowed and conceive by the power of the Holy Ghost" (Alma 7:10). While Luke distinguished the Holy Ghost and the Highest, Alma did not distinguish them in this case, as Matthew did not distinguish by saying "she [Mary] was found with child of the Holy Ghost" (Matthew 1:18).

Signs of His Coming

- ". . . after the Messiah shall come there shall be signs given unto my people of his birth, and also of his death and resurrection; and great and terrible shall that day be unto the wicked" (2 Nephi 26:3, 559–545 BC).
- "There shall be great lights in heaven, insomuch that in the night before he cometh there shall be no darkness . . . as if it was day . . . and it shall be the night before he is born.... there shall a new star arise, such an one as ye never have beheld; and there shall be many signs and wonders in heaven . . . insomuch that ye shall fall to the earth" (Helaman 14:3–7, about 6 BC).

The above prophecies show their plainness by indicating a specific year and the place of the birth of Jesus Christ; they even say that His virgin mother's name will be Mary. Thus, the Book of Mormon has less ambiguity about Jesus's birth. Even though Jesus was born in Bethlehem of Judea, the prophesied sign of no darkness for a night and a day was fulfilled in the Nephite region.[15]

Prophecies about Baptism and John the Baptist

In the Old Testament as Confirmed in the Four Gospels

In the Old Testament, there are no obvious references to baptism performed by John the Baptist. It was apparent that John's baptism was popular but was not received well by the Jewish leadership; they did not know how to answer the question from Jesus when He asked, "The baptism of John, whence was it? From heaven, or of men?" (Matthew 21:25). But there are a couple of prophecies from Isaiah and Malachi about the claims by John the Baptist found in the four Gospels:

- "He shall turn the heart of the fathers to children [and vice versa]" in the spirit and power of Elias (Malachi 4:6; Luke 1:17).

---

[15] Despite such a plain and clear sign, however, there were many (intellectual) skeptics in their society who did not believe the birth of the Savior. Their logic or reasoning for being skeptical was explained in Helaman 16:13–21 (1 BC–AD 1).

- ". . . The voice of one crying in the wilderness, Prepare ye the way of the Lord, make his paths straight" (Luke 3: 4–6; Isaiah 40: 3–5; see also Matthew 3:3; Mark 1:2–3; John 1:23).
- "I will send my messenger and he shall prepare the way before me . . ." (Malachi 3:1; Luke 7:27–28; see also Matthew 11:10; Mark 1:2).

Based on the brief descriptions by the prophets Isaiah and Malachi, it is difficult to interpret whether these prophecies are about John the Baptist, but a close correlation can be drawn between them. Even if there is not a clear trace of baptismal ordinances specifically mentioned in the Old Testament, some Bible scholars have extrapolated water purification activities like mikveh[16] as a baptism-like ordinance.

In the Book of Mormon

In the Book of Mormon, the priesthood ordinance of baptism was taught as early as the days of Lehi and Nephi (600–592 BC). The following shows some of their examples of baptism or teachings on baptism before the birth of Jesus Christ:

John the Baptist

> Lehi spake also concerning a prophet who should come before the Messiah, to prepare the way of the Lord—
> . . . he should go forth and cry in the wilderness: Prepare ye the way of the Lord, and make his paths straight; for there standeth one among you whom ye know not; and he is mightier than I, whose shoe's latchet I am not worthy to unloose. (1 Nephi 10:7–8, 600–592 BC)

Baptisms

> He [Lehi] said he [John] should baptize in Bethabara, beyond Jordan; and he also said he should baptize with water.

---

[16] For a detailed explanation about mikveh, see http://www.setapartpeople.com/mikvah-part-1-spiritual-cleansing

And after he had baptized the Messiah with water, he should behold and bear record that he had baptized the Lamb of God, who should take away the sins of the world. (1 Nephi 10:9–10, 600–592 BC).

I know that if ye shall follow the Son, with full purpose of heart, acting no hypocrisy and no deception before God, but with real intent, repenting of your sins, witnessing unto the Father that ye are willing to take upon you the name of Christ, by baptism—yea, by following your Lord and your Savior down into the water, according to his word, behold, then shall ye receive the Holy Ghost; yea, then cometh the baptism of fire and of the Holy Ghost; and then can ye speak with the tongue of angels, and shout praises unto the Holy One of Israel. (2 Nephi 31:13, 559–545 BC)

. . . they should look forward with one eye, having one faith and one baptism, having their hearts knit together in unity and in love one towards another. . . . (Mosiah 18:21, about 147 BC)

. . . come and go forth, and show unto your God that ye are willing to repent of your sins and enter into a covenant with him to keep his commandments, and witness it unto him this day by going into the waters of baptism. (Alma 7:15, about 83 BC)

Many baptisms were performed by immersion in water throughout the thousand-year history of the Book of Mormon. Unlike the Jews in the Palestine area, the baptism ordinance was an integral part of religious practices for the Nephites both before and after Jesus Christ's ministry. When the resurrected Jesus Christ came to visit them, the first thing He taught about was baptism (see 3 Nephi 11:18–27), and it was not a new ordinance to the Nephites.

Prophecies about the Ministry of Jesus Christ

In the Old Testament as Confirmed in the Four Gospels

There are many prophecies about the ministry of Jesus Christ in the Old Testament that are closely confirmed in the four Gospels. These prophecies are mostly derived from the Psalmist and the prophet Isaiah, but some are from other prophets like Moses, Zechariah, Malachi, Ezekiel, and Hosea. Some prophecies clearly correlate with the ministry of Jesus Christ, but some do not. This section follows a sequence of the four Gospels of Matthew, Mark, Luke, and John, beginning with Matthew.

Prophecies (or Similar Teachings) by the Prophet Moses[17] in the Pentateuch

Love the Lord with all thy heart, and with all thy soul, and with all thy might. (Deuteronomy 6:5; see also Deuteronomy 30:6; Matthew 22:37; Mark 12:30; Luke 10:27)

Thou shalt love thy neighbor as thyself. (Leviticus 19:18; see also Matthew 22:39; Mark 12:31; Luke 10:27)

They offered a pair of turtle doves, or two young pigeons. (Leviticus 12:8; see also Luke 2:24)

I am that I am; Before Abraham was, I am. (Exodus 3:14; John 8:58)

Throughout the New Testament, there are many quotes from the law of Moses pertaining to temple sacrifices or ordinances, the Ten Commandments, and the lineage of Jesus Christ. However, prophecies by Moses about the ministry of Jesus Christ that were confirmed in the four Gospels are somewhat limited.

---

[17] The following are not necessarily prophecies, but quotes. Not included here are quotes from Deuteronomy 8:3, 6:16, 10:12 (6:13) by Jesus when He answered Satan in overcoming the three temptations in Matthew 4:4, 7, 9. Also not included here are quotes from Exodus 20:13–18 (or Deuteronomy 5:17–20) by Jesus on the Ten Commandments in Matthew 19:18 (Mark 10:19, Luke 18:20).

Prophecies (or Similar Teachings) by the Prophet Isaiah

And he said, Go, and tell this people, Hear ye indeed, but understand not; and see ye indeed, but perceive not.

Make the heart of this people fat, and make their ears heavy, and shut their eyes; lest they see with their eyes, and hear with their ears, and understand with their heart, and convert, and be healed. (Isaiah 6:9–10; see also Matthew 13:14–15; Mark 4:12; Luke 8:10; John 12:40)

. . . The land of Zabulon, and the land of Nephthalim, by the way of the sea, beyond Jordan, Galilee of the Gentiles; . . .

The people which sat in darkness saw great light. . . . (Matthew 4:15–16; see also Isaiah 9:1–2)

For unto us a child is born, unto us a son is given: and the government shall be upon his shoulder: and his name shall be called Wonderful, Counsellor, The mighty God, The everlasting Father, The Prince of Peace. (Isaiah 9:6;[18] see also Luke 2:20)

Therefore thus saith the Lord God, Behold, I lay in Zion for a foundation a stone, a tried stone, a precious corner stone, a sure foundation: he that believeth shall not make haste. (Isaiah 28:16; see also Matthew 16:18)

Forasmuch as this people draw near me with their mouth, and with their lips do honour me, but have removed their heart far from me, and their fear toward me is taught by the precept of men. (Isaiah 29:13; see also Matthew 15:9)

. . . mine elect, in whom my soul delighteth; I have put my spirit upon him: he shall bring forth judgment to the Gentiles.

He shall not cry, nor lift up, nor cause his voice to be heard in the street.

---

[18] Right or wrong, some scholars claim that this verse praises a contemporary king and is not a prophecy about Jesus Christ.

A bruised reed shall he not break, and the smoking flax shall he not quench: he shall bring forth judgment unto truth.

He shall not fail nor be discouraged, till he have set judgment in the earth: and the isles shall wait for his law. (Isaiah 42:1–4; see also Matthew 12:18–21)

Who hath believed our report? and to whom is the arm of the Lord revealed? (Isaiah 53:1; see also John 12:38)

But he was wounded for our transgressions, he was bruised for our iniquities: the chastisement of our peace was upon him; and with his stripes we are healed. (Isaiah 53:5; see also Matthew 8:17)

He was oppressed, and he was afflicted, yet he opened not his mouth: he is brought as a lamb to the slaughter, and as a sheep before her shearers is dumb, so he openeth not his mouth. (Isaiah 53:7; see also Mark 14:60)

And all thy children shall be taught of the Lord; and great shall be the peace of thy children. (Isaiah 54:13; see also Jeremiah 31:33–34; John 6:45)

. . . for mine house shall be called an house of prayer for all people. (Isaiah 56:7; see also Jeremiah 7:11; Matthew 21:13; Mark 11:17; Luke 19:46)

The Spirit of the Lord God is upon me; because the Lord hath anointed me to preach good tidings unto the meek; he hath sent me to bind up the brokenhearted, to proclaim liberty to the captives, and the opening of the prison to them that are bound;

To proclaim the acceptable year of the Lord. . . . (Isaiah 61:1–2; see also Isaiah 58:6; Luke 4:18–19)

Even if they are not necessarily cohesive, the above examples show that the Gospel writers in the New Testament confirmed that many prophecies by Isaiah were fulfilled during the ministry of Jesus Christ.

However, the above prophecies by the prophet Isaiah are general and could cover many different situations.

Prophecies (or Similar Teachings) by the Psalmist

> Out of the mouth of babes and sucklings hast thou ordained strength. . . . (Psalms 8:2; see also Matthew 21:16)

> Yea, mine own familiar friend, in whom I trusted, which did eat of my bread, hath lifted up his heel against me. (Psalms 41:9; see also John 13:18)

> They that hate me without a cause are more than the hairs of mine head. . . . (Psalms 69:4; see also Psalms 35:19; John 15:25)

> For the zeal of thine house hath eaten me up. . . . (Psalms 69:9; see also John 2:17)

> I will open my mouth in a parable: I will utter dark sayings of old [secrets from the foundation of the world]. (Psalms 78:2; see also Matthew 13:35)

> I have said, Ye are gods; and all of you are children of the most High. (Psalms 82:6; see also John 10:34–35)

> The Lord said unto my Lord, Sit thou at my right hand, until I make thine enemies thy footstool. (Psalms 110:1; see also Psalms 8:6; Matthew 22:44)

> The stone which the builders refused is become the head stone of the corner.
> This is the Lord's doing; it is marvellous in our eyes. (Psalms 118:22–23; see also Matthew 21:42; Mark 12:10–11; Luke 20:17)

Jesus Christ quoted most of the above prophecies by the Psalmist, and they were all fulfilled during His ministry. Similar to the passages in Isaiah, when Jesus Christ quoted the Psalms, these verses seem to be somewhat circumstantial, depending on particular subjects or persons.

Prophecies (or Similar Teachings) by the Prophets Zechariah and Hosea

> . . . they weighed for my price thirty pieces of silver.
> . . . I took the thirty pieces of silver, and cast them to the potter in the house of the Lord. (Zechariah 11:12–13; see also Matthew 27:9–10)

> . . . saith the Lord of hosts: smite the shepherd, and the sheep shall be scattered: and I will turn mine hand upon the little ones. (Zechariah 13:7; see also Matthew 26:31; Mark 14:27)

> For I desired mercy, and not sacrifice; and the knowledge of God more than burnt offerings. (Hosea 6:6; see also Matthew 12:7)

The above prophecies by Zechariah were fulfilled toward the end of Jesus Christ's ministry during His Crucifixion. The quote from the book of Hosea is more explanatory of the Lord's will concerning the Jews in Hosea's generation, and the same message was delivered to the Jews by Jesus Christ in the days of His ministry.

In the Book of Mormon

There are not as many prophecies about the ministry of Jesus Christ in the Book of Mormon. The following two quotes from King Benjamin and the prophet Alma are related to the overall life of Jesus Christ, including His ministry, mostly focusing on His sufferings in general.

King Benjamin, 124 BC

> And the things which I shall tell you are made known unto me by an angel from God. . . .

*For behold, the time cometh, and is not far distant,
that with power, the Lord Omnipotent who reigneth, who
was, and is from all eternity to all eternity, shall come down
from heaven among the children of men, and shall dwell
in a tabernacle of clay, and shall go forth amongst men,
working mighty miracles, such as healing the sick, raising
the dead, causing the lame to walk, the blind to receive
their sight, and the deaf to hear, and curing all manner of
diseases.*

*And he shall cast out devils, or the evil spirits which
dwell in the hearts of the children of men.*

*And lo, he shall suffer temptations, and pain of body,
hunger, thirst, and fatigue, even more than man can suffer,
except it be unto death; for behold, blood cometh from every
pore, so great shall be his anguish for the wickedness and the
abominations of his people.*

*And he shall be called Jesus Christ, the Son of God, the
Father of heaven and earth, the Creator of all things from
the beginning; and his mother shall be called Mary.*

And lo, he cometh unto his own, that salvation
might come unto the children of men even through
faith on his name; and even after all this they shall consider him a man, and say that he hath a devil, and shall
scourge him, and shall crucify him. (Mosiah 3:2–9; emphasis added)

Alma the Younger, about 83 BC

But behold, the Spirit hath said this much unto me,
. . . .

*And behold, he shall be born of Mary, at Jerusalem
which is the land of our forefathers, she being a virgin, a
precious and chosen vessel, who shall be overshadowed and
conceive by the power of the Holy Ghost, and bring forth a
son, yea, even the Son of God.*

*And he shall go forth, suffering pains and afflictions
and temptations of every kind; and this that the word might*

be fulfilled which saith he will take upon him the pains and the sicknesses of his people.

And he will take upon him death, that he may loose the bands of death which bind his people; and he will take upon him their infirmities, that his bowels may be filled with mercy, according to the flesh, that he may know according to the flesh how to succor his people according to their infirmities.

Now the Spirit knoweth all things; nevertheless the Son of God suffereth according to the flesh that he might take upon him the sins of his people, that he might blot out their transgressions according to the power of his deliverance; and now behold, this is the testimony which is in me. (Alma 7:9–13; emphasis added)

Both prophets said their messages were given to them by either an angel or the Spirit, and these two quotes are similar prophecies from the birth to the death of Jesus Christ.

Prophecies Related to the Crucifixion of Jesus Christ

In the Old Testament as Confirmed in the Four Gospels

Multiple variations on the Crucifixion of Jesus Christ were prophesied by Isaiah, the Psalmist, and Zechariah.

> . . . he was numbered with the transgressors; and he bare the sin of many, and made intercession for the transgressors. (Isaiah 53:12; see also Mark 15:28; Luke 22:37)

> I gave my back to the smiters, and my cheeks to them that plucked off the hair: I hid not my face from shame and spitting [and was delivered to be crucified]. (Isaiah 50:6; see also Matthew 27:26)

> My God, my God, why hast thou forsaken me [Eli, Eli, lama sabachthani]? (Psalms 22:1; see also Matthew 27:46; Mark 15:34)

They part my garments among them, and cast lots upon my vesture. (Psalms 22:18; see also Matthew 27:35; John 19:24)

Into thine hand I commit my spirit: thou hast redeemed me, O Lord God of truth [and having said thus, he gave up the ghost]. (Psalms 31:5; see also Luke 23:46)

He keepeth all his bones: not one of them is broken. (Psalms 34:20; see also Exodus 12:46; Numbers 9:12; John 19:36)

They gave me also gall for my meat; and in my thirst they gave me vinegar to drink. (Psalms 69:21; see also Matthew 27:34)

. . . they shall look upon me whom they have pierced. . . . (Zechariah 12:10; see also Psalms 22:16; John 19:37)

. . . What are these wounds in thine hands? Then he shall answer, Those with which I was wounded in the house of my friends [Jesus saith to Thomas, Reach hither thy finger, and behold my hands; and reach hither thy hand, and thrust it into my side]. (Zechariah 13:6; see also John 20:27)

Though Isaiah's prophecies are general, the prophecies by the Psalmist and Zechariah were mostly quoted by Jesus Christ, even as He hung on the cross.

In the Book of Mormon

Throughout the Book of Mormon, there are so many prophecies and/or teachings on Jesus's suffering, death, and Resurrection that it is not practical to list all of them here. Thus, the quotes in this section are selective. In the Book of Mormon, the words *crucifixion* or *crucifying* are not found, but the words *crucify* or *be crucified* appear nine times.

Nephi

... the God of Abraham, and of Isaac, and the God of Jacob, yieldeth himself, according to the words of the angel, as a man, into the hands of wicked men, to be lifted up, according to the words of Zenock, and to be *crucified*, according to the words of Neum, and to be buried in a sepulchre, according to the words of Zenos, which he spake concerning the three days of darkness, which should be a sign given of his death. ...

And as for those who are at Jerusalem, saith the prophet, they shall be scourged by all people, because they *crucify* the God of Israel, and turn their hearts aside, rejecting signs and wonders, and the power and glory of the God of Israel. (1 Nephi 19:10–13, 588–570 BC; emphasis added)

Nevertheless, the Lord has shown unto me that they should return again ... after he should manifest himself they should scourge him and *crucify* him, according to the words of the angel who spake it unto me. (2 Nephi 6:9, 559–545 BC; emphasis added)

Behold, they will *crucify* him; and after he is laid in a sepulchre for the space of three days he shall rise from the dead. ... (2 Nephi 25:13, 559–545 BC; emphasis added)

Jacob

... for in the last night the angel spake unto me that this should be his name—should come among the Jews, among those who are the more wicked part of the world; and they shall *crucify* him—for thus it behooveth our God, and there is none other nation on earth that would *crucify* their God. ...

But because of priestcrafts and iniquities, they at Jerusalem will stiffen their necks against him, that he be *crucified*. (2 Nephi 10:3–5, 559–545 BC; emphasis added)

King Benjamin

> . . . even after all this they shall consider him a man, and say that he hath a devil, and shall scourge him, and shall *crucify* him. (Mosiah 3:9, about 124 BC; emphasis added)

Abinadi

> Yea, even so he shall be led, *crucified*, and slain, the flesh becoming subject even unto death, the will of the Son being swallowed up in the will of the Father. (Mosiah 15:7, about 148 BC; emphasis added)

1 Nephi 19:10 mentions two prophets, Zenos and Zenock, who are not known in the Bible; both prophesied darkness for three days around the time of death of Jesus. In the Book of Mormon, Zenos was mentioned twelve times, and Zenock was mentioned five times. Even though their names are missing in the Bible, they seemed to belong to a group of major prophets in their days, and their records must have been included on the plates of brass. Their prophecies were esteemed as important by the Nephites.

In 6 BC, not long before Jesus's birth, the Lamanite prophet Samuel elaborated this prophecy about the signs and wonders at the time of death of Jesus Christ:

> But behold, as I said unto you concerning another sign, a sign of his death, behold, in that day that he shall suffer death the sun shall be darkened and refuse to give his light unto you; and also the moon and the stars; and there shall be no light upon the face of this land, even from the time that he shall suffer death, for the space of three days, to the time that he shall rise again from the dead.

Yea, at the time that he shall yield up the ghost there shall be thunderings and lightnings for the space of many hours, and the earth shall shake and tremble; and the rocks which are upon the face of this earth, which are both above the earth and beneath, which ye know at this time are solid, or the more part of it is one solid mass, shall be broken up;

Yea, they shall be rent in twain, and shall ever after be found in seams and in cracks, and in broken fragments upon the face of the whole earth, yea, both above the earth and beneath.

And behold, there shall be great tempests, and there shall be many mountains laid low, like unto a valley, and there shall be many places which are now called valleys which shall become mountains, whose height is great.

And many highways shall be broken up, and many cities shall become desolate.

And many graves shall be opened, and shall yield up many of their dead; and many saints shall appear unto many.

And behold, thus hath the angel spoken unto me; for he said unto me that there should be thunderings and lightnings for the space of many hours.

And he said unto me that while the thunder and the lightning lasted, and the tempest, that these things should be, and that darkness should cover the face of the whole earth for the space of three days.

And the angel said unto me that many shall see greater things than these, to the intent that they might believe that these signs and these wonders should come to pass upon all the face of this land, to the intent that there should be no cause for unbelief among the children of men. (Helaman 14:20–28)

Prophecies about these simultaneous natural disasters and darkness during the three days following the death of Jesus Christ were not recorded in the Bible. These prophecies were recorded uniquely in the regions where the Nephites and Lamanites resided.

Prophecies on the Resurrection of Jesus Christ

From the Bible

John wrote, "For as yet they knew not the scripture, that he must rise again from the dead" (John 20:9). However, the word *resurrection* cannot be found in the present Old Testament.[19] This may be a part of the reason why many Jews had a hard time believing in the resurrection of Jesus after His Crucifixion. Even some of the twelve disciples had a difficult time believing it (see John 20:25–27).

From the Book of Mormon

Unlike its absence in the Old Testament, the word resurrection appears seventy-five times in the record of the six hundred years prior to the birth of Jesus Christ in the Book of Mormon. Out of these seventy-five, the word *resurrection* in association with Christ is mentioned thirty-nine times, as shown below in chronological order (thirty-three times in association with the Christ, three times with the Son of God, two times with the Messiah, and one time with the Holy One of Israel):

Lehi, 588–570 BC

> . . . Holy Messiah, who layeth down his life according to the flesh, and taketh it again by the power of the Spirit, that he may bring to pass the resurrection of the dead, being the first that should rise. (2 Nephi 2:8)

Nephi, 559–545 BC

> And after the Messiah shall come there shall be signs given unto my people of his birth, and also of his death and resurrection. . . . (2 Nephi 6:3)

---

[19] Even if the word *resurrection* is not found in the Old Testament, the following two quotes give indirect indications of resurrection:
Isaiah 25:8 (correlated with John 20:9): "He will swallow up death in victory; and the Lord God will wipe away tears from off all faces; and the rebuke of his people shall he take away from off all the earth: for the Lord hath spoken it."
Ezekiel 37:12 (correlated with Matthew 27:52): "Therefore prophesy and say unto them, Thus saith the Lord God; Behold, O my people, I will open your graves, and cause you to come up out of your graves, and bring you into the land of Israel."

Jacob, 559–545 BC

. . . wherefore, death and hell must deliver up their dead, and hell must deliver up its captive spirits, and the grave must deliver up its captive bodies, and the bodies and the spirits of men will be restored one to the other; and it is by the power of the resurrection of the Holy One of Israel. (2 Nephi 9:12)

Jacob, 544–421 BC

. . . ye may obtain a resurrection, according to the power of the resurrection which is in Christ, and be presented as the first-fruits of Christ unto God, having faith, and obtained a good hope of glory in him before he manifesteth himself in the flesh. (Jacob 4:11)

. . . that the power of the redemption and the resurrection, which is in Christ. . . . (Jacob 6:9)

Abinadi, about 148 BC

And there cometh a resurrection, even a first resurrection; yea, even a resurrection of those that have been, and who are, and who shall be, even until the resurrection of Christ—for so shall he be called. (Mosiah 15:21).

But there is a resurrection, therefore the grave hath no victory, and the sting of death is swallowed up in Christ. (Mosiah 16:8)

Alma, about 147 BC

. . . concerning the resurrection of the dead, and the redemption of the people, which was to be brought to pass through the power, and sufferings, and death of Christ, and his resurrection and ascension into heaven. (Mosiah 18:2)

Alma the Younger

... he shall rise again from the dead, which shall bring to pass the resurrection. ... (Alma 33:22, about 74 BC)

... being filled with great joy because of the resurrection of the dead, according to the will and power and deliverance of Jesus Christ from the bands of death. (Alma 4:14, 84 BC)

Holding forth things which must shortly come; yea, holding forth the coming of the Son of God, his sufferings and death, and also the resurrection of the dead ...
[T]hey were taught that he would appear unto them after his resurrection. ... (Alma 16:19–20, about 78 BC)

... for their hope and views of Christ and the resurrection; therefore, death was swallowed up to them by the victory of Christ over it. (Alma 27:28, between 90 and 77 BC)

... he shall rise again from the dead, which shall bring to pass the resurrection ... (Alma 33:22, about 74 BC).

... that this mortal does not put on immortality, this corruption does not put on incorruption—until after the coming of Christ ... he bringeth to pass the resurrection of the dead. ... (Alma 40:2–3, about 73 BC)
... there is a first resurrection, a resurrection of all those who have been, or who are, or who shall be, down to the resurrection of Christ from the dead. (Alma 40:16, about 73 BC)

... it is requisite and just, according to the power and resurrection of Christ, that the soul of man should be restored to its body, and that every part of the body should be restored to itself. ... (Alma 41:2, about 73 BC)

Aaron, between 90 and 77 BC

> Now Aaron began to open the scriptures unto them concerning the coming of Christ, and also concerning the resurrection of the dead. . . . (Alma 21:9)

Samuel the Lamanite, about 6 BC

> But behold, the resurrection of Christ redeemeth mankind, yea, even all mankind, and bringeth them back into the presence of the Lord. (Helaman 14:17)

Mormon's narration,[20] *AD 29–30*

> . . . testifying unto them concerning the redemption which the Lord would make for his people, or in other words, the resurrection of Christ; and they did testify boldly of his death and sufferings. (3 Nephi 6:20)

Unlike the Jewish prophets in the Bible, many prophets in the Book of Mormon taught the Resurrection repeatedly, and the Nephites believed the Resurrection throughout their history.

An angel showed Nephi a panoramic view of the life of Jesus Christ from before His birth to after His death, and this could be a good summary of many prophecies of Jesus Christ in the Book of Mormon:

> And it came to pass that I looked and beheld the great city of Jerusalem, and also other cities. And I beheld the city of Nazareth; and in the city of Nazareth I beheld a virgin, and she was exceedingly fair and white.
>
> And it came to pass that I saw the heavens open; and an angel came down and stood before me; and he said unto me: Nephi, what beholdest thou?

---

[20] Because the resurrected Jesus did not come to the Nephites until about AD 34, Mormon's narration on 3 Nephi 6:20 (around AD 29–30) is included here even though it was made after the birth of Jesus Christ.

And I said unto him: A virgin, most beautiful and fair above all other virgins.

And he said unto me: Knowest thou the condescension of God?

And I said unto him: I know that he loveth his children; nevertheless, I do not know the meaning of all things.

And he said unto me: Behold, the virgin whom thou seest is the mother of the Son of God, after the manner of the flesh.

And it came to pass that I beheld that she was carried away in the Spirit; and after she had been carried away in the Spirit for the space of a time the angel spake unto me, saying: Look!

And I looked and beheld the virgin again, bearing a child in her arms.

And the angel said unto me: Behold the Lamb of God, yea, even the Son of the Eternal Father! . . .

And I looked, and I beheld the Son of God going forth among the children of men; and I saw many fall down at his feet and worship him. . . .

And I looked and beheld the Redeemer of the world, of whom my father had spoken; and I also beheld the prophet who should prepare the way before him. And the Lamb of God went forth and was baptized of him; and after he was baptized, I beheld the heavens open, and the Holy Ghost come down out of heaven and abide upon him in the form of a dove.

And I beheld that he went forth ministering unto the people, in power and great glory; and the multitudes were gathered together to hear him; and I beheld that they cast him out from among them.

And I also beheld twelve others following him. And it came to pass that they were carried away in the Spirit from before my face, and I saw them not.

And it came to pass that the angel spake unto me again, saying: Look! And I looked, and I beheld the heavens open again, and I saw angels descending upon the children of men; and they did minister unto them.

And he spake unto me again, saying: Look! And I looked, and I beheld the Lamb of God going forth among the children of men. And I beheld multitudes of people who were sick, and who were afflicted with all manner of diseases, and with devils and unclean spirits; and the angel spake and showed all these things unto me. And they were healed by the power of the Lamb of God; and the devils and the unclean spirits were cast out.

And it came to pass that the angel spake unto me again, saying: Look! And I looked and beheld the Lamb of God, that he was taken by the people; yea, the Son of the everlasting God was judged of the world; and I saw and bear record.

And I, Nephi, saw that he was lifted up upon the cross and slain for the sins of the world.

And after he was slain I saw the multitudes of the earth, that they were gathered together to fight against the apostles of the Lamb; for thus were the twelve called by the angel of the Lord. (1 Nephi 11:13-34, between 600 and 592 BC)

In general, prophecies about the resurrection of Jesus Christ made before the birth of Christ are plainer and more specific in the Book of Mormon than those in the Bible. While the Book of Mormon has more prophecies on the Resurrection and Atonement of Jesus Christ, the Old Testament has more prophecies on the ministering life of Jesus Christ. Thus, the Nephites had been anticipating the coming of Jesus with much more clarity regarding His Atonement than the Jews. When the resurrected Jesus came to visit the Nephites, they were the righteous ones who survived tremendous natural disasters, and they readily accepted Him as the Messiah and the Son of God.

Chapter 2

The Ministry of Jesus Christ:
Working with Deity

> BEHOLD, I AM JESUS CHRIST the Son of God. I cre-
> ated the heavens and the earth, and all things that in
> them are. I was with the Father from the beginning. I am
> in the Father, and the Father in me; and in me hath the
> Father glorified his name.
>
> I came unto my own, and my own received me not.
> And the scriptures concerning my coming are fulfilled.
>
> And as many as have received me, to them have I
> given to become the sons of God; and even so will I to
> as many as shall believe on my name, for behold, by
> me redemption cometh, and in me is the law of Moses
> fulfilled.
>
> I am the light and the life of the world. I am Al-
> pha and Omega, the beginning and the end. (3 Nephi
> 9:15–18)

When Jesus Christ began His ministry to both the tribe of Judah
and the tribe of Joseph, the circumstances of the Jewish people (tribe of
Judah) were quite opposite from those of the Nephites (tribe of Joseph).

When Jesus was born, the Jews were able to keep the law of Moses and
traditional temple ceremonies even under Roman rule; His family kept
the law of Moses, as was demonstrated by Jesus being circumcised and
Mary undergoing a purification process (see Luke 2:21–22). However,
only a handful of chosen people were privileged to recognize Jesus as the
Son of God at His birth; some of those included Mary, Joseph, Elizabeth,
Simeon, Anna, a few wise men, and an unknown number of shepherds.

When Jesus began His three-year ministry at the age of thirty, His close acquaintances seemed to be caught by surprise that Jesus became a spiritual teacher, and they had a hard time accepting Him in that role; there were a few exceptions, like Mary and John the Baptist (see Luke 4:22; John 6:42). Three years later, the Jewish leadership arranged Jesus's execution for what they considered His blasphemous claim of being the Son of God. This helped Jesus complete His mission, the Atonement for all mankind, that was planned before the foundation of the world (see John 17:24; 1 Peter 1:20).

For the Nephite society in AD 33–34, the death of Jesus was marked by three days of complete darkness accompanied by multiple unprecedented natural disasters that struck simultaneously, wiping out all but about 2,500 of the more righteous people (see 3 Nephi 8). When the disasters ceased, a voice from heaven explained the reason for the calamity (see 3 Nephi 9–10). After the situation calmed down enough for the survivors to gather at the temple grounds in the city of Bountiful, the Father's voice from heaven introduced His Son by saying, "Behold, my Beloved Son, in whom I am well pleased, in whom I have glorified my name—hear ye him" (3 Nephi 11:7). The resurrected Jesus then descended from heaven and identified Himself to the gathered people as the resurrected Jesus Christ (see 3 Nephi 11:10). He let them feel the wounds in His hands and feet that resulted from His Crucifixion. This event began His three-day ministry among the Nephites (see 3 Nephi 11:1–17).

It is clear, then, that the situations of Jesus's ministry to the Jews and the Nephites were significantly different. The tribe of Judah was not prepared to accept Jesus as the Son of God at His birth nor even after His three-year ministry, a time during which He performed many miracles. Contrary to what happened among the Jews, the wicked people among the tribe of Joseph were cleansed, and the righteous ones who survived were ready to meet and worship Jesus from the beginning of His short, three-day visit.

The three-year ministry of Jesus Christ among the Jews was recorded in the four Gospels in the New Testament. While three synopsists (Matthew, Mark, and Luke) narrated the divine ministry of Jesus Christ in chronological order, the Gospel of John focuses more on the divinity of Jesus Christ during His ministry. While Matthew and Luke started their accounts with the birth of Jesus, Mark and John started theirs with His baptism. The prophet Nephi, the eldest son of Nephi, the son of Helaman, recorded the three-day visit of the resurrected Jesus Christ to the remnant of Joseph; because of his account, some call 3 Nephi 11–27 the fifth Gospel. All five of these accounts testify that Jesus is the Christ, the Son of God, the God of Israel, the Messiah, the Redeemer, the God of earth and heaven, and the Savior.

Analyzing the ministry of Jesus Christ, His roles and missions can be categorized into the following seven areas:

1. He fulfilled the law of Moses and accomplished the Atonement to bring to pass the immortality and eternal life of men.
2. He worked with the Father and the Holy Ghost as a member of the Godhead.
3. He organized His Church by calling the twelve Apostles and the Seventies and by giving them priesthood authority.
4. He ministered to the needy by performing countless miracles.
5. He taught His disciples and people the principles of the gospel.
6. He performed sacred priesthood ordinances.
7. He prophesied the short- and long-term future, including the end of the world.

The first two points show Jesus working with Deity; they will be discussed in this chapter. The last five points show Jesus ministering to people; they will be discussed in the next chapter. In both chapters, we will explore His ministry that is recorded in the Bible and the Book of Mormon.[21]

Jesus fulfilled the law of Moses and accomplished the Atonement to bring to pass the immortality and eternal life of men.

Atonement in the Bible

The Jews in the Old Testament kept the ceremony of sacrifice at their temple very faithfully, as a precursor of the infinite Atonement through their Messiah. Yom Kippur is a reminder of how we can atone for our own sins

---

[21] Some writers of both scriptures confessed that they could only write a small portion of their whole situations or stories (see John 20:30; Words of Mormon 1:5; 3 Nephi 5:8, 26:6; Ether 15:33), but that is always the case for writing any history.

through fasting and prayers. In this discussion, however, reference is to the infinite Atonement by the Savior to redeem mankind from Adam's transgression so that all men have an opportunity to meet their God.

Atonement in the Old Testament

The word *atonement* appears eighty-one times in the Old Testament, but only one time in the New Testament. In the Old Testament, seventy-seven of the references to the Atonement are in three books of Moses: Exodus, Leviticus, and Numbers. The sacrificial offerings of the Atonement are categorized as follows (from verses that contain the word *atonement*, some of which contain it twice).

Purpose of Atoning Rituals	Chapters and verses
Sin offering (animal sacrifice) for consecration and sanctification	Exodus 29:33, 36, 37 Leviticus 4:20, 26, 31, 35
Saving from one's own transgression by offering a sacrificial animal (even paying money in some cases)	Exodus 30:10,15,16, 32:30 Leviticus 1:4; 5:6, 10, 13, 16, 18; 6:7; 7:7; 8:34
Cleansing for women after giving a birth to a child	Leviticus 12:7, 8
Cleansing from leprosy	Leviticus 14:18, 19, 20, 21, 29, 31, 53
Cleansing from unclean issues from the skin	Leviticus 15:15, 30
Aaron's sin offering (one sacrifice, one scapegoat)	Leviticus 16:6, 10, 11, 16, 17, 18, 24, 27
Annual sin offering for Atonement (Yom Kippur on the tenth day of the seventh month)	Leviticus 16:29–30, 32, 33, 34; 23:27–28 Numbers 29:5, 11
Sacrificial blood atones for the souls of men	Leviticus 17:11
Forgiveness of a man who married un-freed bond woman	Leviticus 19:22
When there is no one to recompense for one's trespass, recompense to priests	Numbers 5:8

How to atone when a husband and his wife are separated	Numbers 6:11
Atonement for the Levites	Numbers 8:12, 19, 21
Atonement for those who trespass ignorantly	Numbers 15:25, 28
Atonement from plagues among congregations	Numbers 16:46, 47
The Lord atoned for Phinehas (Aaron's grandson)	Numbers 25:11–13
The tenth offering	Numbers 28:22, 30
Oblations of military praise	Numbers 31:50
Referring to the past Atonement practices in the law of Moses	2 Samuel 21:3, 1 Chronicle 6:49; 29:24 Nehemiah 10:33

Based on the above, it is certain that *atonement* in the Old Testament referred to a ransom offering. There were many types of these offerings, such as sin offerings, meat offerings, burnt offerings, peace offerings, and drink offerings (see, for example, Numbers 15, 28; Ezekiel 45). These are a part of the law of Moses and were made by offering sacrificial animals on an altar of the temple (or tabernacle) to seek mostly for forgiveness, for recompense of sins or trespasses, or for healing from diseases.[22]

Atonement in the New Testament

The Atonement is mentioned only once in the New Testament (see Romans 5:11). The Apostle Paul taught that the purpose of the Atonement of Jesus Christ was to effect an infinite reconciliation between God and people by the Son of God. Even if the word *atonement* was used as in the Old Testament, Paul's usage is in reference to the Atonement wrought by Jesus Christ, not the atonement done for forgiveness of sin in the Old Testament.

---

[22] Sacrificed animals are offered for their owners in a vicarious sin-forgiving nature.

The word *atonement* was translated as "reconciliation" in some versions of the Bible. For example, the King James Version, the New Revised Standard Version, and the New International Version of the Bible have Romans 5:11 as follows (compare the bolded words):

The King James Version:
> "And not only so, but we also joy in God through our Lord Jesus Christ, by whom we have now received the **atonement**."

The New Revised Standard Version:
> "But more than that, we even boast in God through our Lord Jesus Christ, through whom we have now received **reconciliation.**"

The New International Version:
> "Not only is this so, but we also boast in God through our Lord Jesus Christ, through whom we have now received **reconciliation.**"

In the Old Testament, multiple verses also contain the word *reconciliation* or *reconciliate* (see Leviticus 6:30; 8:15; 16:20; 1 Samuel 29:4; 2 Chronicles 29:24; Ezekiel 45:15–20; and Daniel 9:24). These verses refer to animal sacrifices and burnt offerings. In the New Testament, the Apostle Paul used the word *reconciled* in Romans 5:10; 11:15; 1 Corinthians 7:11; 2 Corinthians 5:18–20; Ephesians 2:16; Colossians 1:20–21; and Hebrews 2:17. While the other verses are not related to the Atonement of Jesus Christ, Romans 5:10 and 2 Corinthians 5:18–20 directly refer to the Atonement of Jesus Christ as shown in the following verses in 2 Corinthians 5:18–20:

> And all things are of God, who hath reconciled us to himself by Jesus Christ, and hath given to us the ministry of reconciliation;
> To wit, that God was in Christ, reconciling the world unto himself, not imputing their trespasses unto them; and hath committed unto us the word of reconciliation.
> Now then we are ambassadors for Christ, as though God did beseech you by us: we pray you in Christ's stead, be ye reconciled to God.

The Apostle Paul taught that we need to reconcile with God for our individual Atonement through Christ. However, the Atonement of Jesus Christ was not strongly emphasized in the Bible as whole.

Atonement in the Book of Mormon

In the Book of Mormon, the word *atonement* is used twenty-eight times, and the word *atone, atoneth,* or *atoning* appears eleven times. All these refer to the Atonement of Jesus Christ. The infinite Atonement of Jesus Christ was taught extensively throughout the entire thousand-year history of the Nephites, especially by Jacob, King Benjamin, Amulek, and Alma. Interestingly, they were prophets who lived during the Old Testament period.

Following is a summary of the teachings about the Atonement of Christ in the Book of Mormon. These teachings in the Book of Mormon were thoughtfully written in the future tense before Christ's Resurrection and in the past tense after His Resurrection.

Lehi, 588–570 BC
- There is an opposition in all things to answer the ends of the Atonement (see 2 Nephi 2:10–11).

Nephi, 559–545 BC
- The Jews will believe in Jesus Christ and His Atonement when they shall return from their scattering (see 2 Nephi 6:11; 25:16).

Jacob, 559–545 BC
- Except an infinite Atonement be made, this corruption could not put on incorruption, and the dead can rise no more (see 2 Nephi 9:7).
- The Atonement of Jesus Christ satisfies the demands of justice and enables mercy and grace to obtain eternal life for men (see 2 Nephi 9:25–26).
- God raises men from physical death by the power of resurrection and from everlasting death by the power of the Atonement (see 2 Nephi 10:25; see also Jacob 4:11).
- Through the Atonement of Christ, we can receive a perfect knowledge of Him, of a resurrection, and of the world to come (see Jacob 4:12).

- Without the Atonement of Christ, all mankind shall be lost and perish (see Jacob 7:12; see also Alma 34:9).

Abinadi, about 148 BC
- Salvation does not come by the law of Moses alone, but by the Atonement of Christ (see Mosiah 13:28).

King Benjamin, about 124 BC
- The blood of Christ atones for one's own sins and for the transgression of Adam (see Mosiah 3:11; 4:2; see also Alma 24:13).
- The Atonement of Jesus Christ is effective for the dead who died without knowledge of Jesus Christ and who sinned ignorantly (see Mosiah 3:11).
- The law of Moses availed nothing were it not for the atoning blood of Christ (see Mosiah 3:15).
- The Atonement of Jesus Christ atones little children from their sins. Thus, infant baptism denies the mercy, Atonement, and the power of Christ (see Mosiah 3:16; see also Moroni 8:20).
- The natural man is an enemy to God from the fall of Adam, but man can become a saint through the Atonement of Jesus Christ by yielding to the enticing of the Holy Ghost and by becoming like a little child (see Mosiah 3:19).
- The Atonement was prepared from the foundation of the world for the salvation of all mankind since the fall of Adam (see Mosiah 4:6–7).

Aaron, 90–77 BC
- Through the atoning blood, suffering, and death of Jesus Christ, He will atone for the sins of men (see Alma 21:9; 22:14; see also Alma 33:22; Helaman 5:9).

Amulek, about 74 BC
- It is expedient that the Atonement should be made according to the great plan of the eternal God, or else all mankind must unavoidably perish (see Alma 34:9).
- The Atonement must be a great and last sacrifice that must be infinite and eternal, not just a sacrifice of man, beast, or fowl (see Alma 34:10).

- The Atonement of Jesus Christ is an infinite and eternal sacrifice for all mankind (see Alma 34:10, 13).
- Through the Atonement of the Savior, the law of Moses will be fulfilled, every jot and tittle (see Alma 34:13).

Alma, about 73 BC
- A calling of the holy priesthood is to teach the children of men the commandments of Jesus Christ in and through the Atonement of the Only Begotten Son (see Alma 13:5–6).
- The atoning blood of Christ applies to the forgiveness of our sins and the purification of our hearts (see Alma 36:17; see also Mosiah 4:2).
- The plan of mercy could not be brought about except the Atonement should be made (see Alma 42:15).
- The Atonement brings the resurrection of the dead through mercy (see Alma 42:15).
- The Atonement of Jesus Christ brings to pass resurrection, and men will be judged after resurrection according to their works (see Alma 42:23).

Mormon, written by Moroni sometime during AD 400–421
- One will have hope for the Atonement of Christ and the power of His resurrection. (see Moroni 7:41).

The above shows that the Atonement of the Savior was extensively taught and believed among the Nephites in the Book of Mormon; the first prophet, Lehi, taught it around 588–570 BC. At the same time, the Nephites continued to keep the law of Moses until the resurrected Jesus Christ visited them (see 2 Nephi 25:24; Jacob 4:5; Alma 25:15; Helaman 15:5).

The Atonement references in the Book of Mormon were centered on Jesus Christ and His infinite sacrifice prepared from the foundation of the world (in other words, vicariously by Jesus Christ). Thus, the Nephites from the tribe of Joseph were Christians who believed in Christ. The in-depth teaching of the Atonement of Jesus Christ is a part of the plain and precious parts that are missing from the Bible but provided by the Book of Mormon.

Jesus Christ worked with the Father and the Holy Ghost as a member of the Godhead.

Among Judeo-Christians, one of the major disagreements is whether Jesus of the New Testament is Jehovah (YHWH) of the Old Testament. Even to the present day, the Judeo faction (the Jews) denies that this is the case, but most of the Christian faction believes that Jesus was Jehovah. Each side can argue their points quoting different verses in the Bible. In this section, only the four Gospels in the New Testament will be compared with 3 Nephi 9–28 of the Book of Mormon to avoid citing the controversy between the Jews and Christians.

Jesus Christ Communicated with the Father through Prayer

Prayer by Jesus in the Four Gospels of the New Testament

In all four Gospels, it is apparent that Jesus Christ communicated with His Father through prayer. Following are some of those references to some prayers offered in critical or special situations:

<u>Mark, after Jesus healed many people in the early days of His ministry</u>

> And in the morning, rising up a great while before day, he went out, and departed into a solitary place, and *there prayed*. (Mark 1:35; emphasis added)

<u>Luke, after Jesus called Peter, Andrew, John, and James the first time</u>

> And he withdrew himself into the wilderness, and *prayed*. (Luke 5:16; emphasis added)

<u>Matthew, after Jesus fed five thousand with five loaves of bread</u>

> And when he had sent the multitudes away, he went up into a mountain *apart to pray*: and when the evening was come, he was there alone. (Matthew 14:23; emphasis added; see also Mark 6:46)

Luke, before Jesus organized the Quorum of the Twelve Apostles

> And it came to pass in those days, that *he went out into a mountain to pray, and continued all night in prayer to God*. (Luke 6:12; emphasis added)

Luke, before Jesus asked His disciples, "Whom say the people that I am?"

> And it came to pass, as *he was alone praying*, his disciples were with him: and he asked them, saying, Whom say the people that I am? (Luke 9:18; emphasis added)

Luke, referring to the Transfiguration

> And it came to pass about an eight days after these sayings, he took Peter and John and James, and went up into a mountain to pray.
> And *as he prayed*, the fashion of his countenance was altered, and his raiment was white and glistering.
> And, behold, there talked with him two men, which were Moses and Elias:
> Who appeared in glory, and spake of his decease which he should accomplish at Jerusalem. (Luke 9:28–31; emphasis added; see also Matthew 17:1–13; Mark 9:2–13)

Matthew, Mark, and Luke, referring to the intercessory prayer at Gethsemane

> *Abba, Father, all things are possible unto thee; take away this cup from me: nevertheless, not what I will, but what thou wilt.* (Mark 14:36; emphasis added; see also Matthew 26:39)

> And being in an agony *he prayed more earnestly*: and his sweat was as it were great drops of blood falling down to the ground. (Luke 22:44,[23] emphasis added)

---

[23] It is interesting that Luke 22:44 is missing in the earlier versions of the Greek text of the New Testament, but can be found in later versions. However, King Benjamin

Luke also reported that an angel came from heaven to strengthen Him. John recorded the entire prayer that is known as the intercessory prayer (see John 17).

Luke, referring to Jesus on the cross

Then said Jesus, F*ather, forgive them; for they know not what they do.* And they parted his raiment, and cast lots. (Luke 23:34; emphasis added)

Matthew, referring to Jesus in agony on the cross

And about the ninth hour *Jesus cried with a loud voice, saying, Eli, Eli, lama sabachthani? that is to say, My God, my God, why hast thou forsaken me?* (Matthew 26:46; emphasis added; see also Mark 15:34)

Luke, referring to the last words of Jesus recorded in His earthly mortality

And when Jesus had cried with a loud voice, *he said, Father, into thy hands I commend my spirit:* and having said thus, he gave up the ghost. (Luke 23:46; emphasis added)

The above scriptures describe ten special occasions when Jesus prayed or cried to His Father, even for a whole night on one occasion. Even if other prayers were not recorded in the Bible, it is likely that Jesus prayed to the Father much more during His lifetime.

Prayer by Jesus in the Book of Mormon: 3 Nephi 9–28
The resurrected Jesus also prayed often to His Father during His three-day visit to the Nephites (see, for example, 3 Nephi 17:15, 21;

---

used a similar description of the agony Jesus Christ suffered in His prayer, saying that Jesus would shed blood as if it were sweat during His intercessory prayer (see Luke 22:44; Mosiah 3:7). As such, the Book of Mormon confirms the validity of Luke's statement in the New Testament.

18:18, 19, 24; 19:31). Two unique records relate that His prayers were too marvelous to be recorded:

3 Nephi 17:14–18 (emphasis added)

And it came to pass that when they had knelt upon the ground, Jesus groaned within himself, and said: Father, I am troubled because of the wickedness of the people of the house of Israel.

And when he had said these words, he himself also knelt upon the earth; and behold he prayed unto the Father, and the things which he prayed cannot be written, and the multitude did bear record who heard him.

And after this manner do they bear record: The eye hath never seen, neither hath the ear heard, before, so great and marvelous things as we saw and heard Jesus speak unto the Father;

And no tongue can speak, neither can there be written by any man, neither can the hearts of men conceive so great and marvelous things as we both saw and heard Jesus speak; and no one can conceive of the joy which filled our souls at the time we heard him pray for us unto the Father.

And it came to pass that when Jesus had made an end of praying unto the Father, he arose; but so great was the joy of the multitude that they were overcome.

3 Nephi 19:27–34 (emphasis added)

And he turned from them again, and went a little way off and bowed himself to the earth; and he prayed again unto the Father, saying:

Father, I thank thee that thou hast purified those whom I have chosen, because of their faith, and I pray for them, and also for them who shall believe on their words, that they may be purified in me, through faith on their words, even as they are purified in me.

Father, I pray not for the world, but for those whom thou hast given me out of the world, because of their faith, that they may be purified in me, that I may be in them as thou, Father, art in me, that we may be one, that I may be glorified in them.

And when Jesus had spoken these words he came again unto his disciples; and behold they did pray steadfastly, without ceasing, unto him; and he did smile upon them again; and behold they were white, even as Jesus.

And it came to pass that he went again a little way off and prayed unto the Father;

And tongue cannot speak the words which he prayed, neither can be written by man the words which he prayed.

And the multitude did hear and do bear record; and their hearts were open and they did understand in their hearts the words which he prayed.

Nevertheless, so great and marvelous were the words which he prayed that they cannot be written, neither can they be uttered by man.

In the instance reported in 3 Nephi 17, Jesus seemed to be overcome by the contrast between the righteous, innocent Nephite children who surrounded Him at Bountiful and the wicked Jewish leaders in Jerusalem who crucified Him. In the instance reported in 3 Nephi 19, Jesus started to pray for the newly chosen disciples, a situation much like the intercessory prayer for His disciples in John 17. In both cases, the prophet Nephi could not write what happened when Jesus prayed because it was too sacred and marvelous to describe. These reactions to Jesus's prayers do not occur in the four Gospels of the New Testament.[24]

The resurrected Jesus Christ also taught the Nephites to pray to the Father specifically in His name:

3 Nephi 18:19–23 (emphasis added)

Therefore ye must always pray unto the Father in my name; . . . *Pray in your families unto the Father, always in my name,* that your wives and your children may be

---

[24] However, John 20:30 and 21:25 indicate that many of the signs and things Jesus showed His disciples were not written.

blessed . . . ye shall *pray for them unto the Father, in my name. . . .*

3 Nephi 20:31 (emphasis added)

And they shall believe in me, that I am Jesus Christ, the Son of God, and shall *pray unto the Father in my name.*

People Heard the Father's Voice

Hearing the Father's Voice in the Four Gospels of the New Testament
The Gospels record three occasions when people heard the Father's voice from heaven. This indicates that there was two-way communication between the Father and the Son.

Matthew, after Jesus's baptism

And lo a voice from heaven, saying, *This is my beloved Son, in whom I am well pleased.* (Matthew 3:17; emphasis added; see also Mark 1:11; Luke 3:22)

Luke, referring to the Transfiguration

While he thus spake, there came a cloud, and overshadowed them: and they feared as they entered into the cloud.
And there came a voice out of the cloud, saying, *This is my beloved Son: hear him.* (Luke 9:34–35; emphasis added; see also Matthew 17:5; Mark 9:7)

John, as Jesus was preparing to celebrate His last Passover

Father, glorify thy name. Then came there a voice from heaven, *saying, I have both glorified it, and will glorify it again.*
The people therefore, that stood by, and heard it, said that it thundered: others said, An angel spake to him.

Jesus answered and said, This voice came not because of me, but for your sakes. (John 12:28–30; emphasis added)

Based on the above scriptures, Jesus Christ communicated with His
Father through prayer (assisted by angels in some cases). The Father also
communicated with Jesus and allowed others to hear His confirmation
of Jesus Christ as His beloved Son.

Hearing the Father's Voice in the Book of Mormon (3 Nephi 9–28)
In the Book of Mormon, one occasion was recorded when people
heard a voice from the Father right before Jesus descended:

And it came to pass that while they were thus con-
versing one with another, they heard a voice as if it came
out of heaven; . . .
*Behold my Beloved Son, in whom I am well pleased, in
whom I have glorified my name—hear ye him.*
And it came to pass, as they understood they cast
their eyes up again towards heaven; and behold, they saw
a Man descending out of heaven; and he was clothed in a
white robe; and he came down and stood in the midst of
them; and the eyes of the whole multitude were turned
upon him, and they durst not open their mouths, even
one to another, and wist not what it meant, for they
thought it was an angel that had appeared unto them. (3
Nephi 11:3–8; emphasis added)

Thus, the Nephite people heard a voice from heaven that introduced
Jesus, and they were able to witness His descent from heaven.

Jesus Works under the Father
Jesus used terms like "the Father sent me" in the Gospel of John. In
addition to "the Father sent me," the resurrected Jesus Christ used terms
like, "I must go to the Father" and "the Father commanded me" in 3
Nephi.

Jesus Working under the Father in the Four Gospels of the New Testament

Among the four Gospels, the Gospel of John is the only book that records Jesus saying more than a dozen times that He was sent by the Father.

John 5:30–38 (emphasis added)

> ... I seek not mine own will, but the *will of the Father which hath sent me*. ...
>
> But I have greater witness than that of John: for the works which the Father hath given me to finish, the same works that I do, bear witness of me, *that the Father hath sent me*.
>
> And the Father himself, *which hath sent me*, hath borne witness of me. ...
>
> And ye have not his word abiding in you: for *whom he hath sent*, him ye believe not.

John 6:39–57 (emphasis added)

> And this is *the Father's will which hath sent me*, that of all which he hath given me I should lose nothing, but should raise it up again at the last day. And this is *the will of him that sent me*, that every one which seeth the Son, and believeth on him, may have everlasting life: and I will raise him up at the last day. ...
>
> No man can come to me, except *the Father which hath sent me* draw him: and I will raise him up at the last day. ...
>
> *As the living Father hath sent me*, and I live by the Father: so he that eateth me, even he shall live by me.

John 8:16–42 (emphasis added)

> ... for I am not alone, but I and *the Father that sent me*. ...
>
> I am one that bear witness of myself, and *the Father that sent me* beareth witness of me. ...

Jesus said unto them, If God were your Father, ye would love me: for I proceeded forth and came from God; neither came I of myself, *but he sent me.*

John 14:24 (emphasis added)

He that loveth me not keepeth not my sayings: and the word which ye hear is not mine, but *the Father's which sent me.*

John 17:25 (emphasis added)

O righteous Father, the world hath not known thee: but I have known thee, and these have known that *thou hast sent me.*

John 20:21 (emphasis added)

Then said Jesus to them again, Peace be unto you: *as my Father hath sent me,* even so send I you.

According to the above teachings, Jesus Christ Himself made clear that He was sent by the Father and was carrying out the Father's will.

Jesus Working under the Father in the Book of Mormon (3 Nephi 9–28)
Jesus used phrases like "I go unto the Father" and "I must go unto the Father," as shown below.

3 Nephi 17:4 (emphasis added)

But *now I go unto the Father*, and also to show myself unto the lost tribes of Israel, for they are not lost unto the Father, for he knoweth whither he hath taken them.

3 Nephi 18:27 (emphasis added)

Behold verily, verily, I say unto you, I give unto you another commandment, and *then I must go unto my Father that I may fulfil other commandments which he hath given me.*

3 Nephi 27:28 (emphasis added)

> *And now I go unto the Father.* And verily I say unto
> you, whatsoever things ye shall ask the Father in my name
> shall be given unto you.

During His three-day visit to the Nephites, Jesus went back to His
Father three times, as indicated in the scriptures above. He basically
commuted from heaven to the city of Bountiful for three days. This is a
privilege He had as a resurrected being at the time when He visited the
Nephites.

Another point that the resurrected Jesus emphasized to the Nephites
is that He works under the command of His Father; He frequently said
to the Nephites, "the Father commanded me," as shown below.

3 Nephi 15:15–19 (emphasis added)

> Neither at any time hath *the Father given me com-*
> *mandment* that I should tell unto them concerning the
> other tribes of the house of Israel, whom the Father hath
> led away out of the land.
> This much did *the Father command me*, that I should
> tell unto them:
> . . . therefore *I was commanded to say no more of the*
> *Father concerning this thing unto them.*
> But, verily, I say unto you that *the Father hath com-*
> *manded me*, and I tell it unto you, that ye were separated
> from among them because of their iniquity; therefore it
> is because of their iniquity that they know not of you.

3 Nephi 16:3 (emphasis added)

> But *I have received a commandment of the Father* that I shall
> go unto them, and that they shall hear my voice, and shall be
> numbered among my sheep, that there may be one fold and
> one shepherd; therefore I go to show myself unto them.

3 Nephi 16:10 (emphasis added)

And *thus commandeth the Father that I should say unto you:* . . . and if they shall do all those things, and shall reject the fulness of my gospel, behold, saith the Father, I will bring the fulness of my gospel from among them.

3 Nephi 17:2 (emphasis added)

I perceive that ye are weak, that ye cannot understand all my words which *I am commanded of the Father to speak unto you at this time.*

3 Nephi 18:14 (emphasis added)

Therefore blessed are ye if ye shall keep my commandments, which the *Father hath commanded me that I should give unto you.*

3 Nephi 20:10 (emphasis added)

And it came to pass that when they had all given glory unto Jesus, he said unto them: Behold now *I finish the commandment which the Father hath commanded me concerning this people,* who are a remnant of the house of Israel.

3 Nephi 20:14 (emphasis added)

And the Father hath commanded me that I should give unto you this land, for your inheritance.

3 Nephi 20:46 (emphasis added)

Verily, verily, I say unto you, all these things shall surely come, *even as the Father hath commanded me* . . . and then shall Jerusalem be inhabited again with my people, and it shall be the land of their inheritance.

3 Nephi 26:2 (emphasis added)

> And he saith: These scriptures [Malachi 3 and 4], which ye had not with you, *the Father commanded that I should give unto you*; for it was wisdom in him that they should be given unto future generations.

3 Nephi 27:13–14 (emphasis added)

> . . . that I came into the world to do the will of my Father, *because my Father sent me.*
> And *my Father sent me that I might be lifted up upon the cross.* . . .

In the Gospel of John, Jesus taught His disciples and the Jews that He was sent by the Father. In the Book of Mormon, He taught the Nephites that not only was He sent by the Father, but also that He was commanded to teach them multiple doctrinal points. Thus, Jesus made it plainly known that He worked under the direction of His Father.

Jesus made His subordinate relationship with His Father clearer in the Book of Mormon than in the Bible. If the Book of Mormon had been available in the early centuries of Christianity, it could have been another witness of the true theology of the Godhead and could have helped avoid much confusion about the Trinitarian doctrine.

Jesus Christ and the Holy Ghost

The Holy Ghost was not taught in the Old Testament, but Jesus Christ taught of the Holy Ghost in conjunction with the Father and the Son.

Jesus Christ and the Holy Ghost in the Four Gospels of the New Testament

The Holy Ghost is mentioned ninety times in the New Testament (forty-three times in the book of Acts alone). He is mentioned twenty-five times in the four Gospels in the following six categories or on the following occasions.

Around the time of the birth of Jesus

The Holy Ghost played an important role in the conception and birth of Jesus Christ (see Matthew 1:18–20; Luke 1:15, 35, 41) as well as in the birth of John the Baptist (see Luke 1:67). The Holy Ghost also confirmed to Simeon on the temple grounds that the baby he met was the long-awaited Messiah (see Luke 2:25–26).

At the baptism of Jesus Christ

The Holy Ghost joined with the Father when John the Baptist baptized Jesus (see Matthew 3:11; Mark 1:18; Luke 3:16, 22; John 1:33).

After Jesus's forty-day fast

Luke recorded that Jesus started His ministry filled with the Holy Ghost (see Luke 4:1).

Jesus taught the following about the Holy Ghost

- Blasphemy against the Holy Ghost cannot be forgiven (see Matthew 12:31–32; Mark 3:29; Luke 12:10).
- The Holy Ghost was not given before Jesus was glorified (see John 7:39).
- The Holy Ghost teaches what to say in the same hour it is needed, and it is the Holy Ghost who speaks (see Matthew 10:19; Mark 13:11; Luke 12:12).

The Holy Ghost is the Comforter

Jesus taught His disciples that the Holy Ghost was the Comforter, and Jesus promised His disciples that He would send the Comforter from the Father when He was gone from them (see John 14:16, 26; 15:26; 16:7).

Before Jesus's ascension

Jesus gave the Holy Ghost to His disciples before He ascended to heaven (see John 20:22).[25]

The last commandment Jesus gave His disciples was to go and teach all nations, baptizing them in the name of the Father, and of the Son, and of the Holy Ghost (see Matthew 28:19).

---

[25] Interestingly, it seems that Thomas was missing on this occasion.

The examples above provide ample evidence that Jesus and the Holy Ghost have close ties and that they worked together. After Jesus Christ's ascension, many manifestations of the Holy Ghost are shown in the Acts of the Apostles, starting with the Pentecost under the leadership of the Apostle Peter (see Acts 2).

Jesus Christ and the Holy Ghost in the Book of Mormon (3 Nephi 9–28)

In the Book of Mormon, *Holy Ghost* appears ninety-four times: forty-one times before Jesus's visit to the Nephites in Bountiful and twenty-six times during his visit in 3 Nephi 11–28. This shows that the Nephites were well taught about the Holy Ghost even before the resurrected Jesus came to visit them, and the Holy Ghost was mentioned frequently during the three-day visit by the resurrected Jesus Christ.

The resurrected Jesus mainly taught the Nephites about the Holy Ghost with the following five points:

Bearing witness together

Jesus taught that the Holy Ghost bears record of the Father and the Son (Jesus), and all three are one in this (see 3 Nephi 11:32–36; 28:11).

An ordinance for remission of sin

Jesus taught of the baptism by the Holy Ghost for the remission of sins (see 3 Nephi 12:1–2).

Power to give the Holy Ghost

Jesus gave the disciples the power to give the Holy Ghost (see 3 Nephi 18:37).

A gift from the Father

Jesus thanked the Father for giving the Holy Ghost to the disciples (see 3 Nephi 19:9–22).

Manifestation to the Gentiles

Jesus would not manifest Himself to the Gentiles except through the Holy Ghost (see 3 Nephi 15:23; 16:4; 20:27; 21:2).

The resurrected Jesus taught the Nephites the doctrines of baptism by the Holy Ghost for remission of sins. Jesus gave the Holy Ghost and also gave the power to give the Holy Ghost. Even though Jesus gave the Holy Ghost, the Holy Ghost is from the Father. One unique message that Jesus taught the Nephites is that He would not manifest himself to the Gentiles personally, but only through the Holy Ghost.[26]

Comparing the relationships and dealings of Jesus Christ with the Father and the Holy Ghost in both the Bible and the Book of Mormon, it is clear that the Book of Mormon provides new teachings and/or clarification of divine messages found in the Bible. The infinite Atonement of Jesus Christ was taught in much greater detail in the twenty-five accounts in the Book of Mormon, and Jesus clarified His subordinate relationship to the Father. The Book of Mormon confirms the fulfillment of the law of Moses in Jesus Christ.

---

[26] This literally happened in Israel to Peter and Paul: "While Peter yet spake these words, the Holy Ghost fell on all them which heard the word. And they of the circumcision which believed were astonished, as many as came with Peter, because that on the Gentiles also was poured out the gift of the Holy Ghost" (Acts 10:44-45).

"That I should be the minister of Jesus Christ to the Gentiles, ministering the gospel of God, that the offering up of the Gentiles might be acceptable, being sanctified by the Holy Ghost" (Romans 15:16).

Chapter 3

The Ministry of Jesus Christ

AND YE SHALL OFFER UP unto me no more the shedding of blood; yea, your sacrifices and your burnt offerings shall be done away, for I will accept none of your sacrifices and your burnt offerings.

And ye shall offer for a sacrifice unto me a broken heart and a contrite spirit. And whoso cometh unto me with a broken heart and a contrite spirit, him will I baptize with fire and with the Holy Ghost, even as the Lamanites, because of their faith in me at the time of their conversion, were baptized with fire and with the Holy Ghost, and they knew it not.

Behold, I have come unto the world to bring redemption unto the world, to save the world from sin.

Therefore, whoso repenteth and cometh unto me as a little child, him will I receive, for of such is the kingdom of God. Behold, for such I have laid down my life, and have taken it up again; therefore repent, and come unto me ye ends of the earth, and be saved. (3 Nephi 9:19–22)

The last chapter focused on Jesus Christ working with the Father and the Holy Ghost as a member of Deity. This chapter will focus on the following five categories relating to Jesus's ministry as it pertains to both the tribes of Judah and Joseph:

1. Jesus organized His Church by calling the twelve Apostles and the Seventies and by giving them priesthood authority.

2. Jesus ministered to the needy by performing countless miracles.
3. Jesus taught His disciples and others the principles of His gospel.
4. Jesus performed sacred priesthood ordinances.
5. Jesus prophesied about the imminent, short-, and long-term future, including the end of the world.

The first four of these five categories have many similarities in what Jesus taught the Jews and what He taught the Nephites, so a review of those will be brief. However, the last category contains major differences between what we read in the Bible and what we find in the Book of Mormon, so Jesus's prophecies about the future will be reviewed in greater detail.

1. Jesus organized His Church by calling the twelve Apostles and the Seventy and by giving them priesthood authority.

Jesus organized His Church in two places: Israel (among the Jews) and Bountiful (among the remnant of Joseph).

Among the Jews in Israel

To organize His Church, Jesus called and ordained twelve Apostles and gave them power (in other words, He gave them priesthood authority). Mark recorded this event as follows:

> And he goeth up into a mountain, and calleth unto him whom he would: and they came unto him.
> And he ordained twelve [called them Apostles], that they should be with him, and that he might send them forth to preach,
> And to have power to heal sicknesses, and to cast out devils. (Mark 3:13–15; see also Matthew 10:1; Luke 6:13)

Luke also recorded that Jesus called the Seventy and charged them to preach His gospel two by two:[27] "After these things the Lord appointed

---

[27] Jesus gave the following instructions to the newly called Seventy (Luke 10:2–11): "Therefore said he unto them, The harvest truly is great, but the labourers are few: pray ye therefore the Lord of the harvest, that he would send forth labourers into his harvest. Go your ways: behold, I send you forth as lambs among wolves. Carry neither purse, nor scrip, nor shoes: and salute no man by the way. And into whatsoever house ye enter, first say, Peace be to this house. And if the son of peace be there,

other seventy also, and sent them two and two before his face into every city and place, whither he himself would come" (Luke 10:1).

It is recorded that Jesus used the term church only once, and that was in Matthew:

> And I say also unto thee, that thou art Peter, and upon this rock I will build *my church*; and the gates of hell shall not prevail against it.
>
> And I will give unto thee *the keys of the kingdom of heaven*: and whatsoever thou shalt bind on earth shall be bound in heaven: and whatsoever thou shalt loose on earth shall be loosed in heaven. (Matthew 16:18–19; emphasis added)[28]

He also told the twelve Apostles that they will judge the tribes of Israel (see Matthew 19:27–30; Mark 10:28–31; Luke 18:28–30), and that the Apostle John would tarry on the earth until Jesus's Second Coming (see Matthew 16:28; Mark 9:1; Luke 9:27).[29]

---

your peace shall rest upon it: if not, it shall turn to you again. And in the same house remain, eating and drinking such things as they give: for the labourer is worthy of his hire. Go not from house to house. And into whatsoever city ye enter, and they receive you, eat such things as are set before you: And heal the sick that are therein, and say unto them, The kingdom of God is come nigh unto you. But into whatsoever city ye enter, and they receive you not, go your ways out into the streets of the same, and say, Even the very dust of your city, which cleaveth on us, we do wipe off against you: notwithstanding be ye sure of this, that the kingdom of God is come nigh unto you."

[28] Mark, Luke, and John did not record the above message between Jesus and Peter that happened at Caesarea Philippi.

[29] John 21:20–23: "Then Peter, turning about, seeth the disciple whom Jesus loved following; which also leaned on his breast at supper, and said, Lord, which is he that betrayeth thee? Peter seeing him saith to Jesus, Lord, and what shall this man do? Jesus saith unto him, If I will that he tarry till I come, what is that to thee? follow thou me. Then went this saying abroad among the brethren, that that disciple should not die: yet Jesus said not unto him, He shall not die; but, If I will that he tarry till I come, what is that to thee?"

Among the Nephites (the Josephites) in Bountiful

As He did among the Jews, Jesus called twelve disciples among the Nephites and gave them priesthood authority as He did among the Jews:

> And it came to pass that when Jesus had spoken these words unto Nephi, and to those who had been called, (now the number of them who had been called, and received power and authority to baptize, was twelve) and behold, he stretched forth his hand unto the multitude, and cried unto them, saying: Blessed are ye if ye shall give heed unto the words of these twelve whom I have chosen from among you to minister unto you, and to be your servants; and unto them I have given power that they may baptize you with water; and after that ye are baptized with water, behold, I will baptize you with fire and with the Holy Ghost; therefore blessed are ye if ye shall believe in me and be baptized, after that ye have seen me and know that I am. (3 Nephi 12:1)

Jesus told them, "And know ye that ye shall be judges of this people, according to the judgment which I shall give unto you, which shall be just. Therefore, what manner of men ought ye to be? Verily I say unto you, even as I am" (3 Nephi 27:27). Jesus permitted three of the twelve disciples to tarry on the earth until His Second Coming as he had allowed the Apostle John to do in Israel (see 3 Nephi 28:4–7).[30]

Jesus also answered a question about the name of His Church by saying:

---

[30] 3 Nephi 28:4–7: "And when he had spoken unto them, he turned himself unto the three, and said unto them: What will ye that I should do unto you, when I am gone unto the Father? And they sorrowed in their hearts, for they durst not speak unto him the thing which they desired. And he said unto them: Behold, I know your thoughts, and ye have desired the thing which John, my beloved, who was with me in my ministry, before that I was lifted up by the Jews, desired of me. Therefore, more blessed are ye, for ye shall never taste of death; but ye shall live to behold all the doings of the Father unto the children of men, even until all things shall be fulfilled according to the will of the Father, when I shall come in my glory with the powers of heaven."

And how be it my church save it be called in my
name? For if a church be called in Moses' name then it
be Moses' church; or if it be called in the name of a man
then it be the church of a man; but if it be called in my
name then it is my church, if it so be that they are built
upon my gospel. (3 Nephi 27:8)

Thus, Jesus Christ organized His Church among both tribes of Israel
by calling the twelve Apostles among the Jews in Israel and the twelve
disciples among the Nephites (Josephites) in the Americas. He also
called the Seventy in Jerusalem. He specifically instructed the Nephites
to include His name in the name of His Church.

2. Jesus ministered to the needy by performing countless miracles.

Jesus performed numerous miracles according to the needs of the
people, and it would be beyond the scope of this text to illustrate all
those miracles as discussed in the four Gospels. What follows is a general
overview of ways in which He ministered to the needy.

Among the Jews in Israel

When two disciples of John the Baptist asked Jesus if He was the
Messiah, Jesus provided a good summary description of His ministering
to the needy:

Now when John had heard in the prison the works
of Christ, he sent two of his disciples,
And said unto him, Art thou he that should come,
or do we look for another?
Jesus answered and said unto them, Go and shew
John again those things which ye do hear and see:
The blind receive their sight, and the lame walk, the
lepers are cleansed, and the deaf hear, the dead are raised
up, and the poor have the gospel preached to them.
(Matthew 11:2–5; see also Luke 7:19–22)

Jesus not only healed physical infirmities but also cast out evil spirits
from the possessed. He frequently expressed His compassion to those

who were in need of help. He ministered to the needy even on the Sabbath day, in spite of the strict Jewish custom of keeping the Sabbath day holy, and His actions brought accusations from Pharisees (see, for example, Luke 14:1–2).

One of the most dramatic miracles Jesus performed was raising Lazarus. He had been dead for a few days, and his body was already decaying and giving off a strong scent when Jesus raised him (see John 11).[31]

Among the Nephites (the Josephites)

While Jesus also ministered to people's needs among the Nephites, circumstances there were quite different from those in Israel: Jesus spent a short three days with a limited number of people on the American continent. In this more personal setting, Jesus asked the people to bring all who were suffering with physical infirmities, and He cured them:

> And it came to pass that after he had ascended into heaven—the second time that he showed himself unto them, and had gone unto the Father, after having healed all their sick, and their lame, and opened the eyes of their blind and unstopped the ears of the deaf, and even had done all manner of cures among them, and raised a man from the dead, and had shown forth his power unto them, and had ascended unto the Father. (3 Nephi 26:15)

3. Jesus taught His disciples and others the principles of His gospel.

This section overviews main points of the gospel taught by Jesus as recorded in the New Testament and the Book of Mormon.

Among the Jews in Israel

As the greatest Teacher, Jesus taught His disciples and others throughout His three-year ministry. While there are many examples, the following major events and/or approaches may be good representations of His teachings:

---

[31] Interestingly, even if this may be the epoch of miracles that Jesus performed, three of the Gospel writers did not mention it.

The Sermon on the Mount (See Matthew 5–7; Luke 6:17–49)

This sermon may be one of the most influential messages to Christians. The nine cases of blessed and other lessons in this sermon were higher and holier than what was contained in the law of Moses for the Jews at the time. The resurrected Jesus retaught the Nephites the same sermon with some variations (see 3 Nephi 12–14). This shows that the messages in this sermon must be very important for all.

Teaching through Parables Using Different Metaphors

Jesus explained His frequent use of parables by quoting Isaiah: "By hearing ye shall hear, and shall not understand; and seeing ye shall see, and shall not perceive" (Matthew 13:14). When Jesus taught, He often used objects from nature (such as flowers and birds), children, shepherds, relationships, and others as the metaphorical objects of His parables.

Teaching by the Scriptures

Jesus often quoted the scriptures in His teaching. For example, when He rejected the devil's three temptations at the conclusion of His forty days of fasting, Jesus quoted passages from Deuteronomy (see Matthew 4:1–11; Mark 1:12–13; Luke 4:1–13). He started out His ministry in a synagogue in his hometown, Nazareth, where He quoted Isaiah 61:1–2. Among others, He often quoted Isaiah and the Psalmist. He confirmed that the scriptures would testify of Him (see John 5:39). These examples show that scripture was a critical part of His teaching.

Teaching/Correcting Jewish Leaders When They Challenged/Accused Him

Any new or revolutionary religious movement inevitably creates conflicts between the new leaders and the established ones. The hostility toward Jesus from contemporary leaders, then, is not surprising; Jesus usually rebutted any opposition He faced from Jewish leadership. At the same time, Jesus taught the Pharisees and Sadducees lessons instead of dwelling on arguments with animosity (see, for example, Matthew 15:1–9; 22:41–46; Luke 7:37–50; 14:1–6).

Cleansing the Temple Ground (See Matthew 21; Mark 11; Luke 19)

Jesus addressed the commercial activities on the temple grounds on two separate occasions: the first time was at the Passover in Jerusalem near the beginning of His ministry; then but He physically drove merchants off the temple grounds during His last visit to Jerusalem. His message was that His Father's house should be a holy place, not a commercial place. Some have expressed the opinion that Jesus's motivation for this physical violence in His last visit to the temple was to provoke members of the Sanhedrin so they might have motive to arrest Him.

The Transfiguration with Moses and Elias (See Matthew 17:1–13; Mark 9:2–13; Luke 9:28–36)[32]

Jesus invited only three of His disciples—Peter, James, and John, who might be considered similar to a First Presidency—to this sacred event. After the Transfiguration, Peter suggested it should be made known publicly by making three tabernacles, but Jesus taught Him that he should keep the sacred experience private (at least until after His resurrection).

Private Discourses to Disciples and Others

According to John, Jesus sometimes taught in private. A couple of good examples include teaching Nicodemus, who came to visit him at night (see John 3:1–21), and teaching a Samaritan woman at Jacob's well (see John 4:5–26). John recorded Jesus's private tutoring to His disciples in detail prior to His intercessory prayer, trial, and Crucifixion (see John 13–16).

Overall, the central message of Jesus's teachings is what He called the greatest commandment: to love God and fellow men (see Matthew 22:34–40; Mark 12:28–31; Luke 10:25–37). He also made it clear that His teachings were not just His but were the doctrines of the Father who sent Him (see John 7:16).

Among the Nephites (the Josephites)

During His three-day visit, the resurrected Jesus taught many lesson to the Nephites using the scriptures, including, among others, a sermon nearly identical to the Sermon on the Mount (see 3 Nephi 12-14), quotes from Isaiah 52 and 54 (see 3 Nephi 20 and 22), and quotes from Malachi 3 and 4 (see 3 Nephi 24 and 25). He even gave a commandment to search the words of Isaiah (see 3 Nephi 23:1). He also taught

---

[32] Even though John was present at the Transfiguration, the Gospel of John does not report it at all.

His gospel multiple times in a short three-day visit (see as examples 3 Nephi 15, 27). Moreover, Jesus emphasized to the Nephites that the law of Moses was already fulfilled in Him; after His resurrection, Jesus also taught this to His disciples as recorded in Luke 24:44. He also taught that the land where the Nephites lived (present-day America) was the inheritance for them, and He even prophesied about the roles of the Gentiles in the latter days.

As a great teacher, Jesus began His ministry teaching His doctrines and divine messages through scriptures, and He often quoted the words of Isaiah and Psalms. He taught that the scriptures testify of Him and His messiahship. While some Jews accepted His messages, many Jews rejected them. However, the Nephites—a significantly smaller group composed primarily of righteous people—were unified in accepting Jesus and His teachings with open hearts and arms.

4. He performed sacred priesthood ordinances.

This section lists the ordinances that Jesus initiated and/or performed:

Among the Jews in Israel
The following priesthood ordinances are recorded in the four Gospels:

1. Jesus began His ministry when He was baptized by John the Baptist. He and His disciples also baptized others (as an example, see John 4:1–2).
2. He called and ordained the Twelve Apostles (see Mark 12:15; John 15:16).
3. Jesus instituted an ordinance of offering bread (signifying His body) and wine (signifying His blood) to His disciples at the Last Supper before His trial and Crucifixion (see Matthew 26:26–29; Mark 14:22–25; Luke 22:15–20).

Among the Nephites (the Josephites)
The following priesthood ordinances are recorded in 3 Nephi:

1. The resurrected Jesus gave the prophet Nephi the authority to baptize and taught how baptisms should be performed (see 3 Nephi 11:22–27). Many baptisms were performed by the twelve disciples Jesus called.

2. Jesus broke and blessed bread and blessed wine, and all partook and were filled. He taught that this practice should be done for those who repented and were baptized—that they should do it in remembrance of Him, and that they should keep His commandments. In turn, He promised they would have His Spirit to be with them (see 3 Nephi 18:1–11).

It is interesting to note the following facts about baptism:

- Jesus Christ began His ministry by being baptized by John the Baptist (see Matthew 3:1–17; Mark 1:9–11; Luke 3:21–22; John 1:32–34).
- Jesus's first command to the prophet Nephi was about the authority to baptize, and He taught exactly how to baptize (see 3 Nephi 11:20–28).
- One of Jesus's last commandments to the Nephites was about baptism; He said by way of commandment, "Repent, all ye ends of the earth, and come unto me and be baptized in my name, that ye may be sanctified by the reception of the Holy Ghost, that ye may stand spotless before me at the last day" (3 Nephi 27:20).
- Jesus's last charge to His Apostles right before His ascension was, "Go ye therefore, and teach all nations, baptizing them in the name of the Father, and of the Son, and of the Holy Ghost" (Matthew 28:19; also see Mark 16:15–16).

If the baptismal ordinance was that important to Jesus, it should be critically important to all mankind.[33]

Jesus introduced three critical priesthood ordinances to both the Jews and the Nephites: baptism, ordination, and the sacramental ordinance.[34] He gave the Nephites more instruction pertaining to the method of baptism and the purpose of the sacrament.

---

[33] Some Christians believe that the baptism ordinance is not essential for their salvation, that doing charitable and faithful Christian deeds and being honest and pure in heart is good enough. However, both scriptures equally show that Jesus taught that the baptism ordinance is essential for salvation.

[34] Judeo-Christians commonly call this Eucharist, Holy Communion, or Communion.

5. Jesus prophesied about the imminent, short-, and long-term future, including the end of the world.

In the discussion that follows, the prophecies of Jesus Christ in the New Testament will be limited to His prophecies regarding His death and resurrection (the imminent future), the destruction of Jerusalem (the short-term future), and the end of the world (the long-term future). They are also limited to what is revealed in Chapter 24 of the Gospel of Matthew. The discussion of His prophecies in the Book of Mormon will be limited to the prophecies given to the Nephites in 3 Nephi 11–28.

Among the Jews in Israel

<u>Jesus's Prophecies of His Death and Resurrection Were the Imminent Ones</u>

Toward the end of Jesus's ministry, the following records by the Gospel writers show a crucial chain of events,[35] and Jesus started prophesying to His disciples of His arrest, Crucifixion, and Resurrection.

When Jesus asked His disciples "Whom say ye that I am?" Peter answered, "Thou art the Christ, the Son of the living God." Subsequently, Jesus said the following to Peter and the other disciples:

> And Jesus answered and said unto him, Blessed art thou, Simon Bar-jona: for flesh and blood hath not revealed it unto thee, but my Father which is in heaven.
>
> And I say also unto thee, That thou art Peter, and upon this rock I will build my church; and the gates of hell shall not prevail against it.
>
> And I will give unto thee the keys of the kingdom of heaven: and whatsoever thou shalt bind on earth shall be bound in heaven: and whatsoever thou shalt loose on earth shall be loosed in heaven.
>
> Then charged he his disciples that they should tell no man that he was Jesus the Christ. (Matthew 16:17–20)

After Jesus gave His head Apostle, Peter, the priesthood keys to bind ordinances on both heaven and earth, Jesus prophesied His imminent

---

[35] Mark (chapter 8) and Luke (chapter 9) also recorded these events, but Matthew is more descriptive.

death and Resurrection for the first time: "From that time forth began Jesus to shew unto his disciples, how that he must go unto Jerusalem, and suffer many things of the elders and chief priests and scribes, and be killed, and be raised again the third day" (Matthew 16:21).

When the Apostle Peter disputed this ominous prophecy with all good intention, loyalty, and love, Jesus was displeased to the degree of rebuking Peter sharply by calling him Satan. This response is even more surprising considering that Jesus had just given Peter the priesthood keys to govern the whole Church:

> Then Peter took him, and began to rebuke him, saying, Be it far from thee, Lord: this shall not be unto thee.
> But he turned, and said unto Peter, Get thee behind me, Satan: thou art an offence unto me: for thou savourest not the things that be of God, but those that be of men. (Matthew 16:22–23)

This teaches that Jesus's death and Resurrection were so critically important to Him that even Peter, who had the authority to bind in heaven and earth, was rebuked for opposing God's will. Following His prophecy, Jesus taught His disciples important lessons:

> Then said Jesus unto his disciples, If any man will come after me, let him deny himself, and take up his cross, and follow me.
> For whosoever will save his life shall lose it: and whosoever will lose his life for my sake shall find it.
> For what is a man profited, if he shall gain the whole world, and lose his own soul? or what shall a man give in exchange for his soul? (Matthew 16:24–26)

After teaching this lesson, Jesus explained or prophesied His role and foretold that some of the disciples would not go through the death process:

> For the Son of man shall come in the glory of his Father with his angels; and then he shall reward every man according to his works.

Verily I say unto you, There be some standing here, which shall not taste of death, till they see the Son of man coming in his kingdom. (Matthew 16:27–28)

About a week later,[36] Peter, James, and John witnessed the Transfiguration of Jesus Christ with Moses and Elias and heard the voice of the Father. Afterward, Jesus told His disciples not to talk about the Transfiguration until His Resurrection:[37]

> And after six days Jesus taketh Peter, James, and John his brother, and bringeth them up into an high mountain apart,
>
> And was transfigured before them: and his face did shine as the sun, and his raiment was white as the light.
>
> And, behold, there appeared unto them Moses and Elias talking with him.
>
> Then answered Peter, and said unto Jesus, Lord, it is good for us to be here: if thou wilt, let us make here three tabernacles; one for thee, and one for Moses, and one for Elias.
>
> While he yet spake, behold, a bright cloud overshadowed them: and behold a voice out of the cloud, which said, This is my beloved Son, in whom I am well pleased; hear ye him.
>
> And when the disciples heard it, they fell on their face, and were sore afraid.
>
> And Jesus came and touched them, and said, Arise, and be not afraid.
>
> And when they had lifted up their eyes, they saw no man, save Jesus only.
>
> And as they came down from the mountain, Jesus charged them, saying, Tell the vision to no man, until the Son of man be risen again from the dead. (Matthew 17:1–9)

---

36 Matthew and Mark said it was six days later, but Luke said it was about eight days later (see Matthew 17:1; Mark 9:2; Luke 9:28).

37 Among the four Gospel writers, John was the only one who was present at the Transfiguration. Interestingly, he did not record anything about the Transfiguration, but all of the other Gospel writers recorded it.

In addition to what Matthew recorded, Luke added the content of discussion between Jesus, Moses, and Elias about Jesus's death that would take place in Jerusalem:

> And, behold, there talked with him two men, which were Moses and Elias:
> Who appeared in glory, and spake of *his decease which he should accomplish at Jerusalem*. (Luke 9:30–31; emphasis added)

After this, Jesus prophesied of His death and Resurrection a second time in Galilee:

> And while they abode in Galilee, Jesus said unto them, The Son of man shall be betrayed into the hands of men:
> And they shall kill him, and the third day he shall be raised again. And they were exceeding sorry. (Matthew 17:22–23)

However, both Mark and Luke recorded that the Apostles did not understand what the prophecy was about, and they were afraid to ask:[38] "For he taught his disciples, and said unto them, The Son of man is delivered into the hands of men, and they shall kill him; and after that he is killed, he shall rise the third day. But they understood not that saying, and were afraid to ask him" (Mark 9:31–32).

On His way to Jerusalem for the last time, Jesus prophesied the same thing for the third time, but this time with more specifics (see Matthew 20:17–19; Mark 10:32–34; Luke 18:31–34). Matthew did not mention it, but both Mark and Luke recorded that the Apostles still did not understand the prophecy. Luke recorded:

> Then he took unto him the twelve, and said unto them, Behold, we go up to Jerusalem, and all things that

---

[38] They may have been afraid to ask because Peter was reprimanded earlier (see also Luke 9:43–45).

are written by the prophets concerning the Son of man shall be accomplished.

For he shall be delivered unto the Gentiles, and shall be mocked, and spitefully entreated, and spitted on:

And they shall scourge him, and put him to death: and the third day he shall rise again.

And they understood none of these things: and this saying was hid from them, neither knew they the things which were spoken. (Luke 18:31–34)

His disciples still did not understand when Jesus mentioned the prophecy again two days before Passover: "Ye know that after two days is *the feast of* the Passover, and the Son of man is betrayed to be crucified" (Matthew 26:2; emphasis added).

When the eleven disciples were told of Jesus's Resurrection after His crucifixion and burial, it was apparent that some of them treated it as an idle tale (see Luke 24:11). They finally believed it when the resurrected Jesus showed Himself to them (see John 20:24–28). With that, all of Jesus's prophecies about His trial, death, and Resurrection were fulfilled.

Jesus's Prophecies in Matthew 24

Matthew 24 is known for its many prophecies, which can be divided into short- and long-term prophecies. After making general comments (see verses 1–8), Jesus prophesied the great destruction of Jerusalem (see verses 9–22) and His Second Coming at the end of the world (see verses 29–51). Based on historical records of what happened in Jerusalem around AD 70, it is plausible to separate the entire chapter into categories of short- and long-term prophecies.[39]

Several short-term prophecies are found in verses 2 and 9–22:

> And Jesus said unto them, See ye not all these things? verily I say unto you, There shall not be left here one stone upon another, that shall not be thrown down. (Matthew 24:2)

---

[39] The Joseph Smith Translation of Matthew 24:4 says, "Tell us when shall these things be which thou hast said concerning the destruction of the temple, and the Jews; and what is the sign of thy coming, and of the end of the world, or the destruction of the wicked, which is the end of the world?" In this verse, the question applies to two situations: the end of the temple and Jesus's Second Coming at the end of the world (or destruction of the wicked).

Then shall they deliver you up to be afflicted, and shall kill you: and ye shall be hated of all nations for my name's sake.

And then shall many be offended, and shall betray one another, and shall hate one another.

And many false prophets shall rise, and shall deceive many.

And because iniquity shall abound, the love of many shall wax cold.

But he that shall endure unto the end, the same shall be saved. . . .

Then let them which be in Judæa flee into the mountains:

Let him which is on the housetop not come down to take any thing out of his house:

Neither let him which is in the field return back to take his clothes.

And woe unto them that are with child, and to them that give suck in those days!

But pray ye that your flight be not in the winter, neither on the sabbath day:

For then shall be great tribulation, such as was not since the beginning of the world to this time, no, nor ever shall be.

And except those days should be shortened, there should no flesh be saved: but for the elect's sake those days shall be shortened. (Matthew 24:9–22)

In addition, Jesus also warned the women who followed Him to Golgotha:

And there followed him a great company of people, and of women, which also bewailed and lamented him.

But Jesus turning unto them said, Daughters of Jerusalem, weep not for me, but weep for yourselves, and for your children.

> For, behold, the days are coming, in the which they shall say, Blessed are the barren, and the wombs that never bare, and the paps which never gave suck.
>
> Then shall they begin to say to the mountains, Fall on us; and to the hills, Cover us. (Luke 23:27–30)

At the trial of Jesus in Pilate's court, the Jews shouted to have the blood of Jesus be upon them and their children; in effect, they asked for the terrible calamity to come upon their posterity:

> When Pilate saw that he could prevail nothing, but that rather a tumult was made, he took water, and washed his hands before the multitude, saying, I am innocent of the blood of this just person: see ye to it.
>
> Then answered all the people, and said, His blood be on us, and on our children. (Matthew 27:24–25)

Fulfillment of Jesus's Prophecies of Destruction of Jerusalem and the Herod Temple (AD 70)

Historians recorded the great slaughter in Jerusalem around AD 70. Josephus in particular recorded the scenes of destruction in Jerusalem and of the temple in detail as shown below:

Wars of the Jews, Book V, Chapter 12:3–4

> So all hope of escaping was now cut off from the Jew, together with their liberty of going out of the city. Then did the famine widen its progress, and devoured the family by whole houses and families; the upper rooms were full of women and children that were dying by famine; and the lanes of the city were full of the dead bodies of the aged; the children also and young men wandered about the market-places like shadows, all swelled with famine, and fell down dead wheresoever their misery seized them. As for burying them, those that were sick themselves were not able to do it; and those that were hearty and well were deterred from doing it by the great multitude of those dead bodies, and by the uncertainty there was how soon they should die

themselves; for many died as they were burying others, and many went to their coffins before that fatal hour was come! Nor was there any lamentation made under these calamities, nor were heard any mournful complaints; for those who were just going to die, looked upon those that were gone to their rest before them with dry eyes and open mouths. A deep silence also, and a kind of deadly nigh, had seized upon the city; while yet the robbers were still more terrible than those miseries were themselves; for they brake upon those houses which were no other than graves of dead bodies, and plundered them of what they had; and carrying off the coverings of their bodies, went out laughing, and tried the points of their sword on their dead bodies; and in order to prove what mettle they were made of, they thrust some of those through that still lay alive upon the ground; for those that entreated them to lend them their right hand, and their sword to dispatch them, they were too proud to grant their request, and left them to be consumed by the famine. Now every one of these died with their eyes fixed upon the temple, and left the seditious alive behind them. Now the sedition at first gave orders that the dead should be buried out of the public treasury, as not enduring the stench of their dead bodies. But afterwards, when they could not do that, they had them cast down from the walls into the valleys beneath. However, when Titus [Roman commander to conquer Jerusalem], in going his rounds along those valleys, saw them full of dead bodies, and the thick putrefaction running about them, he gave a groan; and spreading out his hands to heaven, called God to witness that this was not his dong and such was the sad case of the city itself. . . .

Wars of the Jews, Book V, Chapter 13:4

Yet did another plague seize upon those that were thus preserved; for there was found among the Syrian deserters a certain person who was caught gathering pieces of gold out of the excrements of the Jews' bellies; for the deserters used to swallow such pieces of gold, as we told you before, when they came out; and for these did the seditious search them all; for there was a great quantity of gold in the city, insomuch as much was now sold [in the Roman camp] for twelve Attic [drams] as was sold before for twenty-five. . . . Nor does it seem to me that any misery befell the Jews that was more terrible than this, since in one night about two thousands of these deserters were thus dissected.

Wars of the Jews, Book VI, Chapter 4:5–6
> At which time one of the soldiers, without staying for any orders, and without any concern or dread upon him at so great an undertaking, and being hurried on by a certain divine fury, snatched somewhat out of the materials that were on fire, and being lifted up by another soldier, he set fire to a golden window, through which there was a passage to the rooms that were round about the holy house [temple], on the north side of it. As the flames went upward the Jews made a great clamour, such as so mighty an affliction required, and ran together to prevent it, and now they spared not their lives any longer, nor suffered anything to restrain their force, since that holy house was perishing, for whose sake it was that they kept such a guard about it. . . . As for the seditious, they were in too great distress already to afford their assistance, [toward quenching the fire;] they were everywhere slain, everywhere beaten; and as for a great part of the people, they were weak and without arms, and had their throats cut wherever they were caught. Now, round about the alter lay dead bodies heaped one upon another; as at the steps going up to it ran a great quantity of their blood whither also the dead bodies that were slain above [on the alter] fell down.

Josephus estimated that in the small city of Jerusalem about 1.1 million Jews were killed and approximately 97,000 were carried away captive.[40]

---

[40] Josephus, *Wars of the Jews*, Book VI, Chapter 9:3.

Considering the difference of the world population between then[41] and now, this may be equivalent to tens of millions of lives in the present world. Even Titus, the Roman commander who conquered Jerusalem at the time, claimed this horrible and unprecedented devastation in Jerusalem was not because of his army, but because of curses from God.

Josephus's record shows that Jesus's prophecies of the destruction of Jerusalem and the temple of Herod were literally fulfilled one generation after His crucifixion. This could be the Lord's answer to what the Jews cried for in the court of Pilate during the trial of Jesus Christ, asking that "his blood to be upon us, and on our children" (Matthew 27:25).

Long-term Prophecy: Prophecy for the End of the World

> And this gospel of the kingdom shall be preached in all the world for a witness unto all nations; and then shall the end come. . . . (Matthew 24:14).

> Immediately after the tribulation of those days shall the sun be darkened, and the moon shall not give her light, and the stars shall fall from heaven, and the powers of the heavens shall be shaken:
> And then shall appear the sign of the Son of man in heaven: and then shall all the tribes of the earth mourn, and they shall see the Son of man coming in the clouds of heaven with power and great glory.
> And he shall send his angels with a great sound of a trumpet, and they shall gather together his elect from the four winds, from one end of heaven to the other. . . . (Matthew 24:29–31).

> But of that day and hour knoweth no man, no, not the angels of heaven, but my Father only.
> But as the days of Noe were, so shall also the coming of the Son of man be.

---

[41] Some scholars estimate the total population of the entire world during Jesus's days was around 400 million.

For as in the days that were before the flood they were eating and drinking, marrying and giving in marriage, until the day that Noe entered into the ark,

And knew not until the flood came, and took them all away; so shall also the coming of the Son of man be.

Then shall two be in the field; the one shall be taken, and the other left.

Two women shall be grinding at the mill; the one shall be taken, and the other left.

Watch therefore: for ye know not what hour your Lord doth come.

But know this, that if the goodman of the house had known in what watch the thief would come, he would have watched, and would not have suffered his house to be broken up.

Therefore be ye also ready: for in such an hour as ye think not the Son of man cometh.

Who then is a faithful and wise servant, whom his lord hath made ruler over his household, to give them meat in due season?

Blessed is that servant, whom his lord when he cometh shall find so doing.

Verily I say unto you, That he shall make him ruler over all his goods.

But and if that evil servant shall say in his heart, My lord delayeth his coming;

And shall begin to smite his fellowservants, and to eat and drink with the drunken;

The lord of that servant shall come in a day when he looketh not for him, and in an hour that he is not aware of,

And shall cut him asunder, and appoint him his portion with the hypocrites: there shall be weeping and gnashing of teeth. (Matthew 24:36–51)

Based on the above prophecies and other teachings in the Bible, Christians have been anticipating the Second Coming of Jesus Christ and the end of the world with its final judgment. However, interpreting prophecies about the future is difficult without knowing the exact boundary conditions and assumptions at the time they were given. This point was well evidenced when several Christian churches made calculated predictions on the precise date of the Second Coming of Jesus Christ based primarily on the book of Revelation, Matthew 24, Daniel 7–10, and other scriptures. Some Christian churches—for example, the Methodist, Jehovah's Witness, and Seventh-day Adventist churches, among others—even announced their projections publicly. All of them were wrong.

Jesus taught, "But of that day and that hour knoweth no man, no, not the angels which are in heaven, neither the Son, but the Father" (Mark: 13:32). Thus, we learn that Jesus prophesied what will happen around the time of His Second Coming and the end of the world, but the time when these prophecies will be fulfilled is solely Heavenly Father's decision and is known only by Him.

Among the Nephites (the Josephites)[42]

Referring to the prophecies of Isaiah recorded in 3 Nephi 16:18–20 (see also Isaiah 52:8–10), Jesus said,

> And then the words of the prophet Isaiah shall be fulfilled, which say:
> Thy watchmen shall lift up the voice; with the voice together shall they sing, for they shall see eye to eye when the Lord shall bring again Zion.
> Break forth into joy, sing together, ye waste places of Jerusalem; for the Lord hath comforted his people, he hath redeemed Jerusalem. The Lord hath made bare his holy arm in the eyes of all the nations; and all the ends of the earth shall see the salvation of God.

Jesus continued His prophecy about the gathering of Israelites and the land of America being the inheritance of the Josephites:

---

[42] These prophecies from the Book of Mormon will be discussed in more detail in Chapter 9.

> Ye remember that I spake unto you, and said that when the words of Isaiah should be fulfilled—behold they are written, ye have them before you, therefore search them—
>
> And verily, verily, I say unto you, that when they shall be fulfilled then is the fulfilling of the covenant which the Father hath made unto his people, O house of Israel.
>
> And then shall the remnants, which shall be scattered abroad upon the face of the earth, be gathered in from the east and from the west, and from the south and from the north; and they shall be brought to the knowledge of the Lord their God, who hath redeemed them.
>
> And the Father hath commanded me that I should give unto you this land, for your inheritance. (3 Nephi 20:11–14; see also Isaiah 52:8–10)

Jesus then continued His prophecies warning the Gentiles of what would happen if they do not repent after scattering the Lord's covenanted people:

> And I say unto you, that if the Gentiles do not repent after the blessing which they shall receive, after they have scattered my people—
>
> Then shall ye, who are a remnant of the house of Jacob, go forth among them; and ye shall be in the midst of them who shall be many; and ye shall be among them as a lion among the beasts of the forest, and as a young lion among the flocks of sheep, who, if he goeth through both treadeth down and teareth in pieces, and none can deliver.
>
> Thy hand shall be lifted up upon thine adversaries, and all thine enemies shall be cut off.
>
> And I will gather my people together as a man gathereth his sheaves into the floor.
>
> For I will make my people with whom the Father hath covenanted, yea, I will make thy horn iron, and I

will make thy hoofs brass. And thou shalt beat in pieces many people; and I will consecrate their gain unto the Lord, and their substance unto the Lord of the whole earth. And behold, I am he who doeth it.

And it shall come to pass, saith the Father, that the sword of my justice shall hang over them at that day; and except they repent it shall fall upon them, saith the Father, yea, even upon all the nations of the Gentiles. (3 Nephi 20:15–20; see also Micah 4:13; 5:8–9)

Thus, if the Gentiles do not repent, they will be trodden down by the covenant Israelites. Jesus continued His prophecy about the New Jerusalem for the Josephites:

And it shall come to pass that I will establish my people, O house of Israel.

And behold, this people will I establish in this land, unto the fulfilling of the covenant which I made with your father Jacob; and it shall be a New Jerusalem. And the powers of heaven shall be in the midst of this people; yea, even I will be in the midst of you. (3 Nephi 20:21–22)

Jesus also prophesied, quoting the Father, that the Father will remember the Abrahamic covenant, that He will gather His covenant people in Jerusalem in His own due time, and that the fullness of His gospel will be preached to them:

And I will remember the covenant which I have made with my people; and I have covenanted with them that I would gather them together in mine own due time, that I would give unto them again the land of their fathers for their inheritance, which is the land of Jerusalem, which is the promised land unto them forever, saith the Father.

And it shall come to pass that the time cometh, when the fulness of my gospel shall be preached unto them;

And they shall believe in me, that I am Jesus Christ, the Son of God, and shall pray unto the Father in my name.

Then shall their watchmen lift up their voice, and with the voice together shall they sing; for they shall see eye to eye.

Then will the Father gather them together again, and give unto them Jerusalem for the land of their inheritance.

Then shall they break forth into joy—Sing together, ye waste places of Jerusalem; for the Father hath comforted his people, he hath redeemed Jerusalem.

The Father hath made bare his holy arm in the eyes of all the nations; and all the ends of the earth shall see the salvation of the Father; and the Father and I are one. (3 Nephi 20:29–35)

Jesus prophesied that this will fulfill a prophecy of Isaiah:

And then shall be brought to pass that which is written: Awake, awake again, and put on thy strength, O Zion; put on thy beautiful garments, O Jerusalem, the holy city, for henceforth there shall no more come into thee the uncircumcised and the unclean.

Shake thyself from the dust; arise, sit down, O Jerusalem; loose thyself from the bands of thy neck, O captive daughter of Zion.

For thus saith the Lord: Ye have sold yourselves for naught, and ye shall be redeemed without money. (3 Nephi 20:36–38; see also Isaiah 52:13)

Jesus prophesied that the Gentiles who will repent, be baptized, and know the true doctrine will be numbered among His (covenant) people:

For thus it behooveth the Father that it should come forth from the Gentiles, that he may show forth his power unto the Gentiles, for this cause that the Gentiles, if they will not harden their hearts, that they may repent and come unto me and be baptized in my name and know of the true points of my doctrine, that they may be numbered among my people, O house of Israel. (3 Nephi 21:6)

When the remnant of Joseph comes to know the fullness of the gospel through the Book of Mormon, it is a sign that the Father's latter-day work has already commenced to fulfill His covenant with the house of Israel:

> And when these things come to pass that thy seed shall begin to know these things—it shall be a sign unto them, that they may know that the work of the Father hath already commenced unto the fulfilling of the covenant which he hath made unto the people who are of the house of Israel. (3 Nephi 21:7)

Jesus continued with His prophecy that a man—a latter-day prophet—shall declare the fullness of the gospel among the unbelievers, and the work of the Father will be great and marvelous, as prophesied:

> And when that day shall come, it shall come to pass that kings shall shut their mouths; for that which had not been told them shall they see; and that which they had not heard shall they consider.
>
> For in that day, for my sake shall the Father work a work, which shall be a great and a marvelous work among them; and there shall be among them those who will not believe it, although a man shall declare it unto them. (3 Nephi 21:8–9)

Jesus then quoted the entirety of Isaiah 54, in which Isaiah prophesied of joyful restorations with the following promise:

> No weapon that is formed against thee shall prosper; and every tongue that shall revile against thee in judgment thou shalt condemn. This is the heritage of the servants of

the Lord, and their righteousness is of me, saith the Lord.
(Nephi 22:17).

As a summary, Jesus's prophecies in the Book of Mormon show that
the resurrected Jesus prophesied to the Nephites that the covenant Israelites would be scattered by the Gentiles. If the Gentiles stayed righteous,
they would be a part of the covenant people, the Israelites. If the Gentiles
did not continue in righteousness, they would be destroyed by the covenant Israelites. The Lord promised to gather the scattered Israelites in
the Old Jerusalem and the New Jerusalem and to ensure that the gospel
of Jesus Christ would be preached to them. The land of America was
designated to be an inheritance to the Josephites. When the Josephites
are taught the true gospel of Jesus Christ by a man—in other words, a
prophet in the last dispensation—it will signify that the Father has commenced His marvelous work.

Of the five categories discussed in this chapter, the only one with
substantial differences between the Bible and the Book of Mormon is the
one regarding prophecy. Jesus prophesied to the Jews of His imminent
Crucifixion and Resurrection, the destruction of Jerusalem (including
the temple), and the signs of the end of the world. To the Nephites, he
prophesied the fulfillment of Isaiah 52 and 54 for the Josephites in the
latter days.

Chapter 4

The True Nature of Deity

AND NOW ABINADI SAID UNTO them: I would
that ye should understand that God himself shall
come down among the children of men, and shall
redeem his people.

And because he dwelleth in flesh he shall be called
the Son of God, and having subjected the flesh to the
will of the Father, being the Father and the Son—

The Father, because he was conceived by the
power of God; and the Son, because of the flesh;
thus becoming the Father and Son—

And they are one God, yea, the very Eternal Father of heaven and of earth.

And thus the flesh becoming subject to the
Spirit, or the Son to the Father, being one God,
suffereth temptation, and yieldeth not to the temptation, but suffereth himself to be mocked, and
scourged, and cast out, and disowned by his people.
(Mosiah 15:1–5)

Having a correct understanding of the nature of Deity is a critical
aspect of any religion. If one's view of Deity is not correct, the remaining
religious beliefs have little value. Worshiping a misrepresented nature of
the true God may bring some satisfaction with a pious and honorable life
from the human perspective, but it may not have much value from God's
perspective. This may be an example of what Jesus taught in Matthew
7:21–23 (see also 3 Nephi 14:21–23):

Not every one that saith unto me, Lord, Lord, shall enter into the kingdom of heaven; but he that doeth the will of my Father which is in heaven.

Many will say to me in that day, Lord, Lord, have we not prophesied in thy name? and in thy name have cast out devils? and in thy name done many wonderful works?

And then will I profess unto them, I never knew you: depart from me, ye that work iniquity.[43]

The Trinity and Christianity

During most of Christian history, the Trinity has traditionally been the orthodox view of the Godhead. Its basic theology is that the Father, the Son, and the Holy Ghost are consubstantial, meaning one body. This doctrine has been known to exist from the second century, but it became the official doctrine of the Catholic Church at the councils of Nicaea and Constantinople in the fourth century. Following are the creeds from those councils announcing the Trinitarian doctrine.

The Nicene Creed (AD 325)

I [we] believe in one God, the Father Almighty, the Maker of heaven and earth, and of all things visible and invisible. And in one Lord Jesus Christ, the only-begotten Son of God, born of the Father before all ages; God of God, Light of Light, true God of true God; begotten not made; consubstantial with the Father; by whom all things were made. Who for us, men, and for our salvation, came down from Heaven; and was incarnate of the Holy Ghost, of the Virgin Mary, and was made man. He was also crucified for us; suffered under Pontius Pilate, and was buried. The third day He rose again, according to the Scriptures: and ascended into Heaven, sitteth at the right hand of the Father; thence He shall come again with glory to judge both the living and the dead; of whose kingdom there shall be no end. I [we] believe in the Holy Ghost, the Lord and Giver of life, who proceedeth from the

---

[43] The Joseph Smith Translation of this verse reads: "And then will I say, Ye never knew me; depart from me ye that work iniquity."

Father, and the Son; who together with the Father and the Son is adored and glorified; who spoke by the Prophets. And One, Holy, Catholic, and Apostolic Church. I [we] confess one Baptism for the remission of sins. And I [we] look for the resurrection of the dead, and life of the world to come.

The Constantinople Creed (AD 381)

We believe in one God, the Father Almighty, Maker of heaven and earth, and of all things visible and invisible. And in one Lord Jesus Christ, the only-begotten Son of God, begotten of the Father before all worlds (æons), Light of Light, very God of very God, begotten, not made, being of one substance with the Father; by whom all things were made; who for us men, and for our salvation, came down from heaven, and was incarnate by the Holy Ghost of the Virgin Mary, and was made man; he was crucified for us under Pontius Pilate, and suffered, and was buried, and the third day he rose again, according to the Scriptures, and ascended into heaven, and sitteth on the right hand of the Father; from thence he shall come again, with glory, to judge the quick and the dead. Whose kingdom shall have no end. And in the Holy Ghost, the Lord and Giver of life, who proceedeth from the Father, who with the Father and the Son together is worshiped and glorified, who spake by the prophets. In one holy catholic and apostolic Church; we acknowledge one baptism for the remission of sins; we look for the resurrection of the dead, and the life of the world to come. Amen.

These two creeds basically announced the same Trinity doctrine of the Godhead. Athanasius,[44] a bishop of Alexandrea in the fourth century,

---

[44] Bishop of Alexandria, Confessor, and Doctor of the Church, Athanasius was born around 296 and died May 2, 373. He was the greatest champion of Catholic belief on the subject of the incarnation that the church has ever known. In his lifetime, he earned the characteristic title of "Father of Orthodoxy," by which he has been distinguished ever since (adapted from http://www.newadvent.org/cathen/02035a.htm).

explained the Trinitarian doctrine in the following Athanasian Creed with more detail (dogmatic explanations in the *Catholic Encyclopedia*).

The Athanasian Creed[45]

Whosoever will be saved, before all things it is necessary that he hold the Catholic Faith. Which Faith except everyone do keep whole and undefiled, without doubt he shall perish everlastingly. And the Catholic Faith is this, that we worship one God in Trinity and Trinity in Unity. Neither confounding the Persons, nor dividing the Substance. For there is one Person of the Father, another of the Son, and another of the Holy Ghost. But the Godhead of the Father, of the Son and of the Holy Ghost is all One, the Glory Equal, the Majesty Co-Eternal. Such as the Father is, such is the Son, and such is the Holy Ghost. The Father Uncreate, the Son Uncreate, and the Holy Ghost Uncreate. The Father Incomprehensible, the Son Incomprehensible, and the Holy Ghost Incomprehensible. The Father Eternal, the Son Eternal, and the Holy Ghost Eternal and yet they are not Three Eternals but One Eternal. As also there are not Three Uncreated, nor Three Incomprehensibles, but One Uncreated, and One Incomprehensible. So likewise the Father is Almighty, the Son Almighty, and the Holy Ghost Almighty. And yet they are not Three Almighties but One Almighty. So the Father is God, the Son is God, and the Holy Ghost is God. And yet they are not Three Gods, but One God. So likewise the Father is Lord, the Son Lord, and the Holy Ghost Lord. And yet not Three Lords but One Lord. For, like as we are compelled by the Christian verity to acknowledge every Person by Himself to be God and Lord, so are we forbidden by the Catholic Religion to say, there be Three Gods or Three Lords. The Father is made of none, neither created, nor begotten. The Son is of the Father alone; not made, nor created, but begotten. The Holy Ghost is of the Father, and of the Son neither made, nor created, nor begotten, but proceeding. So there is One Father, not Three Fathers; one Son, not Three Sons; One Holy Ghost, not Three Holy

---

[45] http://www.newadvent.org/cathen/02033b.htm

Ghosts. And in this Trinity none is afore or after Other, None is greater or less than Another, but the whole Three Persons are Co-eternal together, and Co-equal. So that in all things, as is afore said, the Unity in Trinity, and the Trinity in Unity, is to be worshipped. He therefore that will be saved, must thus think of the Trinity. Furthermore, it is necessary to everlasting Salvation, that he also believe rightly the Incarnation of our Lord Jesus Christ. For the right Faith is, that we believe and confess, that our Lord Jesus Christ, the Son of God, is God and Man. God, of the substance of the Father, begotten before the worlds; and Man, of the substance of His mother, born into the world. Perfect God and Perfect Man, of a reasonable Soul and human Flesh subsisting. Equal to the Father as touching His Godhead, and inferior to the Father as touching His Manhood. Who, although He be God and Man, yet He is not two, but One Christ. One, not by conversion of the Godhead into Flesh, but by taking of the Manhood into God. One altogether, not by confusion of substance, but by Unity of Person. For as the reasonable soul and flesh is one Man, so God and Man is one Christ. Who suffered for our salvation, descended into Hell, rose again the third day from the dead. He ascended into Heaven, He sitteth on the right hand of the Father, God Almighty, from whence he shall come to judge the quick and the dead. At whose coming all men shall rise again with their bodies, and shall give account for their own works. And they that have done good shall go into life everlasting, and they that have done evil into everlasting fire. This is the Catholic Faith, which except a man believe faithfully and firmly, he cannot be saved.

Controversies with the Trinitarian Doctrine

Of two thousand bishops invited to the Council of Nicaea, about three hundred attended. Of this group, two did not sign the Nicene Creed because of its condemnation of Arianism. *Arianism*[46] (named

---

46 Arianism is often considered to be a form of Unitarian theology in that it stresses God's unity at the expense of the notion of the Trinity, the doctrine that three distinct

after Arius) opposed the Trinitarian doctrine in the late third century, continuing for most of the fourth century. It was popular among some contemporary Christians and even among some political leaders. Many historians confirmed that a politically maneuvering leadership was successful in alienating Arianism in the council. At the end of the Nicaea council, Emperor Constantine issued the following edict to squelch opposition to the Trinitarian doctrine:

> In addition, if any writing composed by Arius should be found, it should be handed over to the flames, so that not only will the wickedness of his teaching be obliterated, but nothing will be left even to remind anyone of him. And I hereby make a public order, that if someone should be discovered to have hidden a writing composed by Arius, and not to have immediately brought it forward and destroyed it by fire, his penalty shall be death. As soon as he is discovered in this offence, he shall be submitted for capital punishment. . . .

As shown above, a controversy over the Trinity had become deep by the fourth century. The Trinity should be a sacred and religious matter; it became the official doctrine of the Catholic Church with political support of the emperor Constantine. This caused some to call the Emperor the first Pope. This controversy resurfaced during the reformation period in the seventeenth century by some anti-Trinitarians, but the reformists kept the Trinity as the official doctrine of their churches.

The Trinitarian doctrine is incomprehensible to many. In general, Catholic theologians have treated it a mystery; as Jerome, translator of *The Vulgate*, wrote, "The true profession of the mystery of the Trinity is to own that we do not comprehend it."[47]

---

persons are united in one Godhead. Arius's basic premise was the uniqueness of God, who is alone self-existent (not dependent for existence on anything else) and immutable; the Son, who is not self-existent, cannot therefore be the self-existent and immutable God. Because the Godhead is unique, it cannot be shared or communicated. Because the Godhead is immutable, the Son, who is mutable, must, therefore, be deemed a creature who has been called into existence out of nothing and has had a beginning. Moreover, the Son can have no direct knowledge of the Father, since the Son is finite and of a different order of existence (http://www.Britannica.com/topic/arianism).

[47] *De mysterio Trinitatus recta confessio est ignoratio scientiae*—"*Proem 1. xviii in Isai.*"

Confusion about the Trinity in the Bible

The word *Trinity* cannot be found in the Bible, but it is found in some Christian records of the second century. Many Catholic and protestant scholars and theologians have tried to prove the Trinity by using scriptures from the Bible, mostly from John's writing in the New Testament. However, the Trinity is controversial, as the following examples show.

Different Versions of the Bible

There are many versions of the Bible, and the same passage can be translated somewhat differently in different versions. Some translations are friendlier to the Trinity doctrine than others. For example, John 1:18 is often quoted to claim that Jesus is the Father as well; following are four examples of the different translations of English Bibles.

> No man hath seen God at any time; the only begotten Son, which is in the bosom of the Father, he hath declared him. (King James Version)

> No one has ever seen God. It is God the only Son, who is close to the Father's heart, who has made him known. (New Revised Standard Version)

> No one has ever seen God. God the only Son, who is at the Father's side, has made God known. (Common English Version)

> No man hath seen God at any time; the only begotten Son, who is in the bosom of the Father, he hath declared [him]. (American Standard Version)

> No one has ever seen God, but the one and only Son, who is himself God and is in closest relationship with the Father, has made him known. (New International Version)

The above examples show that some of the approximate sixty different versions of the English Bible are friendlier to the Trinity doctrine than others.

Controversy over the Passages in the Bible

Some passages in the Bible imply the Trinitarian doctrine; following are a few examples.

<u>The Father, the Word, the Holy Ghost: and these three are one.</u>

This particular statement can be found in 1 John 5:7 of the King James Version, but many other versions do not have this statement, including all of the above-quoted versions (NRSV, CEV, ASV, and NIV). According to some New Testament scholars, this particular statement was added to the Greek text of the New Testament by a scribe of Oxford University in the early sixteenth century, and it started to appear in the Greek text beginning with the third edition of Erasmus's Greek text.[48] Martin Luther's German Bible was translated from the second edition of Erasmus's Greek text, and it does not include this statement. Tyndale's English Bible was translated from the third edition of Erasmus's Greek text—and its sixth edition, the King James Version, consequently has this statement. Many New Testament scholars agree that this statement was copied over to the Greek text to justify the Trinitarian doctrine under the influence of the Catholic Church.

<u>"The Father and I are one."</u>

In the New Testament, some verses state that the Father and Jesus are one. For example, John 10:30 reads, "I and my Father are one." At the same time, if we read the two preceding verses, (John 10:28–29), it is apparent that verse 30 was referring to a case in which no man can pluck Jesus's sheep (followers) out of Jesus's hand, nor can they be plucked from His Father's hand. In this sense (or purpose), it said they are one.

Additionally, Jesus said of His Father in verse 29, "My Father, which gave them me, is greater than all." If one reads all three verses, then, it becomes apparent that the Father and Jesus are one in protecting Jesus's followers.

<u>"I am in the Father and the Father in me."</u>

Some verses said the Father and Jesus are in each other. For example, John 10:38 reads, "the Father is in me, and I in him." At the same time,

---

[48] Erasmus produced five editions of the Greek text of the New Testament: the first edition in AD 1516, the second edition in 1519, the third edition in 1522, the fourth edition in 1527, and the fifth edition in 1535.

Jesus made a point in the preceding verse that He was doing His Father's work in response to the Jews not believing His messages. Because of that, Jesus maintained that the Jews should believe Him through His works and that they should know the Father was in Him and He was in the Father. In other words, Jesus and His Father are together in the work.

John 14:10–11 also reads, "Believest thou not that I am in the Father, and the Father in me? . . . Believe me that I am in the Father, and the Father in me. . . ." After Jesus said this, He said, "Because I go unto my Father" (verse 12), indicating that the Father was in a different place—something that makes it impossible for them to be the same personage.

<u>Calling Jesus Christ "Father"</u>

Many make a point that the Apostle Paul indicated in 1 Corinthians 8:6 that the Father and the Lord Jesus Christ are the same personage: "But to us there is but one God, the Father, of whom are all things, and we in him; and one Lord Jesus Christ, by whom are all things, and we by him." Revelation 21:7 says, "He that overcometh shall inherit all things; and I will be his God, and he shall be my son." Moreover, Isaiah 9:6 says, "For unto us a child is born, unto us a son is given: and the government shall be upon his shoulder: and his name shall be called Wonderful, Counsellor, The mighty God, The everlasting Father, The Prince of Peace."

From these verses, it is difficult to form a concrete conclusion as to whether Jesus is the Father. However, Jesus was called by many different names (or even titles), including, among others, *the Lord*, *Father*, and *the mighty God*.

Thus, the contents of the Bible alone do not provide a clear-cut message of whether the Trinity is a true doctrine. This may be why both doctrines of Athanasianism and Arianism on the Godhead have coexisted with opposite views throughout two thousand years of Christianity. One thing that is certain is that the Trinity is not a clear-cut revelation from heaven.

The Godhead from the Book of Mormon

As mentioned above, Trinitarians justify their Trinity doctrine with biblical passages such as, "the Father, the Son and the Holy Ghost being one"; "the Father in me, and I in the Father"; and various verses in which Jesus is called the Father. Surprisingly, the same descriptions are found more numerously in the Book of Mormon. If we follow the biblical passages that Trinitarians use to prove their doctrine, it seems that the Book of Mormon supports them more strongly than the Bible does. However, there are specific reasons for those statements in both the Bible and the Book of Mormon.

The Father, the Son, and the Holy Ghost are one, or united in a specific purpose

Both in the Bible and the Book of Mormon, each statement saying the Godhead is one provides a specific purpose for that oneness:

In the Bible

John 10:28–30—They are one in protecting the disciples.

John 17:21—The disciples should be united as the Father and Jesus are united as one.

1 John 5:7–8—The Father, the Word, and the Holy Ghost bear record (or witness) as one.

In the Book of Mormon

2 Nephi 31:21—Eternal doctrine has shown the Godhead working in unison.

Mosiah 15:2–4—The Father and Son are a united entity like a team or group.

Alma 11:44—The Godhead is united for the final judgment.

3 Nephi 11:23–27—True baptism must be performed in the three names of the Godhead.

3 Nephi 11:36—The Father and the Holy Ghost bear record of the Son in unison.

3 Nephi 20:35—For salvation, the Father and the Son are in unison.

3 Nephi 28:10—Three specific disciples should be in unison as the Godhead is in unison.

Mormon 7:7—The Godhead is in unison in being happy for redemption.

John is the only one who described in the Bible that the Father, the Son, and the Holy Ghost are one. As shown above, the same description was taught more in the Book of Mormon than in the Bible.

The Father, the Son, and the Holy Ghost are in each other for a particular work

Each statement of the Father and the Son being "in each other" explains that they are working together for a specific work (for example, creation or the plan of salvation). Each statement shows that they are laboring with one heart and one mind. In both the Bible and the Book of Mormon, Jesus also prayed to the Father that His followers could be one as He and His Father are one.

In the Bible

John 10:34–38—Jesus's work manifests the work of the Father (see also John 14:10–12).

John 14:20—The Father, Jesus, and the disciples are in this work together.

In the Book of Mormon

3 Nephi 9:15—The Father and Jesus worked in unison in the Creation.

3 Nephi 19:23—Jesus prayed to the Father that His followers will be with Him as one.

3 Nephi 19:29—Being unified with faithful people, all can be sanctified and glorified in one.

Both the Bible and the Book of Mormon confirm that the Father and Jesus work as one, and Jesus prayed that His disciples would be one as He was one with the Father.

Jesus Christ has been called the Father

In worshiping their God, the Nephites in the Book of Mormon were monotheistic, as were the Jews worshiping Jehovah. The Nephites called Jesus (who was their God) the Father in various ways. The following shows the different ways Jesus was called *Father* in the Bible and the Book of Mormon.

In the Bible

Isaiah 9:6—"The mighty God, the everlasting Father"

Revelation 21:7—"He that overcometh shall inherit all things; and I will be his God, and he shall be my son."

In the Book of Mormon
    2 Nephi 26:12—"The Eternal God"
    Mosiah 16:15—"The very Eternal Father"
    Mosiah 3:8—"The Father of heaven and earth"
    Mosiah 15:2—"Being the Father and the Son"
    Mosiah 15:4—"The Father of heaven and of the earth"
    Alma 11:39—"The very eternal Father of heaven and earth"
    Helaman 14:12—"The Father of heaven and earth"
    Helaman 16:18—"The Father of heaven and earth"
    3 Nephi 11:14—"God of Israel, and the God of the whole earth"
    Mormon 9:12—"The Father and Son"

The above shows that Jesus was called *Father* in various ways in the Book of Mormon, more than in the Bible. As just one example, see Revelation 21:7: "He that overcometh shall inherit all things; and I will be his God, and he shall be my son." Moroni quoted Jesus explaining the reason He was called the Father: "Behold, I am he who was prepared from the foundation of the world to redeem my people. Behold, I am Jesus Christ. I am the Father and the Son. In me shall all mankind have life, and that eternally, even they who shall believe on my name; and they shall become my sons and my daughters" (see Ether 3:14). In this sense, Jesus is our Father as the Savior because of His Atonement, and we are His sons and daughters.

Thus, both the Bible and the Book of Mormon have common descriptions of the Father and the Son being one, the Father and the Son being in each other, and Jesus being called the Father in multiple ways. Both scriptures explain reasons for these descriptions.

A subordinate relationship exists between the Father and the Son

Of the four Gospels in the New Testament, the Apostle John recorded that Jesus called Heavenly Father "my Father" thirty-seven times, particularly during Jesus's discourse to His disciples (see John 13–16). He also recorded that Jesus confirmed that He was sent by the Father (see John 6:57; 12:49; 20:17), and that He prayed to the Father (see John 11:41; 14:16; 16:26; 17:1, 5, 11, 21, 24, 25). The other Gospel writers also recorded that Jesus called Heavenly Father "my Father" on numerous occasions (for example, sixteen times by Matthew and eight times by Luke). These passages have been the scriptural sources for the anti-Trinitarians.

The Book of Mormon strongly confirms a subordinate relationship between the Father and the Son. As shown in the following verses, the resurrected Jesus said frequently, "I go unto the Father," "I pray unto the Father," "given by the Father," "the Father commanded me," "will of the Father," "the Father gave me," "the Father sent," "saith the Father," and so forth. These do not leave any room to doubt that Jesus was working under the direction of the Father, and they clearly describe Jesus's subordinate relationship with the Father.

Subordination descriptions by Jesus	Related verses in 3 Nephi
I (Jesus) go to the Father	16:3; 17:4; 18:15
Jesus prayed to the Father	17:14, 15, 17, 21; 19:20–24, 27–29, 31
The Father commanded me (Jesus)	15:18–19; 16:16; 17:2; 18:14; 20:10, 14, 46; 26:2
Jesus was sent by the Father	15:16; 16:3, 10; 18:14; 20:10, 14, 46; 26:2; 27:14
The Father gave me	11:32; 15:13, 14, 24
The Father saith (quoting the Father)	15:18, 19; 16:10, 14; 20:20, 29; 21:2, 14
Ascend or go to the Father	15:1; 26:15; 27:28; 28:1, 4

The above verses confirm that Jesus clearly taught that He is the Father's Son, not the Father Himself.

Abinadi's discourse on the Godhead in Mosiah 15:1–5

One of the best discourses on the relationship between the Father and the Son is the prophet Abinadi's teachings in the Book of Mormon. When Abinadi taught King Noah's priests, he explained this relationship in Mosiah 15:1–5. While profound, Abinadi's teachings can easily be misinterpreted. Possible interpretations are discussed below.

There are two possible interpretations of the prophet Abinadi's discourse. One interpretation is that one (consubstantial) God is both the Father and the Son (which is the concept of the Trinity). According to this interpretation, there is only one God who is both the Father and the Son: the eternal God of heaven and of earth. He self-conceived to be born in the flesh, lived among the children of men, and submitted His will to His own self to suffer through the intercession process for His people.

Another interpretation is that two Gods are united in one Godhead (or an entity of Deity). According to this interpretation, there are two Gods, the Father and the Son. The Son was conceived by the Father, was born in the flesh, lived among the children of men, and submitted His will to that of His Father. The Son suffered through the intercession process for His people.

If we read these five verses casually, it sounds like Trinitarian doctrine. However, if we analyze them more carefully, we can see that the prophet Abinadi does not teach the Trinity, but teaches the relationship between the Father and the Son as separate beings.

Following are two analyses of the above passage taught by the prophet Abinadi.

Analysis One

These words of Abinadi are a case of chiasmus (emphasis added):

> And now Abinadi said unto them: I would that ye should understand that
> [A] ***God himself*** shall come down among the children of men, and shall redeem ***his people***. And because he dwelleth in flesh he shall be called
>   [B] ***the Son of God***, and
>   [C] having subjected ***the flesh to the will of the Father***,
>   [D] being ***the Father and the Son***—
>   [E] The Father, ***because*** he was conceived
>   [F] by ***the power of God*** [compare with Luke 1:35];

[E] and the Son, **because** of the flesh; thus

[D] becoming **the Father and Son**—And they are one God [compare with John 10:30] yea, the very Eternal Father of heaven and of earth.

[C] And thus the **flesh becoming subject to the Spirit**, or

[B] **the Son to the Father**,

[A] being **one God**, suffereth temptation, and yieldeth not to the temptation, but suffereth himself to be mocked, and scourged, and cast out, and disowned by **his people**.

The above chiasmus reveals that the Son shall be conceived by the power of God, which is the key message confirming what the angel Gabriel told Mary: that the son to whom she would give birth would be the Son of the Highest (God), as recorded by Luke:

> And the angel answered and said unto her, The Holy Ghost shall come upon thee, and *the power of the Highest* shall overshadow thee: therefore also that holy thing which shall be born of thee shall be called the Son of God. (Luke 1:35; emphasis added)

Analysis Two

[1] And now Abinadi said unto them:
I would that ye should understand that
God himself
    shall come down among the children of men, and
    shall redeem **his people**.
[2] And because he dwelleth in flesh
    he shall be called **the Son of God**,

[Note: The prophet Abinadi taught that the Son of God is the God in flesh, and He shall redeem His people among the children of men]

and having subjected the flesh to the will of **the Father**,
    <u>**being the Father and the Son**</u>—
    [3] **The Father**,
        because he was conceived by the power of God; and
    the Son,
        because of the flesh; thus
    <u>**becoming the Father and Son**</u>—
    [4] And **they are one God**, yea,
        the very **Eternal Father** of heaven and of earth.

[Note: "<u>The Father</u> and <u>the Son</u>" (two separate personages) become one entity ("the Father and Son") as one God. Thus, one God is a singular entity consisting of two separate personages of the Father and the Son. In this sense, one God can be thought of as a "family" in which a singular entity represents multiple people. In other words, "they are one God" in verse 4 can be interpreted as "they are one God family or Godhead." This confirms a statement by John "I [Jesus] and my Father are one" (John 10:30). The statement in verse 4 also shows that either one can be called the very Eternal Father of heaven, and the other the very Eternal Father of earth, or both can jointly be called the very Eternal Father of heaven and of earth. This implies that Father and Son are co-creators of heaven and of earth.]

    [5] And thus the flesh
        becoming subject to the Spirit, or
            the Son to the Father,
            being one God,
                suffereth temptation, and
                yieldeth not to the temptation, but
                suffereth himself to be
                    mocked, and
                    scourged, and
                    cast out, and
                    disowned
                        by his people.

[Note: The Son in the flesh is subject to the Father, and the Son in the Godhead (one God in verse 5) suffered the Crucifixion by his own people. The above analysis shows that "one God" in verse 4 means one entity of Deity or Godhead as a unit, but "one God" in verse 5 refers to "God himself" in verse 1 and "the Son of God" in verse 2, which is a singular God, the Son of God.]

Summary of the above analyses and their interpretation

As shown through chiasmus in the first analysis, the central theme of the prophet Abinadi's teaching reinforces the angel Gabriel's message to Mary in Luke 1:35: Jesus is the Son of the Highest, the Father. This clarifies a somewhat confusing description in Matthew 1:20–21, where an angel announced to Joseph in his dream, "Joseph, thou son of David, fear not to take unto the Mary thy wife: for that *which is conceived in her is of* [49] *the Holy Ghost. And she shall bring a son, and thou shalt call his name JESUS: for he shall save his people from their sins*" (emphasis added). This can be interpreted that Jesus is the Son of the Holy Ghost (see Matthew 1:19). Between Matthew and Luke's records, the prophet Abinadi confirmed that Luke's description in Luke 1:35 is correct, and he also explained John's statement in John 10:30 with clarity.

In the cascade method of the second analysis, it shows that the Prophet Abinadi taught a polytheistic nature of Deity, explaining that a singular entity of ONE GOD in verse 4 consists of TWO SEPARATE GODS, the FATHER GOD and the SON GOD. He also taught that the SON GOD in verses 1, 2, and 5 shall be conceived by the power of the FATHER GOD and shall go through the intercession process in flesh on the earth to redeem His people. In verse 5, one criterion for the Son is that He submits totally to the Father's will. This may even imply that we can be gods if we are totally submissive to the Father's will as is the Son.

As discussed earlier, the canonized Bible contains passages that can be used to argue both for and against the Trinity, and neither side can prove its argument convincingly through the Bible alone. The Book of Mormon clarifies confusion on the traditional Trinitarian theology through teachings by the resurrected Jesus Christ and by the prophet Abinadi, who both teach that the Trinitarian doctrine is incorrect.

---

[49] The New Revised Standard Version used the word *from* instead of *of.*

The Holy Ghost has a spiritual body

The Apostle Paul taught that there is a natural (earthly) body and a spiritual body (see 1 Corinthians 15:44). Moroni elaborated this teaching as he quoted a dialog between Jesus and the brother of Jared around the time of the Tower of Babel, long before Jesus was born: "Behold, this body, which ye now behold, is the body of my spirit; and man have I created after the body of my spirit; and even as I appear unto thee to be in the spirit will I appear unto my people in the flesh" (Ether 3:16).

This teaches that the image of Jesus's spiritual body was like His earthly image after His birth, and His physical body has the same image as His spiritual body.[50] Thus, we can conclude that the Holy Ghost, the third member of the Godhead, is a spirit with a spiritual body.

Additional Revelations on the Godhead in The Church of Jesus Christ of Latter-day Saints

During the 1840s, more revelations were given to Joseph Smith on the nature of the Godhead. These are available through records of The Church of Jesus Christ of Latter-day Saints; they include D&C 130 and 131 and the King Follett address.

Joseph Smith received the following revelation on the character of God:

> The Father has a body of flesh and bones as tangible as man's; the Son also; but the Holy Ghost has not a body of flesh and bones, but is a personage of Spirit. Were it not so, the Holy Ghost could not dwell in us. A man may receive the Holy Ghost, and it may descend upon him and not tarry with him. (D&C 130:22)

Joseph Smith also received the following revelation on the spirit:

> There is no such thing as immaterial matter. All spirit is matter, but it is more fine or pure, and can only be discerned by purer eyes; We cannot see it; but when

---

[50] This could imply that the shapes and genders are the same between our physical body and spiritual body. If so, this means our shapes and genders are eternal from our pre- to post-mortal lives.

our bodies are purified we shall see that it is all matter. (D&C 131:7–8)

In the last public sermon given by Joseph Smith before his martyrdom in 1844, he addressed the nature of the Godhead. The following are excerpts from that sermon, commonly known as the King Follett address.[51]

> God himself was once as we are now, and is an exalted man, and sits enthroned in yonder heavens! . . . I say, if you were to see him today, you would see him like a man in form—like yourselves in all the person, image, and very form as a man; for Adam was created in the very fashion, image and likeness of God, and received instruction from, and walked, talked and conversed with Him, as one man talks and communes with another. . . . It is the first principle of the gospel to know for a certainty the character of God, and to know that we may converse with Him as one man converses with another, and that He was once a man like us; yea, that God himself, the Father of us all, dwelt on an earth, the same as Jesus Christ Himself did. . . .

Joseph Smith revealed much more about the character of the Godhead than what the Bible and the Book of Mormon teach. Not only did these revelations break the Trinitarian doctrine that has been the *de facto* doctrine of Christianity for fifteen to sixteen hundred years,[52] but they also teach the characters of the Father and the Holy Ghost with much more new knowledge. Through these revelations we learn that the Father was once a man and has a tangible physical body as we do and that the Holy Ghost is a pure, materialistic substance. These revelations

---

[51] http://www.ldslearning.org/lds-king-follett-discourse-a-newly-amalgamated-text-byu.pdf

[52] It is interesting to see that tens of thousands (if not millions) of well-learned theologians and professors have not broken the Trinitarian doctrines for centuries, but an unlearned young prophet of God, Joseph Smith, broke it through revelations from God.

add significant new knowledge of the Godhead to all Christianity. These revelations given to Joseph Smith add significant new knowledge of the Godhead to all Christianity, and might be an example of what the Apostle Paul eluded to the Corinthians when he wrote, "But God hath revealed them unto us by his Spirit: for the Spirit searcheth all things, yea, the deep things of God" (see 1 Corinthians 2:10).

Chapter 5

Connecting the Bible and the Book of Mormon

WHEREFORE, THE FRUIT OF THY loins shall write; and the fruit of the loins of Judah shall write; and that which shall be written by the fruit of thy loins, and also that which shall be written by the fruit of the loins of Judah, shall grow together, unto the confounding of false doctrines and laying down of contentions, and establishing peace among the fruit of thy loins, and bringing them to the knowledge of their fathers in the latter days, and also to the knowledge of my covenants, saith the Lord. (2 Nephi 3:12)

The canonized Bible has been the only scripture for the Judeo-Christian community for thousands of years. The Old Testament is basically a historical record of Israel written by Jewish scribes and prophets starting from the prophet Moses. The New Testament is a compilation of selected documents and epistles about Jesus's life and teaching written in the first century AD by some of the Apostles and a few other followers of Jesus Christ.

Some of these records started to be available and were used in the Mediterranean Sea area in the first and second centuries; during subsequent centuries, they have spread to the rest of the world. The canonized Bible has been one of the main instigators for leading Christianity to become the largest religion in the world.

The Book of Mormon has been available since AD 1830. It is a historical record of a small group of the tribe of Joseph who migrated from Jerusalem to what we know as the American continent; they recorded their history for about one thousand years, beginning in 600 BC and continuing to AD 421. They were divided into two groups: the Nephites and the Lamanites.

The Nephites were annihilated and disappeared from the face of the earth around AD 400. Their last surviving prophet, Moroni, completed this record on golden plates that he buried in the ground at the Lord's direction. The Lord provided the means to translate this buried record from a dead ancient language to English through Joseph Smith, a modern-day prophet. This translated record is the Book of Mormon.

The Plates of Brass

With special guidance from the Lord, the prophet Lehi's family obtained a set of plates of brass in Jerusalem before their migration to the present American continent, which they knew as the promised land. The plates of brass were a set of records containing the Pentateuch of Moses, the history of the Jews to the time of King Zedekiah, a genealogy of their forefathers, a genealogical line of Joseph in Egypt, and many prophecies up to the days of Jeremiah (see 1 Nephi 5:10–13).

The prophet Nephi mentioned that the plates of brass contained what Joseph in Egypt prophesied of his posterity (see 2 Nephi 4:2). Nephi also mentioned that he quoted many scriptures from the plates of brass in his writing (see 2 Nephi 4:15). He confirmed that the things written on the plates are true (see 1 Nephi 22:30).

Since the plates of brass contain records made before the canonization and Ezra's restructuring of the Old Testament around 500 to 450 BC, it presumably was a more authentic document than the present Old Testament; it was also presumably more accurate than the Septuagint that was translated from Hebrew to Greek in the fourth century BC. The plates of brass were the main link between the Hebrew scripture and the Book of Mormon and were the main source of Hebrew records for the Book of Mormon writers. Five Book of Mormon writers quoted the plates of brass in their records; the quotes from the Bible that are used in the Book of Mormon constitute about 7 percent of the Book of Mormon. The law of Moses and the book of Isaiah particularly seem to be very influential to many prophets in the Book of Mormon.

About 35 percent of the book of Isaiah is quoted in the Book of Mormon, though some quotations do not match exactly with our current

Jewish scriptures, such as the Old Testament and the Septuagint. It is apparent that both the first and last writers in the Book of Mormon, Nephi and Moroni, loved the book of Isaiah (see 2 Nephi 11:2; Mormon 8:23).

After Jesus's ascension to heaven in Judea, the resurrected Jesus visited and taught the Nephite people for three days, explaining that they were the "other sheep" He talked about to the Jews (see John 10:16). During His visit, Jesus quoted from the book of Isaiah, the book of Malachi, the book of Micah, and the book of Zechariah. He also retaught the Sermon on the Mount that is recorded in the book of Matthew (see Matthew 5–7) with some variations (see 3 Nephi 12–14).

The Book of Isaiah Quoted in the Book of Mormon[53]

Hugh Nibley, Victor Ludlow, and other scholars have done much work on this subject. In this chapter, some of the meaningful differences between the Book of Mormon and the Bible will be highlighted.

In the Book of Mormon, twenty-one entire chapters and more than twenty additional verses of the book of Isaiah are quoted. Nephi quoted seventeen chapters, and Nephi's brother Jacob also quoted two chapters. Abinadi and the resurrected Jesus Christ quoted a chapter each. While the nineteen chapters of the book of Isaiah were quoted very closely as entire chapters, Isaiah 29 and 52 were quoted mostly with some paraphrases in a different order than they appeared in the book of Isaiah. Jacob's quote from chapters 50 and 51 of the book of Isaiah includes four more verses than these two chapters in our present Bible, inclusive of Isaiah 49:25–26 and Isaiah 52:1–2. This indicates that the plates of brass were not divided by chapters and verses as the present Bible has been.

The following table shows entire chapters of the book of Isaiah quoted in the Book of Mormon (in chronological order in the Book of Mormon):

---

[53] Of the 433 verses from the book of Isaiah that are quoted in the Book of Mormon, 199 are quoted word for word; 234 verses have some differences.

Book of Mormon	Book of Isaiah	Number of Chapters	Writer Who Quoted
1 Nephi 20–21	Chapters 48–49	2	Nephi
2 Nephi 6:17–8:25	Chapter 49:25–52:2	2	Jacob (under direction from Nephi)
2 Nephi 12–24	Chapter 2–14	13	Nephi
2 Nephi 26:15–16	Chapter 29:3–4	Virtually one Chapter	Paraphrased by Nephi
2 Nephi 27:2–6, 15–19, 25–34	Chapter 29:6–10, 11–12, 13–24		Nephi
Mosiah 14	Chapter 53	1	Abinadi
Mosiah 12:21–24	Chapter 52:7–10	Virtually one Chapter	King Noah's priest (a question to Abinadi)
Mosiah 15:29–31	Chapter 52:8–10		Abinadi (in answering King Noah's priest)
3 Nephi 20:36–38, 39–40, 41–45	Chapter 52:1–3, 6–7, 11–15		Jesus Christ (verses are not sequentially quoted following the verses of the book of Isaiah)
3 Nephi 22	Chapter 54	1	Jesus Christ

For whole chapter quotations, Isaiah 48–49 is the first group. Chapters and verses from Isaiah 49:24 to 52:2 are the second group. Isaiah 2–14 are the third group, Isaiah 29 is the fourth group, Isaiah 53 is the fifth group, and Isaiah 52 and 54 are the sixth group. King Noah's priest and the prophet Abinadi quoted from Isaiah 52 twice (see verses 7–10), and Jesus Christ also quoted ten verses of the chapter. The last prophet, Moroni, also quoted a part of Isaiah 54:2 as a part of his last words (see Moroni 10:31).

Group 1: Isaiah 48–49 Compared to 1 Nephi 20–21

Nephi explained why he was quoting the words of Isaiah from these chapters by saying that these quotes are for the broken-off branch of Israel. By so doing, he hoped that they might have the same hope as the main branch from which they were broken off (see 1 Nephi 19:24).

Isaiah 48:1 and 1 Nephi 20:1

Nephi 20:1 adds a phrase, "or out of the waters of baptism," to Isaiah 48:1.

> Hearken and hear this, O house of Jacob, who are called by the name of Israel, and are come forth out of the waters of Judah, *or out of the waters of baptism*, who swear by the name of the Lord, and make mention of the God of Israel, yet they swear not in truth nor in righteousness. (Emphasis added)

Adding the phrase "or out of the waters of baptism" makes it clear that both the tribe of Judah (blood lineage) and converts to Christ through baptism are entitled to the blessing of the house of Israel. Thus, this addition combined or equalized two groups of the Jewish blood descendants and the converts to Christ.[54]

Isaiah 48:14 and 1 Nephi 20:14

The following compares the Bible, the Septuagint, and the Book of Mormon (emphasis added):

---

[54] The Apostle Paul also implied the same understanding in Galatians 3:29: "And if ye be Christ's, then are ye Abraham's seed, and heirs according to the promise."

Bible	Septaugint	Book of Mormon
All ye, assemble yourselves, and hear; which among them hath declared these things? The Lord hath loved him: he will do his pleasure on Babylon, and *his arm shall be on the Chaldeans.*	And they shall all be gathered together and shall hear. Who announced these things to them? Loving thee I have done what thou desirest concerning Babylon to the *taking away of the seed of the Chaldeans.*	All ye, assemble yourselves, and hear; who among them hath declared these things unto them? The Lord hath loved him, yea, and he will fulfill his word which he hath declared by them; and he will do his pleasure on Babylon, and *his arm shall come upon the Chaldeans.*

In the above comparison, the message of a prophecy about the Chaldeans in both the Book of Mormon and the Septuagint is negative, while it is the opposite in the Bible.

Isaiah 49:1 and 1 Nephi 21:1

The following addition to Isaiah 49:1 in 1 Nephi 21:1 also reemphasizes that the message of this chapter in the Book of Mormon is for the broken-off and scattered branches of Israel (emphasis added to show what is different in the Book of Mormon).

> *And again: Hearken, O ye house of Israel, all ye that are broken off and are driven out because of the wickedness of the pastors of my people; yea, all ye that are broken off, that are scattered abroad, who are of my people, O house of Israel.* Listen, O isles, unto me, and hearken ye people from far; the Lord hath called me from the womb; from the bowels of my mother hath he made mention of my name.

Without these passages that the Book of Mormon adds to what is in the Bible and the Septuagint, the messages in these sections of the book of Isaiah were for only the blood descendants of Judah. The Book of

Mormon makes it clear that these messages are not only for the tribe of Judah, but also for converts to Christ and the broken-off and scattered branches of Israel.

Isaiah 49:13 and 1 Nephi 21:13

> Sing, O heavens; and be joyful, O earth; *for the feet of those who are in the east shall be established*; and break forth into singing, O mountains; for they shall be smitten no more; for the Lord hath comforted his people, and will have mercy upon his afflicted. (Emphasis added to show what is different in the Book of Mormon.)

This added sentence in the Book of Mormon provides an additional message to that given by Isaiah in the Bible.

Group 2: Isaiah 49:24–52:2 Compared to 2 Nephi 6:16–8:25

The plates of brass were more ancient than the present Old Testament and the Septuagint. As mentioned earlier, the quotes of this section from Isaiah 49:24 to 52:2 indicate that the plates of brass were not divided into chapters and verses as is the material in the present Bible.

Isaiah 49:25 and 2 Nephi 6:17

There is one major difference between the Bible and the Book of Mormon in Isaiah 49:25, as shown in the following table in italics.

Bible	Septuagint	Book of Mormon
Isaiah 49:25	**Isaiah 49:25**	**2 Nephi 6:17**
But thus saith the LORD, Even the captives of the mighty shall be taken away, and the prey of the terrible shall be delivered: for I will contend with him that contendeth with thee, and I will save *thy children.*	For thus saith the Lord, If one should take a giant captive, he shall take spoils, and he who takes them from a mighty man shall be delivered: for I will plead thy cause, and I will deliver *thy children.*	But thus saith the Lord: Even the captives of the mighty shall be taken away, and the prey of the terrible shall be delivered; for the Mighty God shall deliver *his covenant people.* For thus saith the Lord: I will contend with them that contendeth with thee—

One major difference in this verse is "thy children" in the Bible and the Septuagint, while the Book of Mormon says "his covenant people." The Book of Mormon indicates that all who make covenants will be delivered, while the Bible indicates that only blood descendants will be delivered. This teaching in the Book of Mormon is in accordance with the same message discussed previously: the people who covenant through baptism are equal to those covenanted by bloodline.

Group 3: Isaiah 2–14 Compared to 2 Nephi 12–24

This is the longest consecutive quote from the book of Isaiah in the Book of Mormon: thirteen chapters of the book of Isaiah as contained in the present Bible are quoted in the Book of Mormon. These thirteen chapters of the book of Isaiah cover many important prophecies, such as the Lord's temple in the latter days, the future of the kingdom of Judah and Jerusalem, the scattering and gathering of the Jews, the birth of the Savior, the Second Coming of the Savior, the Millennium, and so forth. Noticeable differences are shown in the following.

Bible	Septuagint	Book of Mormon
13 [B1] And upon all the cedars of Lebanon, that are high and lifted up, and [B2] upon all the oaks of Bashan, 14 [B3] And upon all the high mountains, and [B4] upon all the hills that are lifted up, 15 [B5] And upon every high tower, and [B6] upon every fenced wall, 16 [B7] And upon all the ships of Tarshish, and [B8] upon all pleasant pictures. 17 And the loftiness of man shall be bowed down, and the haughtiness of men shall be made low: and the LORD alone shall be exalted in that day.	13 [S1] and upon every cedar of Libanus, of them that are high and towering, and [S2] upon every oak of Basan, 14 [S3] and upon every high mountain, and [S4] upon every high hill, 15 [S5] and upon every high tower, and [S6] upon every high wall, 16 [S7] upon every ship of the sea, and [S8] upon every display of fine ships 17 And every man shall be brought low, and the pride of men shall fall: and the Lord alone shall be exalted in that day.	13 Yea, and the day of the Lord shall come [M1] upon all the cedars of Lebanon, for they are high and lifted up; and [M2] upon all the oaks of Bashan; 14 [M3] And upon all the high mountains, and [M4] upon all the hills, and [M5] upon all the nations which are lifted up, and [M6] upon every people; 15 [M7] And upon every high tower, and [M8] upon every fenced wall; 16 [M9] And upon all the ships of the sea, and [M10] upon all the ships of Tarshish, and [M11] upon all pleasant pictures. 17 And the loftiness of man shall be bowed down, and the haughtiness of men shall be made low; and the Lord alone shall be exalted in that day.

Isaiah 2:13–16 and 2 Nephi 12:12–16

This section contains a list of the lofty and high being brought low and made humble. There are different lists between the Bible and the Septuagint. Italics are used in the table above to indicate additional items in the Book of Mormon that are not in the Bible and the Septuagint. There are eight different items of "upon" in the Bible and the Septuagint (verse 16 is not the same between them), but there are eleven in the Book of Mormon—two items are added in verse 14 (M5 and M6; see italicized phrases). In addition, verse 16 adds a phrase from the Septuagint (M9; see italicized phrase) to the ones from the Bible (M10 and M11). These differences do not impose any doctrinal significance, but they do imply that the plates of brass contained more information than both the Old Testament and the Septuagint.[55]

Isaiah 9:1 and 2 Nephi 19:1

Nevertheless the dimness shall not be such as was in her vexation, when at the first he lightly afflicted the land of Zebulun and the land of Naphtali, and afterward did more grievously afflict her by the way of the [Red] sea, beyond Jordan, in Galilee of the nations.

The Book of Mormon specifies "the sea" as "the Red Sea."

Isaiah 13:15 and 2 Nephi 23:15

"Every one that is found shall be thrust through; and every one that is joined *unto them* [the wicked] shall fall by the sword" (emphasis added).

In this verse, "unto them" in the Bible is replaced with "to the wicked" in the Book of Mormon.

Isaiah 14:2 and 2 Nephi 24:2

And the people shall take them and bring them to their place; *yea, from far unto the ends of the earth; and they*

---

[55] The English version of the Septuagint was not commonly available in the United States in the nineteenth century. Thus, it is quite likely that Joseph Smith, who translated the Book of Mormon from April to June of 1829, never saw a copy of the English Septuagint while he was translating the Book of Mormon.

shall return to their lands of promise. And the house of Israel shall possess them, and the land of the Lord shall be for servants and handmaids; and they shall take them captives unto whom they were captives; and they shall rule over their oppressors. (Emphasis added.)

In this verse of the Book of Mormon, "yea, from far unto the ends of the earth; and they shall return to their lands of promise" is added to the verse in the Bible.

Group 4: Multiple verses of Isaiah 29, and Their Quotations and Paraphrasing in 2 Nephi 25–28

After Nephi quoted the thirteen chapters of Isaiah (Isaiah 2–14), he recorded his sermon from 2 Nephi 25 to the end of his writing in 2 Nephi 33. In his sermon, he delivered his messages by quoting many verses of Isaiah 29 (in a somewhat random fashion). In this sermon, he mainly prophesied the coming of Christ, the establishment of a Gentile church and its apostasy, the coming forth of a book from the dust (the Book of Mormon), and so forth. Nephi also prophesied that people will reject the Book of Mormon because of the Bible, and all would get access to both scriptures from both tribes of Judah and Joseph in the latter days.

Group 5: Isaiah 53 and Mosiah 14

This chapter is a quote from the prophet Abinadi, and there are no major differences in this chapter. However, two changes may be noteworthy: "he had done no violence" is changed to "he had done no evil" in verse 9, and "he bare the sins of many" to "he bore the sins of many" in verse 12. In both cases, *he* refers to the Son of God.

Group 6: Isaiah 52, 54 and 3 Nephi 16, 20, 22

The resurrected Jesus quoted Isaiah 52:1–3, 6–15, and all of Isaiah 54. The different parts of Isaiah 52 were quoted or paraphrased in 3 Nephi 16:18–20, especially throughout the whole chapter of 3 Nephi 20. These verses are not quoted in the same order as they appear in Isaiah 52, but are quoted in a random fashion. The whole chapter of Isaiah 54 was quoted in 3 Nephi 22. There are no significant differences except the phrase "and the Father and I are one" is added to Isaiah 52:10 in 3 Nephi 20:35. After the resurrected Jesus quoted these, He commanded the Nephites to search the words of Isaiah (see 3 Nephi 23:1).

It is noticeable that significant teachings follow the quoted word of Isaiah:

After Nephi quoted Isaiah 48–49 in 1 Nephi 20–21, in the next chapter (1 Nephi 22) he prophesied the future of the Israelites. After Jacob quoted Isaiah 50–51 in 2 Nephi 7–8, he taught in the next chapter (2 Nephi 9) a significant discourse on the Atonement of Jesus Christ. After Nephi quoted Isaiah 2–14 in 2 Nephi 12–24, he provided significant discourses as his last words in the subsequent chapter (2 Nephi 2:25–33). After the prophet Abinadi quoted Isaiah 53 in Mosiah 14, he taught a significant lesson on Deity in the next chapter, Mosiah 15. The resurrected Jesus Christ quoted Isaiah 54 in 3 Nephi 22. In the next chapter (3 Nephi 23), He taught the Nephites the importance of the message from Samuel the Lamanite concerning the resurrection of many deceased Saints that occurred right after the Resurrection of Jesus Christ.

Quotes of Multiple Verses (Not an Entire Chapter) from the Book of Isaiah

In addition to the entire chapters that are quoted, many verses from different chapters in Isaiah are quoted throughout the Book of Mormon, as shown in the table below. Following is an order of chapters and verses of the book of Isaiah.[56]

Book of Isaiah	Book of Mormon	Quoted by
Isaiah 5:26	2 Nephi 29:2	paraphrased by Nephi
Isaiah 9:12–13	2 Nephi 28:32	quoted by Nephi
Isaiah 11:4	2 Nephi 30:9	quoted by Nephi
Isaiah 11:5–9	2 Nephi 30:11–15	quoted by Nephi
Isaiah 11:11	partially in 2 Nephi 25:17; 29:1	quoted by Nephi

---

[56] Updated from Book of Mormon Reference Companion (Salt Lake City: Deseret Book Company, 2003), 344.

Isaiah 22:13	2 Nephi 28:7–8	paraphrased by Nephi
Isaiah 28:10, 13	2 Nephi 28:30	paraphrased by Nephi
Isaiah 29:3–4	2 Nephi 26:15–16	rephrased by Nephi
Isaiah 29:5	2 Nephi 26:18	paraphrased by Nephi
Isaiah 29:6	2 Nephi 6:15	paraphrased by Jacob
Isaiah 29:6–10	2 Nephi 27:2–5	quoted by Nephi (with a few added words)
Isaiah 29:11–12	2 Nephi 27:15–19	paraphrased by Nephi
Isaiah 29:13–25	2 Nephi 27:25–34	quoted by Nephi (with some paraphrasing)
Isaiah 40:3	1 Nephi 10:8	paraphrased by Nephi
Isaiah 45:18	1 Nephi 17:36	paraphrased by Nephi
Isaiah 49:22	1 Nephi 22:6	quoted by Nephi paraphrased by Nephi
	1 Nephi 22:8; 2 Nephi 6:6	quoted by Jacob
Isaiah 49:23	2 Nephi 6:7	
	2 Nephi 10:9	partially paraphrased by Nephi
Isaiah 49:24–26	2 Nephi 6:16–18	quoted by Jacob[57]

---

57 These verses are also included in the quotes from the entire chapter.

Isaiah 52:1	Moroni10:31	partially paraphrased by Moroni
Isaiah 52:1–2	2 Nephi 8:24–25	quoted by Jacob
Isaiah 52:1–3	3 Nephi 20:36–38	quoted by Jesus Christ
Isaiah 52: 6–7	3 Nephi 20:39–40	paraphrased/quoted by Jesus Christ
Isaiah 52:7	1 Nephi 13:37; Mosiah 15:14–18	paraphrased by Nephi and Abinadi
Isaiah 52:7–9	3 Nephi 16:18–20	quoted by Jesus Christ
Isaiah 52:8	3 Nephi 20:32	paraphrased by Jesus Christ
Isaiah 52:7–10	Mosiah 12:21–24	quoted by a priest of King Noah
Isaiah 52:8–10	Mosiah 15:29–31	quoted by Abinadi
Isaiah 52:9–10	3 Nephi 20:34–35	quoted by Jesus Christ
Isaiah 52:10	1 Nephi 22:10–11	paraphrased by Nephi
Isaiah 52:11–15	3 Nephi 20:41–45	quoted by Jesus Christ
Isaiah 52:12	3 Nephi 21:29	quoted by Jesus Christ
Isaiah 52:15	3 Ne. 21:8	quoted by Jesus Christ

Isaiah 53:7, 10	Mosiah 15:6, 10	partially quoted by Abinadi
Isaiah 54:2	Moroni10:31	partially quoted by Moroni
Isaiah 55:1	2 Nephi 26:25	partially paraphrased by Nephi
Isaiah 55:1–2	2 Nephi 9:50–51	quoted by Jacob

Additional Quotes by the Resurrected Christ from the Bible in the Book of Mormon

In addition to quoting the book of Isaiah, Jesus Christ quoted Malachi 3–4, Micah 4:13 and 5:8–9, and part of Zechariah 12:6. He also retaught the Sermon on the Mount recorded in Matthew 5–7.

Malachi 3–4 and 3 Nephi 24–25

After Jesus quoted these scriptures, he expounded on them in depth and said, "These scriptures, which ye had not with you, the Father commanded that I should give unto you; for it was wisdom in him that they should be given unto future generations" (3 Nephi 26:2). Since the book of Malachi was written about 150 years after Lehi's family had obtained the plates of brass, it could not have been included in the plates of brass.

Jesus taught the main messages of the importance of ordinances and offerings and tithing in Malachi 3 (see 3 Nephi 24), and the coming of Elijah in Malachi 4 (see 3 Nephi 25). Since these messages were so important that the Father specifically commanded Jesus to teach these principles for future generations, they must be critically important in our day.

One interesting difference between Malachi 4:2 and 3 Nephi 25:2 is shown in bold italics.

Bible	Septuagint	Book of Mormon
But unto you that fear my name shall the **Sun** of righteousness arise with healing in his wings; and ye shall go forth, and grow up as calves of the stall.	But to you that fear my name shall the **Sun** of righteousness arise, and healing shall be in his wings: and ye shall go forth, and bound as young calves let loose from bonds.	But unto you that fear my name, shall the **Son** of Righteousness arise with healing in his wings; and ye shall go forth and grow up as calves in the stall.

As shown above, the Bible and the Septuagint have "the Sun of righteousness," but the Book of Mormon has "the Son of Righteousness."

After the resurrected Jesus Christ quoted Malachi 3–4 as shown above, He taught the Nephites that He was commanded by the Father to teach the messages in this quote for future generations, not necessarily for the Nephites. In the quote, He taught the importance of priesthood ordinances, tithes and offering, and the coming of the prophet Elijah and his roles (temple work) for future generations, the present dispensation (see 3 Nephi 26:2).

Other Quotes from the Old Testament

- The resurrected Jesus quoted Micah 4:13 partially in 3 Nephi 20:19 and Micah 5:8–9 in 3 Nephi 20:16–17. There are no noticeable differences in these quotes. Micah gave a stern warning to people of his day in Micah 4 and 5: they would be in great danger if they did not repent. Jesus pronounced much the same warning to the future generations of Gentiles in 3 Nephi 20.
- The resurrected Jesus quoted Deuteronomy 18:15 in 3 Nephi 20:23.
- The resurrected Jesus taught about the Abrahamic covenant when He quoted (or paraphrased) Genesis 12:2 (also see Galatians 3:8) in 3 Nephi 20:27.
- The resurrected Jesus paraphrased a part of Zechariah 12:6 by saying, "and then shall Jerusalem be inhabited again with my people," and added, "and it shall be the land of their inheritance" (3 Nephi 20:46).

- The prophet Abinadi quoted the Ten Commandments (see Exodus 20:3–17) in his teaching to King Noah's priests with some explanations (see Mosiah 12:34–36, 13:12–24).[58]

Matthew 5–7 (Sermon on the Mount) and 3 Nephi 12–14 (Sermon on the Temple)

Jesus retaught the Sermon on the Mount recorded in Matthew 5–7 to the Nephites. Some call the teachings of Jesus Christ recorded in 3 Nephi 12–14 the Sermon at the Temple. The content in 3 Nephi 12–14 is comparable to the content in Matthew 5–7 with some variations, as shown in the following:

- Verse 3: "Yea, blessed are the poor in spirit who come unto me, for theirs is the kingdom of heaven" (the underlined phrase is added in the Book of Mormon).
- Verse 6: "And blessed are all they who do hunger and thirst after righteousness, for they shall be filled with the Holy Ghost" (the underlined phrase is added in the Book of Mormon).
- Verse 12: "Rejoice, and be exceeding glad" is replaced in the Book of Mormon with "For ye shall have great joy and be exceedingly glad."
- Verse 13: "Ye are salt of the earth" is replaced in the Book of Mormon with "Verily, verily, I say unto you, I give unto you to be the salt of the earth."
- Verse 14: "Ye are the light of the world" is replaced in the Book of Mormon with "verily, verily, I say unto you, I give unto you to be the light of this people."
- Verse 18: "For verily I say unto you, Till heaven and earth pass, one jot or one tittle shall in no wise pass from the law, till all be fulfilled" is changed in the Book of Mormon to "For verily I say unto you, one jot nor one tittle hath not passed away from the law, but in me it hath all been fulfilled." In the Bible, the verse is in future tense; in the Book of Mormon, it is in past tense. This shows it was mentioned before the Atonement process in the Bible but was mentioned after the Atonement process in the Book of Mormon.

---

[58] The prophet Abinadi also taught that the time will come when the law of Moses will no more be expedient to keep (see Mosiah 13:27).

- Verses 19–20: There are quite different messages in these two verses, as shown in the following table.

Bible	Book of Mormon
19 Whosoever therefore shall break one of these least commandments, and shall teach men so, he shall be called the least in the kingdom of heaven: but whosoever shall do and teach them, the same shall be called great in the kingdom of heaven. 20 For I say unto you, That except your righteousness shall exceed the righteousness of the scribes and Pharisees, ye shall in no case enter into the kingdom of heaven.	19 And behold, I have given you the law and the commandments of my Father, that ye shall believe in me, and that ye shall repent of your sins, and come unto me with a broken heart and a contrite spirit. Behold, ye have the commandments before you, and the law is fulfilled. 20 Therefore come unto me and be ye saved; for verily I say unto you, that except ye shall keep my commandments, which I have commanded you at this time, ye shall in no case enter into the kingdom of heaven.

- Verse 21: The underlined phrase in "Ye have heard that it was said by them of old time <u>before you</u>" is added in the Book of Mormon.
- Verse 22: The underlined phrase in "But I say unto you, That whosoever is angry with his brother <u>without a cause </u>shall be in danger of the judgment" is omitted in the Book of Mormon.
- Verses 23–26: Messages in these four verses are rephrased differently. Also, the monetary unit *farthing* was changed to *senine*.

Bible	Book of Mormon
23 Therefore if thou bring thy gift to the altar, and there rememberest that thy brother hath ought against thee; 24 Leave there thy gift before the altar, and go thy way; first be reconciled to thy brother, and then come and offer thy gift. 25 Agree with thine adversary quickly, whiles thou art in the way with him; lest at any time the adversary deliver thee to the judge, and the judge deliver thee to the officer, and thou be cast into prison. 26 Verily I say unto thee, Thou shalt by no means come out thence, till thou hast paid the uttermost <u>farthing</u>.	23 Therefore, if ye shall come unto me, or shall desire to come unto me, and rememberest that thy brother hath aught against thee— 24 Go thy way unto thy brother, and first be reconciled to thy brother, and then come unto me with full purpose of heart, and I will receive you. 25 Agree with thine adversary quickly while thou art in the way with him, lest at any time he shall get thee, and thou shalt be cast into prison. 26 Verily, verily, I say unto thee, thou shalt by no means come out thence until thou hast paid the uttermost senine. And while ye are in prison can ye pay even one <u>senine</u>? Verily, verily, I say unto you, Nay.

- Verse 27: "Ye have <u>heard</u> by them of old time, Thou shalt not commit adultery:" is replaced with "Verily, it is <u>written</u> by them of old time, that thou shalt not commit adultery." Thus, *heard* is changed to *written* in the Book of Mormon.
- Verse 31: "It has been said" is changed to "It hath been written." This is basically the same change as in verse 27.
- Verse 33: "Again, ye have heard" is changed to "And again it is written." This is the same kind of change as in verses 27 and 31.
- Verse 35: The biblical phrase "neither by Jerusalem; for it is the city of the great King" is omitted from the Book of Mormon.
- Verse 38: "Ye have heard that it hath been said, An eye for an eye, and a tooth for a tooth;" is changed to "And behold, it is written, an eye for an eye, and a tooth for a tooth." This is the same change as made in verses 27, 31, and 33.

- Verse 45: The biblical phrase "and sendeth rain on the just and on the unjust" is omitted from the Book of Mormon.
- Verses 46–47: Different messages are taught. In the Book of Matthew, comparing the audience with the publicans is the main message. In the Book of Mormon, the main message emphasizes that the old law was fulfilled and all things are new.

Bible	Book of Mormon
46 For if ye love them which love you, what reward have ye? do not even the publicans the same? 47 And if ye salute your brethren only, what do ye more than others? do not even the publicans so?	46 Therefore those things which were of old time, which were under the law, in me are all fulfilled. 47 Old things are done away, and all things have become new.

- Verse 48: "Be ye therefore, be perfect, even as your Father which is in Heaven is perfect" is changed to "Therefore, I would that ye should be perfect <u>even as I</u>, or your Father who is in heaven is perfect." By adding the underlined phrase "even as I" in the Book of Mormon, Jesus might have indicated that after His resurrection, He became perfect as Heavenly Father is perfect.

The following are noticeable variations between Matthew 6 and 3 Nephi 13:

The Lord's Prayer in Matthew 6:9–13 was recorded somewhat differently from how it was recorded in Luke 11:2–4. In the Book of Mormon, the noticeable differences are the omissions of "Thy kingdom come" and "Give us our daily bread," as shown in the table below:

Matthew 6:9–13	Luke 11:2–4	3 Nephi 13:9–13
9 After this manner therefore pray ye: Our Father which art in heaven, Hallowed be thy name. **10** Thy kingdom come. Thy will be done in earth, as it is in heaven. **11** Give us this day our daily bread. **12** And forgive us our debts, as we forgive our debtors. **13** And lead us not into temptation, but deliver us from evil: For thine is the kingdom, and the power, and the glory, for ever. Amen.	**2** And he said unto them, When ye pray, say, Our Father which art in heaven, Hallowed be thy name. Thy kingdom come. Thy will be done, as in heaven, so in earth. **3** Give us day by day our daily bread. **4** And forgive us our sins; for we also forgive every one that is indebted to us. And lead us not into temptation; but deliver us from evil.	**9** After this manner therefore pray ye: Our Father who art in heaven, hallowed be thy name. **10** Thy will be done on earth as it is in heaven. **11** And forgive us our debts, as we forgive our debtors. **12** And lead us not into temptation, but deliver us from evil. **13** For thine is the kingdom, and the power, and the glory, forever. Amen.

- Verse 25: In the Book of Mormon, "And now it came to pass that when Jesus had spoken these words he looked upon the twelve whom he had chosen, and said unto them: Remember the words which I have spoken. For behold, ye are they whom I have chosen to minister unto this people" is added in the front of verse 25 in the Bible: "take no thought for your life, what you shall eat, or what ye shall drink; nor yet for your body, what ye shall put on. Is not the life more than meat, and the body than raiment?" Thus, the Book of Mormon indicates these messages were for the chosen twelve disciples.

Following is a noticeable variation between Matthew 7 and 3 Nephi 14:

- Verse 1: In Matthew, "Judge not, that ye be not judged" is changed with an addition (indicated by italics) in 3 Nephi: "*And now it came to pass that when Jesus had spoken these words he turned again to the multitude, and did open his mouth unto them again, saying: Verily, verily, I say unto you,* Judge not, that ye be not judged."

Additional Bible-Related Information in the Book of Mormon

Throughout the Book of Mormon, there are some passages that are directly or indirectly related to the Bible but not found in the Bible. These were new to the world when the Book of Mormon was published in AD 1830. Following are some examples of clarity provided by the Book of Mormon:

- According to the book of Ether in the Book of Mormon, a family headed by Jared and his brother were spared from the confounding of the languages and from being scattered as consequence for the Tower of Babel (see Genesis 11:1–9). Their families ended up crossing the sea and migrating to the promised land (the American continent) under the Lord's direction (see Ether 6). After many centuries, their descendants destroyed themselves due to many internal wars and political conspiracies among their royal families (see Ether 15).

- Contrary to the Old Testament records claiming that all the sons of King Zedekiah were killed by Babylonians (see 2 Kings 25:21; Jeremiah 39:6, 52:10), the Book of Mormon shows that Mulek (the youngest son) was not slain. Instead, he and his group migrated to the land of America under the Lord's direction. His descendants lived at a place called Zerahemla. They ended up merging with the Nephites sometime during 279–130 BC (see Omni 1:15–18; see also Helaman 8:21).

- Lehi taught around 588–570 BC that Joseph in Egypt prophesied that the record from the loins of Judah and the record from his loins would grow together in the latter days to confound false doctrines, lay down contentions, establish peace among the remnant of Joseph, and bring them knowledge of their forefathers (see 2 Nephi 3:12).

- Contrary to the belief about the so-called original sin of Adam that is extrapolated from the Pauline doctrine (for example, 1 Corinthian 15:22), Lehi taught around 588–570 BC that Adam's transgression was done under the wisdom of the all-knowing God. He said, "Adam fell that men might be; and men are, that they might have joy" (2 Nephi 2:24–25).

- The first writer in the Book of Mormon, Nephi taught during 600–592 BC that the original Bible from the Jews and the twelve Apostles contained the fullness of the gospel and covenants of the Lord. He prophesied that after the Bible would go forth in purity from the Jews to the Gentiles, a great and abominable Gentile church would remove many plain and most precious parts from the Bible. Thus, he prophesied that many Gentiles would stumble and that Satan would have great power over them (see 1 Nephi 13:21–29).

- Nephi also taught during 600–592 BC that the Book of Mormon will establish the truth of the Bible, will make known the plain and precious things taken away from the Bible, will make known to all that the Lamb of God is the Son of the Eternal Father and the Savior of the world, and that all men must come unto Him or they cannot be saved (see 1 Nephi 13:40).

- Nephi taught around 559–545 BC that the book of Isaiah is plain to understand for those who have the spirit of prophecy (see 2 Nephi 25:4). The resurrected Jesus also taught in AD 34 that searching the words of Isaiah is a commandment (see 3 Nephi 23:1).

- Nephi taught around 559–545 BC that the Gentiles will say in the latter days, "A Bible! A Bible! We have got a Bible, and there cannot be any more Bible" (2 Nephi 29:3). This prophecy predicts that people would have a hard time accepting the Book of Mormon as additional scripture.

- Among the twelve Apostles, only the Apostle John was mentioned in the Book of Mormon (and he was mentioned twice). Around 600–592 BC, Nephi taught that John would write revelations about the end of the world (see 1 Nephi 14:27). Moroni taught around AD 400–421 that the time for fulfillments of those revelations would be at hand when this information from the Book of Mormon became known (see Ether 4:16–17). Even if the authenticity of the canonized the Revelation of John is not clear, and it has been somewhat controversial among some Christian branches, the Book of Mormon confirms that the Apostle John was assigned to write this apocalyptic revelation long before he was born.

- As there are some lost records, such as the book of Jasher (see Joshua 10:13, 2 Samuel 1:18), the book of Wars of the Lord (see Numbers 21:14), and many others, there are some lost prophets who are not known in the Bible, but that are known in the Book of Mormon. As an example, the ancient prophets Zenos and Zenock and their teachings are quoted multiple times in the Book of Mormon: Zenos appears twelve times and Zenock five times. They were new to the world when the Book of Mormon was published. Even though their life periods are not specified in the Book of Mormon, they seem to belong to a group of the major prophets in their days.

- The Catholic Church used passages from the Bible to defend its belief of geocentrism against heliocentrism in the Galileo inquisition in AD 1633. The church prosecutors defended geocentrism by quoting 1 Chronicles 16:30; Psalms 93:1; 96:10; 104:5; and Ecclesiastes 1:5, among others. The prophet Nephi in the Book of Mormon taught heliocentrism in 6 BC, long before Galileo and other scientists did. He taught, "And thus, according to his [the Lord's] word the earth goeth back, and it appeareth unto man that the sun standeth still; yea, and behold, this is so; for surely it is the earth that moveth and not the sun" (Helaman 12:15).

- The prophet Mormon prophesied around AD 385 that if the remnants of Joseph believe the Bible, they will also believe the Book of Mormon. He prophesied that the Book of Mormon will teach them concerning their forefathers and marvelous works among their forefathers (see Mormon 7:8–9).

Many faithful Judeo-Christians have put enormous effort in preserving the Bible throughout many centuries to the present time, and countless people have been blessed by the Bible; they have accepted Jesus as their Christ and have lived righteous lives keeping the commandments as taught in the Bible. But for some Christians who believe that the Bible is an infallible collection of divine words of God, it may not be easy to accept the fact that the Book of Mormon provides additional knowledge (and/or correct words of God) to the Bible.

Traditional Belief of Infallibility of the Bible

During the reformation period, some church leaders started a concept of infallibility of the Bible, and many Christians believe in this teaching. For example, John Wesley, the founder of the Methodist Church, used the word *infallible* to describe the Bible. In his sermon on "The Means of Grace," Wesley said,

> The same truth (namely, that this is the great means God has ordained for conveying his manifold grace to man) is delivered, in the fullest manner that can be conceived, in the words which immediately follow: *All Scripture is given by inspiration of God*; consequently, **all Scripture is infallibly true**; *and is profitable for doctrine, for reproof, for correction, for instruction in righteousness; to the end that the man of God may be perfect, thoroughly furnished unto all good works* (2 Tim. 3:16, 17; emphasis added). As such, 'orthodox, evangelical, and traditionalist United Methodists believe in the infallibility of Scripture. Article V—Of the Sufficiency of the Holy Scriptures for Salvation' in the <u>Articles of Religion</u> states that "The Holy Scripture containeth all things necessary to salvation; so that whatsoever is not read therein, nor may be proved thereby, is not to be required of any man that it should be believed as an article of faith, or be thought requisite or necessary to salvation.

> In the name of the Holy Scripture we do understand those
> canonical books of the Old and New Testament of whose
> authority was never any doubt in the Church. (*The Articles
> of Religion of the Methodist Church V–VIII*, The United
> Methodist Church, 2004)

At the same time, many seem to doubt that the Bible is so perfect that it can be considered infallible. For example, Erasmus, one of the most respected and recognized Bible translators and an authority in Greek language during the sixteenth century,[59] made the following poignant statement, with which many have agreed:

> But one thing the facts cry out, and it can be clear, as
> they say, even to a blind man, that often through the translator's clumsiness or inattention the Greek has been wrongly
> rendered; often the true and genuine reading has been corrupted by ignorant scribes, which we see happen every day,
> or altered by scribes who are half-taught and half-asleep.
> ("Epistle 337," *Collected Works of Erasmus*, Vol. 3, 134)

In the process of the transcribing and translating of ancient scriptures throughout many centuries, there inevitably seems to be many human errors. Even today, there are around sixty different versions of the English Bible, and they contain variations.[60] Infallibility or inerrancy of

---

[59] Some records show that copies of the Bible translated by Erasmus accounted for around 20 percent of the book sales in Europe during his day; during his lifetime, fewer than 300,000 copies of his Greek/Latin Bible were sold.

[60] Some of the easily noticeable discrepancies in the canonized New Testament may be as follows:
- Mark 14:12 and 15:25 do not agree with John 19:14 regarding whether Jesus's crucifixion was done before or after the Passover.
- Luke 2:39 and Matthew 2:14–22 do not agree about whether the baby Jesus went to Egypt.
- Acts 9:26 and Galatians 1:16–17 do not agree regarding whether the Apostle Paul went to Jerusalem right after his conversion on the way to Damascus.
- Examples of some verses not found the early text include Mark 16:9–20; Luke 22:40; Luke 22:43–44; Luke 24:51; John 5:4; John 7:23–8:11; and 1 John 5:7.

the Bible has been a very controversial topic since the eighteenth century. In recent decades, some New Testament scholars in the field of textual criticism have reported many problems with the authenticity of multiple sections of the canonized New Testament, including, but not limited to, Mark 1:41, 16:9–20; John 7:53–8:11; 1 John 5:7–8; and Revelation 13:18, 22:16–21. Some liberal Bible scholars have even argued that the Bible should be rewritten because new information from archeological records has been discovered in the twentieth century, such as the Dead Sea Scrolls, the Nag Hammadi Text, and so on. Thus, opinions about the canonized Bible range from infallibility to the necessity to rewrite it. The Prophet Joseph Smith addressed this aspect of the Bible in the following statements:

> We believe the Bible to be the word of God as far as it is translated correctly; we also believe the Book of Mormon to be the word of God. (Articles of Faith 1:8)

> From sundry revelations which had been received, it was apparent that many important points touching the salvation of man had been taken from the Bible, or lost before it was compiled. (D&C 76 heading; see also History of the Church 1:245)

According to Nephi, the present Bible misses plain and precious parts as well as covenants, and it is not the same as the original records

---

- Thirteen verses are not found in the New Standard Revised Version but are found in the King James Version:
  Matthew 17:21; Matthew 20:14; Matthew 20:16 (partially), 23:14; Mark 11:26, 15:28; Luke 17:36, 23:17; Acts 8:37, 15:34, 24:7, 28:29; Romans 16:24.
- Exemplary verses with noticeable differences between different versions of the New Testament:
  Matthew 3:16, 6:13, 11:19, 27:49; Mark: 1:1, 4:40, 10:24, 10:29, 14:68; Luke 6:35, 8:43, 8:45, 9:35, 11:11, 15:21, 23:34; John 1:18, 3:13, 9:35, 10:29; Acts 9:12, 11:20, 20:4, 24:6, 24:8; Romans 26:24; 1 Corinthians 14:38; 2 Corinthians 13:4; Ephesians 3:9; Colossians 3:6; Hebrews 2:7; 1 Peter 3:18; 2 John 1:12; Revelation 21:3, 22:19, 22:21.
- Revelation 11:3 of the King James Version has the word *power* added.

written by the Apostles. As evidenced in this chapter, the Book of Mormon provides some additional teachings that are not in the Bible (even correcting the Bible in some cases).

The Book of Mormon rarely has discrepancies throughout the book, and it is remarkably consistent with its messages and information,[61] making it more infallible than the Bible.

---

[61] This may be because Mormon and Moroni edited the book before it was compiled.

Chapter 6

Two Priesthoods of God

AND IT WAS THIS SAME Melchizedek to whom Abraham paid tithes; yea, even our father Abraham paid tithes of one-tenth part of all he possessed. . . .

Now this Melchizedek was a king over the land of Salem; and his people had waxed strong in iniquity and abomination; yea, they had all gone astray; they were full of all manner of wickedness;

But Melchizedek having exercised mighty faith, and received the office of the high priesthood according to the holy order of God, did preach repentance unto his people. And behold, they did repent; and Melchizedek did establish peace in the land in his days; therefore he was called the prince of peace, for he was the king of Salem; and he did reign under his father.

Now, there were many before him, and also there were many afterwards, but none were greater; therefore, of him they have more particularly made mention. (Alma 13:15–19)

Priesthood of God

According to the Bible, there are two priesthoods: the Levitical Priesthood and the Melchizedek Priesthood (see as examples Exodus 40, Numbers 1, and Hebrews 5–8).

Levitical Priesthood

The well-known Levitical Priesthood originated from the Lord's commandment to the prophet Moses. The Lord commanded Moses to confer the priesthood to Aaron and his sons, and He directed that this priesthood should continue with their posterity from generation to generation:

> And thou shalt put upon Aaron the holy garments, and anoint him, and sanctify him; that he may minister unto me in the priest's office.
>
> And thou shalt bring his sons, and clothe them with coats:
>
> And thou shalt anoint them, as thou didst anoint their father, that they may minister unto me in the priest's office: for their anointing shall surely be an everlasting priesthood throughout their generations.
>
> Thus did Moses: according to all that the Lord commanded him, so did he. (Exodus 40:13–16)

The Lord also commanded Moses that the Levites were to oversee the priestly affairs in the tabernacle:

> But thou shalt appoint the Levites over the tabernacle of testimony, and over all the vessels thereof, and over all things that belong to it: they shall bear the tabernacle, and all the vessels thereof; and they shall minister unto it, and shall encamp round about the tabernacle.
>
> And when the tabernacle setteth forward, the Levites shall take it down: and when the tabernacle is to be pitched, the Levites shall set it up: and the stranger that cometh nigh shall be put to death.
>
> And the children of Israel shall pitch their tents, every man by his own camp, and every man by his own standard, throughout their hosts.
>
> But the Levites shall pitch round about the tabernacle of testimony, that there be no wrath upon the congregation of the children of Israel: and the Levites shall keep the charge of the tabernacle of testimony.
>
> And the children of Israel did according to all that the Lord commanded Moses, so did they. (Numbers 1:50–54)

This was also confirmed by the prophet Joshua: "But the Levites have no part among you; for the priesthood of the Lord is their inheritance" (Joshua 18:7). Thus, the responsibility of the Levitical Priesthood was to take care of sacred affairs in their tabernacle (and later in temples).

Melchizedek Priesthood

The Old Testament contains no specific explanations about the responsibilities of Melchizedek Priesthood holders. However, Melchizedek's name was mentioned two times in the Old Testament, once in Genesis and once in Psalms:

> And Melchizedek king of Salem brought forth bread and wine: and he was the priest of the most high God.
> And he blessed him, and said, Blessed be Abram of the most high God, possessor of heaven and earth:
> And blessed be the most high God, which hath delivered thine enemies into thy hand. And he gave him tithes of all. (Genesis 14:18–20)

> The Lord hath sworn, and will not repent, Thou art a priest for ever after the order of Melchizedek. (Psalms 110:4)

Since Abraham paid his tithes to Melchizedek, we can presume that Melchizedek held the high priesthood office. The Psalmist basically confirmed the existence of the Melchizedek Priesthood.

The Melchizedek Priesthood was explained in detail by the Apostle Paul in the New Testament (written around AD 60) and by the prophet Alma in the Book of Mormon (written around 82 BC).

Apostle Paul's Teaching on the Levitical and Melchizedek Priesthoods (Hebrews 5:5–10, 6:20–8:2)

> So also Christ glorified not himself to be made an high priest; but he that said unto him, Thou art my Son, to day have I begotten thee.
> As he saith also in another place, Thou art a priest for ever after the order of Melchisedec. . . .

And being made perfect, he became the author of eternal salvation unto all them that obey him;

Called of God an high priest after the order of Melchisedec. (Hebrews 5:5–10)

Whither the forerunner is for us entered, even Jesus, made an high priest for ever after the order of Melchisedec.

For this Melchisedec, king of Salem, priest of the most high God, who met Abraham returning from the slaughter of the kings, and blessed him;

To whom also Abraham gave a tenth part of all; first being by interpretation King of righteousness, and after that also King of Salem, which is, King of peace;

Without father, without mother, without descent, having neither beginning of days, nor end of life; but made like unto the Son of God; abideth a priest continually.

Now consider how great this man was, unto whom even the patriarch Abraham gave the tenth of the spoils.

And verily they that are of the sons of Levi, who receive the office of the priesthood, have a commandment to take tithes of the people according to the law, that is, of their brethren, though they come out of the loins of Abraham. . . .

And as I may so say, Levi also, who receiveth tithes, payed tithes in Abraham.

For he was yet in the loins of his father, when Melchisedec met him.

If therefore perfection were by the Levitical priesthood, (for under it the people received the law,) what further need was there that another priest should rise after the order of Melchisedec, and not be called after the order of Aaron? . . .

For it is evident that our Lord sprang out of Juda; of which tribe Moses spake nothing concerning priesthood.

And it is yet far more evident: for that after the si-
militude of Melchisedec there ariseth another priest, . . .

For he testifieth, Thou art a priest for ever after the
order of Melchisedec. . . .

Now of the things which we have spoken this is the
sum: We have such an high priest, who is set on the
right hand of the throne of the Majesty in the heavens.
(Hebrews 6:20–8:1)

Based on the above scriptures, the Apostle Paul taught the Hebrew
(or Jewish) Christians of his day that there are two priesthoods: the Levitical Priesthood and the Melchizedek Priesthood. He called Melchizedek
a priest of the most High God, and explained the Melchizedek Priesthood by quoting Psalms 110:4 "Thou art a priest forever after the order of
Melchizedek." He taught that the Melchizedek Priesthood is of the Son of
God, proclaiming that Jesus has an unchangeable High Priesthood.

Prophet Alma's Teaching on the Melchizedek Priesthood

Now, as I said concerning the holy order, or this
high priesthood, there were many who were ordained
and became high priests of God; and it was on account
of their exceeding faith and repentance, and their righteousness before God, they choosing to repent and work
righteousness rather than to perish;

Therefore they were called after this holy order, and
were sanctified, and their garments were washed white
through the blood of the Lamb. .. . .

Yea, humble yourselves even as the people in the
days of Melchizedek, who was also a high priest after
this same order which I have spoken, who also took
upon him the high priesthood forever.

And it was this same Melchizedek to whom Abraham paid tithes; yea, even our father Abraham paid
tithes of one-tenth part of all he possessed. . . .

Now this Melchizedek was a king over the land of
Salem; and his people had waxed strong in iniquity and

abomination; yea, they had all gone astray; they were full of all manner of wickedness;

But Melchizedek having exercised mighty faith, and received the office of the high priesthood according to the holy order of God, did preach repentance unto his people. And behold, they did repent; and Melchizedek did establish peace in the land in his days; therefore he was called the prince of peace, for he was the king of Salem; and he did reign under his father.

Now, there were many before him, and also there were many afterwards, but none were greater; therefore, of him they have more particularly made mention. (Alma 13:10–19)

Alma taught people in the city of Ammonihah, a wicked city, that Melchizedek was a high priest after the order of the Son of God. He said that Melchizedek preached repentance to wicked people in the land of Salem, and they repented such that Melchizedek was able to establish peace. Using the people of Salem as an example, Alma taught the people in Ammonihah to humble themselves, to repent of their sins, to call on the holy name of Jesus, and to watch and pray continually so that they could hope to have eternal life through faith. By doing so, he taught, they might be lifted up at the last day and enter into His rest through the love of God.

Thus, the Apostle Paul tried to convince the Hebrew Christians that Jesus was the foundation of the High Priesthood. The prophet Alma admonished people to be sanctified like the people of Salem by following Melchizedek, who was the high priest after the order of the Son of God. Both Paul and Alma taught that this high priesthood does not have a starting nor ending point, and it has existed from eternity to eternity.

Priesthood Ordinances in the Bible and the Book of Mormon

In the Old Testament, the Creation and a history of the patriarchs from Adam to Jacob and his twelve sons are recorded in Genesis. In that record, we learn that the patriarchs built altars, offered sacrifices to God, and gave patriarchal blessings to their sons. As a part of those blessings, they gave the birthright to the chosen son from generation to generation. However, priesthood ordinances were not mentioned much other than as offerings on the sacred altars.

From Moses's day, there were priesthood ordinances of sacrificing animals in the tabernacle or in their temple, and the practice of sacrificing animals lasted until the destruction of Jerusalem in AD 70, with some interruptions due to foreign invasions. The Levites were assigned to perform these ordinances in the tabernacle and temples, but the Sadducees (presumably the Zadokites) were in charge of the affairs of the Herodian temple during the time of Jesus's ministry.

In the New Testament, the first recorded priesthood ordinance was the baptism ordinance by John the Baptist. Other sacred ordinances recorded in the New Testament include Jesus Christ's calling and ordaining His Apostles and the Seventy, baptizing, conferring the Holy Ghost, breaking the bread that signified His flesh, and giving the wine that signified His blood. His Apostles also baptized and conferred the Holy Ghost by the laying on of hands.

In the Book of Mormon, those in charge of the sacred plates were the prophets, with a few exceptions. Many priesthood ordinances are recorded in the Book of Mormon. The first patriarch and prophet, Lehi, built an altar and offered sacrifices. His son, Nephi, built a temple after the manner of Solomon's temple. The baptism ordinance by water and the Holy Ghost as a part of the doctrine of Christ was taught as early as 589–559 BC (see 2 Nephi 31). The first record of baptism was of 204 souls baptized by water in about 147 BC (see Mosiah 18). Unlike the Jews, the Nephites practiced baptism by immersion in water long before Jesus was born.

Nephi consecrated his younger brothers, Jacob and Joseph, to be teachers and priests around 570 BC. Alma established a church in Zarahemla and ordained teachers, priests, and elders about 120 BC. The resurrected Jesus Christ taught the exact manner of baptism in AD 34. He also conferred the Holy Ghost and offered the sacramental bread and wine as He had done for His Apostles in Jerusalem. Moroni, the last prophet in the Book of Mormon, recorded the exact manner of several priesthood ordinances around AD 400, including how to confer the Holy Ghost, how to ordain teachers and priests, and how to administer the sacramental bread and wine.

Following are some details of the priesthood ordinances associated with Jesus Christ. In a comparison of teachings on the priesthood ordinances between the Bible and the Book of Mormon, it is evident that the Book of Mormon teaches the priesthood ordinances and covenants with much more exactness.

Baptism by Water

In the Bible

Matthew recorded the baptism of Jesus Christ by John the Baptist[62] in Matthew 3 (see also Mark 1; Luke 3; John 1). We will discuss John's encounter with the Pharisees and Sadducees, who were contemporary religious leaders, and the actual baptism of Jesus Christ. Matthew recorded that this fulfilled a prophecy by Isaiah: "prepare ye the way of the Lord, make his paths straight" (Isaiah 40:3).

John's proclamation to the Pharisees and Sadducees was recorded in Matthew:

> Then went out to him Jerusalem, and all Judæa, and all the region round about Jordan,
>
> And were baptized of him in Jordan, confessing their sins.
>
> But when he saw many of the Pharisees and Sadducees come to his baptism, he said unto them, O generation of vipers, who hath warned you to flee from the wrath to come.
>
> Bring forth therefore fruits meet for repentance:
>
> And think not to say within yourselves, We have Abraham to our father: for I say unto you, that God is able of these stones to raise up children unto Abraham.
>
> And now also the axe is laid unto the root of the trees: therefore every tree which bringeth not forth good fruit is hewn down, and cast into the fire.
>
> I indeed baptize you with water unto repentance: but he that cometh after me is mightier than I, whose shoes I am not worthy to bear: he shall baptize you with the Holy Ghost, and with fire:

---

62 John's father, Zacharias, was a priest working in the temple; his mother, Elisabeth, was a descendant of Aaron (see Luke 1).

Whose fan is in his hand, and he will throughly purge his floor, and gather his wheat into the garner; but he will burn up the chaff with unquenchable fire. (Matthew 3:5–12)

Through this proclamation, John the Baptist announced the start of the new era with the following points:

- By performing baptisms in an unclean public place outside the temple, like the Jordan River, he announced the legitimacy of his priesthood authority[63] and baptism for remission of sins over the sin-forgiving sacrifices by the Sadducees, which were done only in the temple (see Matthew 3:7).
- He institutionalized baptism for anyone who repents and will bring fruit of their works, regardless of whether they keep the law of Moses (see Matthew 3:8, 10).
- He taught that his baptism supersedes the blood lineage of Abraham (see Matthew 3:9).
- He introduced a new priesthood authority who is mightier than him (see Matthew 3:11).
- He taught that Jesus will baptize with the Holy Ghost (see Matthew 3:11).
- He pronounced that Jesus will be the final judge (see Matthew 3:12).

With the above points, John the Baptist literally prepared for the start of a new era in which Jesus could establish His kingdom (in other words, His Church).[64] John the Baptist proclaimed and prepared this

---

[63] The Doctrine and Covenants indicates that John was ordained by the angel of God at his infancy: "For he was baptized while he was yet in his childhood, and was ordained by the angel of God at the time he was eight days old unto this power, to overthrow the kingdom of the Jews, and to make straight the way of the Lord before the face of his people, to prepare them for the coming of the Lord, in whose hand is given all power" (D&C 84:28).

[64] Because of purification-in-water practices like mikveh during the days of John and Jesus, purification by a complete immersion in water was a familiar practice for the Jews. John might have chosen the Jordan River because of all its water, and his

new era for Jesus Christ with a new priesthood ordinance of baptism, replacing the sacrificial ordinances performed by the priests and Levites only in the temple, which Moses had started about fifteen centuries earlier.

Baptism of Jesus Christ[65]

In the Bible

John the Baptist baptized Jesus in the following way:

> Then cometh Jesus from Galilee to Jordan unto John, to be baptized of him.
>
> But John forbad him, saying, I have need to be baptized of thee, and comest thou to me?
>
> And Jesus answering said unto him, Suffer it to be so now: for thus it becometh us to fulfil all righteousness. Then he suffered him.
>
> And Jesus, when he was baptized, went up straightway out of the water: and, lo, the heavens were opened unto him, and he saw the Spirit of God descending like a dove, and lighting upon him:
>
> And lo a voice from heaven, saying, This is my beloved Son, in whom I am well pleased. (Matthew 3:13–17)

This record shows many things: Jesus came to the John the Baptist at the Jordan River (see verse 13), Jesus and John discussed whether John was qualified to baptize Jesus (see verses 14–15), Jesus was baptized (see verse 16), and Jesus went straightway up out of the water (see verse 16). Following His baptism, the heavens were opened, and Jesus saw the Spirit of God like a dove lighting on Him (see verse 16) and heard a voice from heaven saying, "This is my beloved Son, in whom I am well pleased." (verse 17).

But it does not describe in what manner Jesus was baptized. As a result, there are consequently multiple manners of baptism among Christian

---

baptisms quite likely required the complete immersion in water like Mikveh for one's repentance and remission of sins.

[65] A similar descriptions of Jesus's baptism can be found in Mark 1:9–11, Luke 3:21–22, and John 1:32–34.

churches today, including submersion (or total immersion), partial immersion, affusion, and aspersion.

After Jesus was baptized, Jesus and His disciples also baptized their followers (see John 3:22, 3:26, 4:1–2[66]), and they established a church (see John 16:18). Peter added three thousand souls to the Church through baptism at the Pentecost (see Acts 2:41). Philip baptized men and women (see Acts 18:12), including a eunuch (see Acts 8:38); Ananias baptized Paul (see Acts 9:18); Peter baptized Cornelius (see Acts 10:48); and Paul baptized certain disciples (see Acts 19:5) as well as the household of Stephanas (see 1 Corinthians 1:16). These are only some of the examples showing that the baptism ordinance was commonly practiced by the Apostles.

In the Book of Mormon

As mentioned, the record of Matthew (see Matthew 3:13–17) does not specify the exact manner in which Jesus was baptized. In the Book of Mormon, however, the resurrected Jesus specifically instructed the Nephites how to baptize:

> And the Lord said unto him [Nephi]: I give unto you power that ye shall baptize this people when I am again ascended into heaven.
>
> And again the Lord called others, and said unto them likewise; and he gave unto them power to baptize. And he said unto them: On this wise shall ye baptize; and there shall be no disputations among you.
>
> Verily I say unto you, that whoso repenteth of his sins through your words, and desireth to be baptized in my name, on this wise shall ye baptize them—Behold, ye shall go down and stand in the water, and in my name shall ye baptize them.
>
> And now behold, these are the words which ye shall say, calling them by name, saying:

---

[66] Some scholars indicated that John 4:2 was mistranslated, saying, "This might be a bad translation of an Aramaic statement that Jesus baptized nobody but his disciple" (Morton Smith, The Secret Gospel [Lower Lake, CA: The Dawn Horse Press, 1960], 94).

Having authority given me of Jesus Christ, I baptize you in the name of the Father, and of the Son, and of the Holy Ghost. Amen.

And then shall ye immerse them in the water, and come forth again out of the water.

And after this manner shall ye baptize in my name; for behold, verily I say unto you, that the Father, and the Son, and the Holy Ghost are one; and I am in the Father, and the Father in me, and the Father and I are one. (3 Nephi 11:21–27)

With this specific instruction, there should be no disputation on how to baptize by water as Jesus told in verse 22:

- One who is going to be baptized must repent and must desire to be baptized in Jesus's name (in other words, the person must desire to make a covenant).
- Baptism should be done with authority given from Jesus Christ.
- Jesus taught the specific baptismal words in 3 Nephi 11:25 (this coincides with the instruction to His disciples in Matthew 28:19: "baptizing them in the name of the Father, and of the Son, and of the Holy Ghost").
- Baptism by water requires being completely immersed in the water and coming back out of the water.

The resurrected Jesus Christ taught the exact manner of baptism. He also taught that a condition or covenant for baptism is repentance and a desire to be baptized in His name.

Teachings about Baptism Ordinances for the Dead

In the Bible

Baptism for the dead was mentioned to the Corinthians by the Apostle Paul.[67] While he was explaining to the Corinthians the subject

---

[67] This ordinance was not taught directly in the Book of Mormon. But as the resurrected Jesus Christ taught, this was revealed in a future generation to Joseph Smith in

of resurrection, emphasizing that Jesus was the first to be resurrected, the Apostle Paul brought up the subject of baptism for the dead:

> For since by man came death, by man came also the resurrection of the dead.
>
> For as in Adam all die, even so in Christ shall all be made alive.
>
> But every man in his own order: Christ the first-fruits; afterward they that are Christ's at his coming. . . .
>
> And when all things shall be subdued unto him, then shall the Son also himself be subject unto him that put all things under him, that God may be all in all.
>
> Else what shall they do which are baptized for the dead, if the dead rise not at all? why are they then baptized for the dead? (1 Corinthians 15:21–29)

There are many different views and interpretations of this statement about baptism for the dead. However, not knowing much about what was being done with this particular practice in Paul's day, it is hard to know the exact reason why and how they practiced it. Nonetheless, it seems clear that the Apostle Paul had enough knowledge of this subject to mention it to the Corinthians.

In the Book of Mormon
Baptism for the dead was not taught in the Book of Mormon directly, but the resurrected Jesus taught it indirectly to the Nephites at Bountiful by quoting Malachi 4:5–6:

> *Behold, I will send you Elijah the prophet before the coming of the great and dreadful day of the Lord;*
>
> *And he shall turn the heart of the fathers to the children, and the heart of the children to their fathers,* lest I come and smite the earth with a curse. (3 Nephi 25:5–6; emphasis added)

1841–1842 (see D&C 124:29–39; 127:6; 128:12, 16–18).

The angel Gabriel delivered to Zacharias the same message of turning the heart of the fathers to the children in conjunction with the work of his son John the Baptist.[68] Moroni quoted Malachi 4:6 to Joseph Smith somewhat differently: "And he shall plant in the hearts of the children the promises made to the fathers, and the heart of the children shall turn to their fathers" (Joseph Smith—History 1:39).[69] Thus, Moroni explained that turning the heart of the fathers to the children means that children (including non-Hebrews like the Gentiles) will be blessed with the Abrahamic covenant through the baptism that John the Baptist introduced.[70] Turning the children's hearts to the fathers also indicates children could provide means for the same blessings to their forefathers (the dead), and that all on both sides of veil can be blessed with the Abrahamic covenant and linked as a family before the end of the world.

After he quoted Malachi 3 and 4, the resurrected Jesus taught the Nephites that this prophecy was for a future generation: "And he saith: These scriptures, which ye had not with you, the Father commanded that I should give unto you; for it was wisdom in him that they should be given unto future generations" (3 Nephi 26:2).

When the prophet Elijah comes, it will be the time when the future generations will turn their hearts to their deceased forefathers through baptism. Thus, baptism for the dead was indirectly taught to the Nephites, but it was for future generations,[71] not for the Nephites.

---

[68] When the angel Gabriel visited with Zacharias, the father of John the Baptist, in the temple prior to the conception of John, Gabriel told him that John would go before the Lord in the spirit and power of Elias to turn the heart of the fathers to the children (see Luke 1:17). Thus, Gabriel taught that all those who are baptized (including the Gentiles) would be blessed with the Abrahamic covenant through John's work (in other words, baptism by water).

69 Doctrine and Covenants 2:2 and 138:47 have the same message as the one from Moroni to Joseph Smith.

[70] This is the same line of teachings: When Nephi quoted Isaiah 48:1 in 1 Nephi 20:1, he added a phrase, "waters of baptism," and the Apostle Paul taught the same principle to the Galatians (see Galatians 3:29).

71 The Doctrine and Covenants gives more revelations to Joseph Smith on baptism for the dead in section 124 (received on January 19, 1841) and section 128 (received on September 6, 1842). Thus, the "future generation" turned out to be this dispensation, the dispensation in which the Book of Mormon was translated and published and the fullness of the gospel was restored.

Teachings on Infant Baptism

Infant baptism has been commonly practiced among many Christian churches, and it is a familiar practice even today. However, it was never mentioned in the Bible, and the practice of infant baptism started after the New Testament time. Interestingly, people in the Book of Mormon also practiced infant baptism around AD 400, and the prophet Mormon warned against it:

> For, if I have learned the truth, there have been disputations among you concerning the baptism of your little children. . . .
>
> For immediately after I had learned these things of you I inquired of the Lord concerning the matter. And the word of the Lord came to me by the power of the Holy Ghost, saying:
>
> Listen to the words of Christ, your Redeemer, your Lord and your God. Behold, I came into the world not to call the righteous but sinners to repentance; the whole need no physician, but they that are sick; wherefore, little children are whole, for they are not capable of committing sin; wherefore the curse of Adam is taken from them in me, that it hath no power over them; and the law of circumcision is done away in me.
>
> And after this manner did the Holy Ghost manifest the word of God unto me; wherefore, my beloved son, I know that it is solemn mockery before God, that ye should baptize little children. . . .
>
> And he that saith that little children need baptism denieth the mercies of Christ, and setteth at naught the atonement of him and the power of his redemption. (Moroni 8:5–20)

The prophet Mormon received a confirmation against infant baptism through the Holy Ghost, and he even called infant baptism "mockery before God." He asked his son, Moroni, to remove this gross error from the church.[72]

---

[72] King Benjamin taught a similar principle to his people around 124 BC: "And even

Baptism by the Holy Ghost (Conferring the Holy Ghost)

<u>In the Bible</u>

In the Old Testament, the name *Holy Ghost* is not found, but *Holy Spirit* is found in Psalms 51:11 and Isaiah 63:10–11. In the New Testament, the Holy Ghost was first mentioned in the explanation of Mary's conception (see Matthew 1:18–20, Luke 1:35). John the Baptist announced the ordinance of baptism by the Holy Ghost as shown in the previous section. After His Resurrection, Jesus conferred the Holy Ghost on His disciples in the following manner:

> Then said Jesus to them again, Peace *be* unto you: as *my* Father hath sent me, even so send I you. And when he had said this, *he breathed on them, and saith unto them, Receive ye the Holy Ghost: Whose soever sins ye remit, they are remitted unto them; and whose soever sins ye retain, they are retained.* (John 20:21–23; emphasis added)

Interestingly, Jesus conferred the Holy Ghost on the Apostles as a group (in the absence of Judas Iscariot and Thomas), and He taught that they could remit sins through baptism by the Holy Ghost. The Apostles also conferred the Holy Ghost by the laying on of hands: "Then laid they [Peter and John] their hands on them, and they [Samarians] received the Holy Ghost" (Acts 8:17). The Apostle Paul re-baptized a group of disciples in the name of Jesus Christ who had previously been baptized in John's name, and he conferred the Holy Ghost by laying his hands upon them:

if it were possible that little children could sin they could not be saved; but I say unto you they are blessed; for behold, as in Adam, or by nature, they fall, even so the blood of Christ atoneth for their sins. And moreover, I say unto you, that there shall be no other name given nor any other way nor means whereby salvation can come unto the children of men, only in and through the name of Christ, the Lord Omnipotent. For behold he judgeth, and his judgment is just; and the infant perisheth not that dieth in his infancy; but men drink damnation to their own souls except they humble themselves and become as little children, and believe that salvation was, and is, and is to come, in and through the atoning blood of Christ, the Lord Omnipotent" (Mosiah 3:16–18). The prophet Abinadi also taught that little children have eternal life (see Mosiah 15:25). Modern-day revelation taught that children who die under the age of accountability are saved in the celestial kingdom of heaven (see D&C 137:10).

And it came to pass, that, while Apollos was at Corinth, Paul having passed through the upper coasts came to Ephesus: and finding certain disciples,

He said unto them, Have ye received the Holy Ghost since ye believed?

And they said unto him, We have not so much as heard whether there be any Holy Ghost. And he said unto them, Unto what then were ye baptized? And they said, Unto John's baptism.

Then said Paul, John verily baptized with the baptism of repentance, saying unto the people, that they should believe on him which should come after him, that is, on Christ Jesus.

When they heard this, they were baptized in the name of the Lord Jesus.

And *when Paul had laid his hands upon them, the Holy Ghost came on them; and they spake with tongues, and prophesied.*

And all the men were about twelve. (Acts 19:1–7; emphasis added)

In the Book of Mormon

Nephi recorded that the resurrected Jesus Christ gave His Nephite disciples the power to give the Holy Ghost by touching them one by one with His hand:

> And it came to pass that when Jesus had made an end of these sayings, *he touched with his hand the disciples whom he had chosen, one by one, even until he had touched them all, and spake unto them as he touched them.*
>
> And the multitude heard not the words which he spake, therefore they did not bear record; but *the disciples bare record that he gave them power to give the Holy Ghost. And I will show unto you hereafter that this record is true.* (3 Nephi 18:36–37; emphasis added)

Moroni recorded how Jesus gave the Holy Ghost to His disciples:

The words of Christ, which he spake unto his disciples, the twelve whom he had chosen, as he laid his hands upon them—

And he called them by name, saying: *Ye shall call on the Father in my name, in mighty prayer; and after ye have done this ye shall have power that to him upon whom ye shall lay your hands, ye shall give the Holy Ghost; and in my name shall ye give it, for thus do mine apostles.*

Now Christ spake these words unto them at the time of his first appearing; and the multitude heard it not, but the disciples heard it; and *on as many as they laid their hands, fell the Holy Ghost.* (Moroni 2:1–3; emphasis added)

From the above, we learn how to confer the Holy Ghost:

- In mighty prayer, call on the Father in Jesus's name.
- Call the recipient's name.
- Lay hands on the recipient.
- Give the Holy Ghost in the name of Jesus Christ.

Calling and/or Ordaining to Priesthood Offices

In the Bible

In the Old Testament, there seemed to be multiple ways of calling prophets. For example, Moses was chosen by God directly to be a prophet (see Exodus 3:2–6). Joshua was ordained by Moses (see Deuteronomy 34:9), Samuel was called by the Lord in the temple at the age of a young lad (see 1 Samuel 3:4-14), Elijah started to work under the direction of God (see 1 Kings 17:12), Elisha became a prophet by taking over Elijah's mantle (see 2 Kings 2:12-15), Jeremiah was chosen to be a prophet by God even before he was born (see Jeremiah 1:4–5), Ezekiel started his ministry as a prophet after seeing a vision (see Ezekiel 1:1-3), and so forth.

In Solomon's temple, a Levite named Zadok was the high priest in charge of the temple. By the time of Jesus's ministry, the Sadducees (presumably a line of Zadokites) were in charge of temple affairs, but they disappeared after the second temple was destroyed in AD 70.

In the New Testament, as Jesus began His ministry, He called and ordained His disciples first (see Mark 3:14). He called the first four disciples as follows:

> And Jesus, walking by the sea of Galilee, saw two brethren, Simon called Peter, and Andrew his brother, casting a net into the sea: for they were fishers.
>
> And he saith unto them, Follow me, and I will make you fishers of men.
>
> And they straightway left their nets, and followed him.
>
> And going on from thence, he saw other two brethren, James the son of Zebedee, and John his brother, in a ship with Zebedee their father, mending their nets; and he called them.
>
> And they immediately left the ship and their father, and followed him. (Matthew 4:18–22)

After Jesus Christ's Crucifixion, there was a vacancy among the twelve Apostles because of Juda Iscariot. The Apostles filled that vacancy in the following way:

> And they [eleven Apostles] appointed two, Joseph called Barsabas, who was surnamed Justus, and Matthias.
>
> And they prayed, and said, Thou, Lord, which knowest the hearts of all men, shew whether of these two thou hast chosen,
>
> That he may take part of this ministry and apostleship, from which Judas by transgression fell, that he might go to his own place.
>
> And they gave forth their lots; and the lot fell upon Matthias; and he was numbered with the eleven apostles. (Acts 1:23–26)

Thus, it seems that there were multiple approaches to calling to the office of Apostle as well.

<u>In the Book of Mormon</u>

Nephi called his younger brothers Jacob and Joseph to be teachers and priests (see 2 Nephi 5:26; Jacob 1:18). Alma consecrated teachers and priests (see Mosiah 23:17). Alma the Younger organized the Church of God in the land of Zarahemla, ordained priests and elders by the laying on of hands according to the order of God, and instructed them to preside and watch over the Church (see Alma 4:7, 6:1). Aaron and his brethren consecrated teachers and priests among the Lamanites (see Alma 23:4). Helaman and his brethren also consecrated teachers and priests (see Alma 45:22–23). However, none of them recorded how they ordained teachers, priests, or elders.

Moroni recorded how to ordain priests and teachers:

> The manner which the disciples, who were called the elders of the church, ordained priests and teachers—
>
> *After they had prayed unto the Father in the name of Christ, they laid their hands upon them, and said:*
>
> *In the name of Jesus Christ I ordain you to be a priest (or if he be a teacher, I ordain you to be a teacher) to preach repentance and remission of sins through Jesus Christ, by the endurance of faith on his name to the end. Amen.*
>
> And after this manner did they ordain priests and teachers, according to the gifts and callings of God unto men; and they ordained them by the power of the Holy Ghost, which was in them. (Moroni 3:1–4; emphasis added)

Thus, Moroni taught that an ordination of teachers and priests must be done by the power of the Holy Ghost according to the following:

- Pray unto the Father in the name of Christ.
- Lay hands upon the recipient.
- Say these words: "In the name of Jesus Christ, I ordain you to be a priest [or teacher] to preach repentance and remission of sins through Jesus Christ, by the endurance of faith on his name to the end. Amen."

Administration of the Sacramental Bread and Wine

In the Bible

Jesus Christ blessed the bread and wine and gave them to His disciples at the Last Supper, as recorded by Matthew:

> And as they were eating, Jesus took bread, and blessed it, and brake it, and gave it to the disciples, and said, Take, eat; this is my body.
>
> And he took the cup, and gave thanks, and gave it to them, saying, Drink ye all of it;
>
> For this is my blood of the new testament, which is shed for many for the remission of sins. (Matthew 26:26–28; see also Mark 14:22–25; Luke 22:19–20)

In the Book of Mormon

The resurrected Jesus Christ twice performed the same ordinances with bread and wine for the Nephites (see 3 Nephi 18:1–4; 20:2–8). Just as all four writers of the Gospels in the New Testament did not record the exact manner of administering the sacramental bread and wine, Nephi did not record it either. However, Moroni recorded how to administer the sacramental bread and wine. Elders and priests administering the flesh and blood of Christ are to kneel down with the Church and pray to the Father in the name of Christ with the following sacramental prayers:

For bread:

> O God, the Eternal Father, we ask thee in the name of thy Son, Jesus Christ, to bless and sanctify this bread to the souls of all those who partake of it; that they may eat in remembrance of the body of thy Son, and witness unto thee, O God, the Eternal Father, that they are willing to take upon them the name of thy Son, and always remember him, and keep his commandments which he hath given them, that they may always have his Spirit to be with them. Amen. (Moroni 4:3)

For wine by taking the cup:

> O God, the Eternal Father, we ask thee, in the name of thy Son, Jesus Christ, to bless and sanctify this wine to the souls of all those who drink of it, that they may do it in remembrance of the blood of thy Son, which was shed for them; that they may witness unto thee, O God, the Eternal Father, that they do always remember him, that they may have his Spirit to be with them. Amen. (Moroni 5:2)

As shown in the above prayers, both priesthood ordinances should be done for the following purposes:

- In remembrance of the sacrificed body and blood of the Son of God.
- As a covenant to witness His name, to keep His commandments, and to remember Him always.
- To have His Spirit with them.

For those who keep these covenants as they partake of the sacramental bread and wine, the Lord covenants that His Spirit will be with them.

Priesthood Leadership

During the patriarch days in the Old Testament (as recorded in Genesis), there was no record of the priesthood and its authorities other than mentions of Melchizedek, the king of Salem. Their records were more focused on the patriarchal blood lineage and birthrights. After a brief period during the reign of the Judges, there was a separation between political and religious leadership in general, and prophets from Samuel to Malachi were the religious and spiritual leaders. As far as their priestly work was concerned, their main ordinances were done by the Levites and their descendants in the tabernacle and/or temple.

John the Baptist challenged the contemporary religious leadership with an announcement that a new leader, Jesus of Nazareth, would have a higher (priesthood) authority, and the new baptismal ordinances by water and the Holy Ghost would replace all the priesthood works in the temple (see Matthew 3:7–12). Later, the Apostle Paul confirmed that Jesus Christ has the power for eternal life as a priest after the order of Melchizedek forever (see Hebrews 7:15–17). Jesus established His Church by calling His twelve Apostles, and they performed the new priesthood ordinances of baptism by water and the Holy Ghost (see, for example, Acts 2:41–42).

Thus, the prophets of God, the Levites, and the Apostles have historically been the priesthood leaders chosen by the Lord in the Bible.

Leadership of the Judeo-Christian Churches of the Modern Days
Rabbinical Leadership

After the second temple in Jerusalem was destroyed and the Jews were scattered around the world in AD 70, some types of new rabbinical leadership were developed. Even during the ministry of Jesus Christ, it is noticeable that respectable and wise teachers in a community were called rabbi, meaning "master." For example, Nicodemus, a Pharisee, called Jesus Rabbi to show his respect for Jesus as a great teacher (see John 3:2).

In modern days, there are formal rabbinical training institutes, and their graduates become rabbis. The rabbinical leadership gradually became more than just teachers, and today they fill religious leadership roles like Christian priests or clergies who minister to the needs of their congregations. In a way, the priesthood leadership and authority has now been replaced by formally and professionally trained rabbis among the Jews.

Leadership of Christian Churches

After the ascension of the resurrected Jesus Christ, the Apostle Peter and James (brother of Jesus) seemed to be the body of authority of the Church (see Galatians 2:9). The beginning of the book of Acts recorded the Apostle Peter's leadership and ministry, but the book finished with the Apostle Paul's proselyting works to the Gentiles.

After this generation of Apostles, multiple Christian groups developed in different regions like Jerusalem, Rome, Antioch, Alexandria, and other places around the Mediterranean Sea. It is not certain how long there was direct succession with the apostolic priesthood authority in the early days of Christianity.

Emperor Constantine ordered the formation of a unified Christian church, and the Catholic Church headed by a Pope was born at the

Council of Nicaea in AD 325. Until the College of Cardinals started to elect the next Pope as a body of the College from AD 1059, the Popes were usually chosen from among the Roman cardinals.[73] The Papal authority was so absolute during the midcenturies that some even promoted a concept of the Pope's infallibility.[74] The church announced officially in the nineteenth century that the Apostle Peter was the first Pope.

Opinions on the legitimacy of a Pope truly representing Christ vary from acknowledgment that Emperor Constantine practically appointed (or approved) the first Pope to the belief that the Apostle Peter was the first Pope. Nonetheless, it seems that the Papal authority is quite different from the authority of the Levite and Melchizedek priesthoods as taught in the Bible.

During the reformation period in the sixteenth century, Martin Luther introduced a new view of the priesthood, maybe in an effort to minimize (or even nullify) Papal authority. As an example, he promoted a theological concept that everyone is a priest by citing the specific passages in the New Testament, such as "But ye are a chosen generation, a royal priesthood, an holy nation, a peculiar people; that ye should shew forth the praises of him who hath called you out of darkness into his marvelous light" (1 Peter 2:9) and "And hath made us kings and priests unto God and his Father; to him be glory and dominion for ever and ever. Amen" (Revelation 1:6).

After the Calvinists started a council of elders to represent a congregation of laymen in each church unit, it became a common practice for the council to hire their ministers from those ordained ministers

---

[73] The newly selected Popes were often sanctioned by powerful kings in Europe.

[74] For the doctrine of infallibility of the Pope, see https://www.catholic.com/tract/papal-infallibility (also see http://www.catholicfaithandreason.org/papal-infallibility.html). Vatican II explained the doctrine of infallibility as follows: "Although the individual bishops do not enjoy the prerogative of infallibility, they can nevertheless proclaim Christ's doctrine infallibly. This is so, even when they are dispersed around the world, provided that while maintaining the bond of unity among themselves and with Peter's successor, and while teaching authentically on a matter of faith or morals, they concur in a single viewpoint as the one which must be held conclusively. This authority is even more clearly verified when, gathered together in an ecumenical council, they are teachers and judges of faith and morals for the universal Church. Their definitions must then be adhered to with the submission of faith" (Lumen Gentium 25).

with seminary education. In most cases, a newly hired minister must be ratified by the higher church council of his or her denomination.[75] The responsibility of a minister is to teach and minister to the laymen of the church unit within the guidelines of his or her denomination. This professional clergy leadership system does not seem to have any relationship with the Levite and Melchizedek priesthoods.

However, the Jewish rabbinical and Christian clergy leaderships in the Judeo-Christian churches have become very common, and so much goodness has come from their leadership and service to billions of people collectively that it is hard to imagine not having them in most Judeo-Christian communities around the world. In spite of their good works and sacrifices, the leadership of the Judeo-Christian churches do not seem to have any priesthood connections with the Levites and Melchizedek that was taught and practiced in the Bible.

Priesthood Leaderships of The Church of Jesus Christ of Latter-day Saints

The first prophet of The Church of Jesus Christ of Latter-day Saints, Joseph Smith, received the following revelation on the Aaronic (or Levitical) and Melchizedek priesthoods in AD 1835:

> There are, in the church, two priesthoods, namely, the Melchizedek and Aaronic, including the Levitical Priesthood.
>
> Why the first is called the Melchizedek Priesthood is because Melchizedek was such a great high priest.
>
> Before his day it was called *the Holy Priesthood, after the Order of the Son of God.*
>
> But out of respect or reverence to the name of the Supreme Being, to avoid the too frequent repetition of his name, they, the church, in ancient days, called that priesthood after Melchizedek, or the Melchizedek Priesthood.
>
> All other authorities or offices in the church are appendages to this priesthood. . . .

---

[75] Since the protestant churches are organized by different denominations, most denominations have their own administrative control system in place.

The second priesthood is called the Priesthood of Aaron, because it was conferred upon Aaron and his seed, throughout all their generations.

Why it is called the lesser priesthood is because it is an appendage to the greater, or the Melchizedek Priesthood, and has power in administering outward ordinances.

The bishopric is the presidency of this priesthood, and holds the keys or authority of the same.

No man has a legal right to this office, to hold the keys of this priesthood, except he be a literal descendant of Aaron.

But as a high priest of the Melchizedek Priesthood has authority to officiate in all the lesser offices, he may officiate in the office of bishop when no literal descendant of Aaron can be found, provided he is called and set apart and ordained unto this power by the hands of the Presidency of the Melchizedek Priesthood.

The power and authority of the higher, or Melchizedek Priesthood, is to hold the keys of all the spiritual blessings of the church—

To have the privilege of receiving the mysteries of the kingdom of heaven, to have the heavens opened unto them, to commune with the general assembly and church of the Firstborn, and to enjoy the communion and presence of God the Father, and Jesus the mediator of the new covenant.

The power and authority of the lesser, or Aaronic Priesthood, is to hold the keys of the ministering of angels, and to administer in outward ordinances, the letter of the gospel, the baptism of repentance for the remission of sins, agreeable to the covenants and commandments. (D&C 107:1–20)

Restoration of the Aaronic and Melchizedek Priesthoods

As an angel, John the Baptist came to visit Joseph Smith and Oliver Cowdery near Harmony, Pennsylvania, on May 15, 1829. There he conferred the Aaronic Priesthood upon them by saying the following:

Upon you my fellow servants, in the name of Messiah I confer the Priesthood of Aaron, which holds the keys of the ministering of angels, and of the gospel of repentance, and of baptism by immersion for the remission of sins; and this shall never be taken again from the earth, until the sons of Levi do offer again an offering unto the Lord in righteousness. (D&C 13:1)

As angels, the three chief Apostles of Jesus Christ—Peter, James, and John—came to visit Joseph Smith and Oliver Cowdery not long after John the Baptist visited. They ordained Joseph and Oliver to the apostleship with the same priesthood authority as theirs, which they had received directly from Jesus Christ:

And also with Peter, and James, and John, whom I [Jesus Christ] have sent unto you [Joseph Smith and Oliver Cowdrey] by whom I have ordained you and confirmed you to be apostles, and especial witnesses of my name, and bear the keys of your ministry and of the same things which I revealed unto them;

Unto whom I have committed the keys of my kingdom, and a dispensation of the gospel for the last times; and for the fulness of times, in the which I will gather together in one all things, both which are in heaven, and which are on earth;

And also with all those whom my Father hath given me out of the world. (D&C 27:12–14)

Thus, both the Aaronic (Levitical) and Apostolic (Melchizedek) priesthoods were restored to The Church of Jesus Christ of Latter-day Saints.

Three Priesthood Keys

In addition to the restoration of these priesthoods, additional priesthood keys were restored to the Church. In a vision at the Kirtland

Temple[76] on April 3, 1836,[77] Joseph Smith and Oliver Cowdery received three priesthood keys: the gathering of Israel, from Moses; the gospel of Abraham, from Elias; and the Spirit of Elijah, from Elijah:

> After this vision closed, the heavens were again opened unto us; and Moses appeared before us, and committed unto us the keys of the gathering of Israel from the four parts of the earth, and the leading of the ten tribes from the land of the north.
>
> After this, Elias appeared, and committed the dispensation of the gospel of Abraham, saying that in us and our seed all generations after us should be blessed.
>
> After this vision had closed, another great and glorious vision burst upon us; for Elijah the prophet, who was taken to heaven without tasting death, stood before us, and said:
>
> Behold, the time has fully come, which was spoken of by the mouth of Malachi—testifying that he [Elijah] should be sent, before the great and dreadful day of the Lord come—
>
> To turn the hearts of the fathers to the children, and the children to the fathers, lest the whole earth be smitten with a curse—
>
> Therefore, the keys of this dispensation are committed into your hands; and by this ye may know that the great and dreadful day of the Lord is near, even at the doors. (D&C 110:11–16)

Thus, both the Aaronic (Levitical) and Melchizedek priesthoods as well as three priesthood keys were restored to The Church of Jesus Christ of Latter-day Saints.

---

[76] It is interesting to compare the following contrast between the old Jewish and the new modern-day temples:
- The sacred old Jewish temple was operated by Sadducees, who did not believe in resurrection.
- The new modern-day temples are the sacred edifices of vicarious ordinances for the resurrection of the dead.

[77] This day was an Easter Sunday as well as the second day of Passover week in 1836.

The ecclesiastic leadership of the Church is organized in line with the Aaronic (Levitical) and Melchizedek priesthoods. Priests, teachers, and deacons are ordained to their offices in the Aaronic Priesthood. High priests (including the sustained prophets and Apostles), seventies, and elders are ordained to their offices in the Melchizedek Priesthood. Thus, the organizational structure of the ecclesiastic leadership is similar to that in the primitive Church organization and in line with the Aaronic (Levitical) and Melchizedek priesthoods.

Chapter 7

Joint Teaching Examples

THEREFORE REPENT, AND BE BAPTIZED in the name of Jesus, and lay hold upon the gospel of Christ, which shall be set before you, not only in this record but also in the record which shall come unto the Gentiles from the Jews, which record shall come from the Gentiles unto you.

For behold, this is written for the intent that ye may believe that; and if ye believe that ye will believe this also; and if ye believe this ye will know concerning your fathers, and also the marvelous works which were wrought by the power of God among them.

And ye will also know that ye are a remnant of the seed of Jacob; therefore ye are numbered among the people of the first covenant; and if it so be that ye believe in Christ, and are baptized, first with water, then with fire and with the Holy Ghost, following the example of our Savior, according to that which he hath commanded us, it shall be well with you in the day of judgment. Amen. (Mormon 7:8–10)

As shown above, the prophet Mormon said that the Book of Mormon was written for the intent that the remnant of Joseph may believe the Bible. If they believe the Bible, they will believe the Book of Mormon, and they can be numbered among the people of the first covenant. If they repent and are baptized and follow the example of the Savior, they will be well in the day of judgment.

In this chapter, we will discuss ten exemplary joint teachings by both the Bible and the Book of Mormon:

1. The doctrine of Christ.
2. Faith, hope, meekness, and charity.
3. Justification by faith versus judgment according to works.
4. The parable of the sower and the analogy of the seed.
5. Adam's transgression and the Atonement of Jesus Christ
6. Examples of dramatic conversions.
7. The prophecy of "the first being last, and the last being the first."
8. An example of the hand-and-glove fit point by point (see John 1:1–18 and 3 Nephi 9:15–22).
9. The discipleship of Jesus Christ.
10. A unique teaching example from the Book of Mormon.

The Doctrine of Christ

Both the Bible and the Book of Mormon teach the doctrine[78] of Christ. The word doctrine is mentioned fifty-six times in the Bible and twenty-nine times in the Book of Mormon (including one in the heading of the book of Jacob), but there are only a few cases that explain what the doctrine of Christ is.

In the Bible

The word *doctrine* appears six times in the Old Testament and fifty times in the New Testament (fourteen times in the four Gospels, twenty-three times in the epistles written by the Apostle Paul, and thirteen times in additional text).

Jesus maintained that what He taught was not His doctrine, but it was from His Father who sent Him:

> Now about the midst of the feast Jesus went up into the temple, and taught.
>
> And the Jews marvelled, saying, How knoweth this man letters, having never learned?
>
> *Jesus answered them, and said, My doctrine is not mine, but his that sent me.*

---

[78] The Merriam-Webster dictionary defines the word doctrine as "a set of ideas or beliefs that are taught or believed to be true."

*If any man will do his will, he shall know of the doc-
trine, whether it be of God, or whether I speak of myself.*

He that speaketh of himself seeketh his own glory:
but he that seeketh his glory that sent him, the same is
true, and no unrighteousness is in him. (John 7:14–18;
emphasis added)

In most cases, the contents of the doctrine were not explicitly explained in the Bible. For example, Matthew and Luke did not say the
parable of the sower was the doctrine (see Matthew 13:3–9; Luke 8:4–
8), but Mark recorded that Jesus taught the parable of the sower as a part
of His doctrine: "And he taught them many things by parables, and said
unto them in his doctrine" (Mark 4:2).

The Apostle Paul admonished that we should become perfect like Jesus Christ by living beyond the basic doctrine. For this, he used an analogy of adults eating meat instead of drinking milk like little children:

Therefore leaving the principles of the doctrine of
Christ, let us go on unto perfection; not laying again the
foundation of repentance from dead works, and of faith
toward God,

Of the doctrine of baptisms, and of laying on of
hands, and of resurrection of the dead, and of eternal
judgment. (Hebrews 6:1–2)

In this quote, the Apostle Paul teaches that the doctrine includes repentance, faith, baptism, laying on of hands, resurrection, and the eternal (final) judgment.

In the Book of Mormon

The word *doctrine* appears twenty-nine times in the Book of Mormon. The content of the doctrine is explicitly taught in only a couple
of cases: in 2 Nephi 31 by Nephi and in 3 Nephi 11 by the resurrected
Jesus.

The following is Nephi's teaching on the doctrine of Christ (2 Nephi
31):

Doctrine of Christ (see verses 2–4): Beginning statement

"Wherefore, the things which I have written sufficeth me, save it be a few words which I must speak concerning the *doctrine of Christ*; wherefore, I shall speak unto you plainly, according to the plainness of my prophesying" (2 Nephi 31:2; emphasis added).

Baptism by Water (see verses 5–7)

"And now, if the Lamb of God, he being holy, should have need to be baptized by water, to fulfil all righteousness, O then, how much more need have we, being unholy, to be baptized, yea, even by water!" (2 Nephi 31:5).

Baptism by the Holy Ghost (see verses 8–13)

> Wherefore, after he was baptized with water the Holy Ghost descended upon him in the form of a dove.
> . . .
> *And also, the voice of the Son came unto me, saying: He that is baptized in my name, to him will the Father give the Holy Ghost, like unto me; wherefore, follow me, and do the things which ye have seen me do* . . . by baptism—yea, by following your Lord and your Savior down into the water, according to his word, behold, *then shall ye receive the Holy Ghost; yea, then cometh the baptism of fire and of the Holy Ghost*; and then can ye speak with the tongue of angels, and shout praises unto the Holy One of Israel. (2 Nephi 31:8–13; emphasis added)

Endure to the End (see verses 14–17)

> But, behold, my beloved brethren, thus came the voice of the Son unto me, saying: After ye have repented of your sins, and witnessed unto the Father that ye are willing to keep my commandments, by the baptism of water, and have received the baptism of fire and of the Holy Ghost, and can speak with a new tongue, yea, even with the tongue of angels, and after this should deny

me, it would have been better for you that ye had not known me.

And I heard a voice from the Father, saying: Yea, *the words of my Beloved are true and faithful. He that endureth to the end, the same shall be saved. And now, my beloved brethren, I know by this that unless a man shall endure to the end, in following the example of the Son of the living God, he cannot be saved.* (2 Nephi 31:14–15; emphasis added)

Eternal Life (see verses 18–20)

Wherefore, *ye must press forward with a steadfastness in Christ, having a perfect brightness of hope, and a love of God and of all men. Wherefore, if ye shall press forward, feasting upon the word of Christ, and endure to the end,* behold, thus saith the Father: Ye shall have eternal life. (2 Nephi 31:20; emphasis added)

The Doctrine of Christ (see verse 21): Ending Statement

And now, behold, my beloved brethren, this is the way; and there is none other way nor name given under heaven whereby man can be saved in the kingdom of God. And now, behold, *this is the doctrine of Christ*, and the only and true doctrine of the Father, and of the Son, and of the Holy Ghost, which is one God, without end. Amen. (2 Nephi 31:21)

Nephi simply taught that the doctrine of Christ includes baptism by water (with humility and repentance), baptism by the Holy Ghost, enduring to the end, and living with the power of the Holy Ghost to obtain eternal life. He also taught that the Holy Ghost will guide one's life if he or she follows the doctrine of Christ.

The Resurrected Jesus Christ Taught His Doctrine (3 Nephi 11)

During His three-day visit to the Nephites, Jesus taught the following about His doctrine:

Behold, verily, verily, I say unto you, *I will declare unto you my doctrine.*

And this is my doctrine, and it is the doctrine which the Father hath given unto me; and I bear record of the Father, and the Father beareth record of me, and the Holy Ghost beareth record of the Father and me; and I bear record that the Father commandeth all men, everywhere, to repent and believe in me.

And whoso *believeth in me, and is baptized, the same shall be saved;* . . .

[The Father] will visit him with fire and with the Holy Ghost.

And thus will the Father bear record of me, and the Holy Ghost will bear record unto him of the Father and me; for the Father, and I, and the Holy Ghost are one.

And again I say unto you, ye must *repent*, and become *as a little child*, and be baptized in my name, or ye can in nowise receive these things . . .

. . . *[t]his is my doctrine, and whoso buildeth upon this buildeth upon my rock, and the gates of hell shall not prevail against them* (3 Nephi 11:31–39; emphasis added).

Jesus Christ taught the Nephites that to inherit the kingdom of God, they must be humble as little children, have faith in Christ, repent of their sins, and be baptized by water and by the Holy Ghost. He called this way of living building upon His rock. He confirmed that the Father, Jesus Himself, and the Holy Ghost are in this together as one.

The resurrected Jesus Christ also taught the Nephites His gospel with the following definition and admonition:

Behold I have given unto you my gospel, and *this is the gospel* which I have given unto you—that I came into the world to do the will of my Father, because my Father sent me. . . .

Verily, verily, I say unto you, *this is my gospel*; and ye know the things that ye must do in my church; for the works which ye have seen me do that shall ye also do; for that which ye have seen me do even that shall ye do. (3 Nephi 27:13–21; emphasis added)

As shown above, the Nephites were taught a much plainer and clearer definition of the doctrine and the gospel of Christ than the Judeo-Christians have been through the Bible.

Faith, Hope, Meekness, and Charity (or Love)

Jesus Christ taught the importance of charity and love very clearly. Both the Bible and the Book of Mormon provide very inspirational teachings on this subject. However, while the Apostle Paul taught of faith, hope, and charity in the Bible, the prophet Mormon taught of faith, hope, meekness, and charity in the Book of Mormon.

<u>In the Bible</u>
What Jesus Taught
The synopsists recorded Jesus's teaching on charity and love for God and neighbor with some variations. Matthew recorded two greatest commandments by Jesus Christ succinctly:

> Then one of them, which was a lawyer, asked him a question, tempting him, and saying,
> Master, which is the great commandment in the law?
> Jesus said unto him, Thou shalt love the Lord thy God with all thy heart, and with all thy soul, and with all thy mind.
> This is the first and great commandment.
> And the second is like unto it, Thou shalt love thy neighbour as thyself.
> On these two commandments hang all the law and the prophets. (Matthew 22:35–40)

Mark added to Matthew's report (above) that a scribe confirmed what Jesus taught (since they knew the scriptures well) by responding, "Well, Master, thou hast said the truth: for there is one God; and there is none other but he: And to love him with all the heart, and with all the understanding, and with all the soul, and with all the strength, and to love his neighbour as himself, is

more than all whole burnt offerings and sacrifices" (Mark 12:32–33). However, Luke recorded that the lawyer who asked the question was willing to
justify, and asked Jesus who his neighbor was (see Luke 10:29). In answering,
Jesus taught the parable of the good Samaritan.[79]

What Moses and Joshua Taught

The law of Moses taught the same lessons and commandments
about love of God and neighbor, and the Pharisees and scribes had to be
very familiar with what Jesus said about loving God and their neighbors
(see Leviticus 19:18; Deuteronomy 6:5–6; 10:12–13; 11:1; 3:16 and 20;
Joshua 22:5).[80] Jesus basically retaught the Jewish leaders some parts of

---

[79] The parable of the good Samaritan: "And Jesus answering said, A certain man
went down from Jerusalem to Jericho, and fell among thieves, which stripped him of
his raiment, and wounded him, and departed, leaving him half dead. And by chance
there came down a certain priest that way: and when he saw him, he passed by on
the other side. And likewise a Levite, when he was at the place, came and looked
on him, and passed by on the other side. But a certain Samaritan, as he journeyed,
came where he was: and when he saw him, he had compassion on him, And went
to him, and bound up his wounds, pouring in oil and wine, and set him on his own
beast, and brought him to an inn, and took care of him. And on the morrow when
he departed, he took out two pence, and gave them to the host, and said unto him,
Take care of him; and whatsoever thou spendest more, when I come again, I will
repay thee. Which now of these three, thinkest thou, was neighbour unto him that
fell among the thieves? And he said, He that shewed mercy on him. Then said Jesus
unto him, Go, and do thou likewise" (Luke 10: 30–37).

[80]"Thou shalt not avenge, nor bear any grudge against the children of thy people,
but thou shalt love thy neighbour as thyself: I am the Lord" (Leviticus 19:18).

"And thou shalt love the Lord thy God with all thine heart, and with all thy soul,
and with all thy might. And these words, which I command thee this day, shall be in
thine heart" (Deuteronomy 6:5–6).

"And now, Israel, what doth the Lord thy God require of thee, but to fear the Lord
thy God, to walk in all his ways, and to love him, and to serve the Lord thy God with all
thy heart and with all thy soul, To keep the commandments of the Lord, and his statutes,
which I command thee this day for thy good?" (Deuteronomy 10:12–13).

"Therefore thou shalt love the Lord thy God, and keep his charge, and his statutes, and his judgments, and his commandments, alway" (Deuteronomy 11:1).

"In that I command thee this day to love the Lord thy God, to walk in his ways,
and to keep his commandments and his statutes and his judgments, that thou mayest live and multiply: and the Lord thy God shall bless thee in the land whither thou
goest to possess it. . . . That thou mayest love the Lord thy God, and that thou mayest obey his voice, and that thou mayest cleave unto him: for he is thy life, and the

the law of Moses that they already knew at an expert level.

What the Apostle Paul Taught

In his letter to the Corinthians, the Apostle Paul correlated the three attributes of faith, hope, and charity (or love) in such a profound and inspiring way that it may be one of the most influential as well as most-quoted scriptural verses for Christians:

> Though I speak with the tongues of men and of angels, and have not *charity*, I am become as sounding brass, or a tinkling cymbal.
>
> And though I have *the gift of* prophecy, and understand all mysteries, and all knowledge; and though I have all faith, so that I could remove mountains, and have not *charity*, I am nothing.
>
> And though I bestow all my goods to feed *the poor*, and though I give my body to be burned, and have not *charity*, it profiteth me nothing.
>
> *Charity* suffereth long, *and* is kind; charity envieth not; *charity* vaunteth not itself, is not puffed up,
>
> Doth not behave itself unseemly, seeketh not her own, is not easily provoked, thinketh no evil;
>
> Rejoiceth not in iniquity, but rejoiceth in the truth;
>
> Beareth all things, believeth all things, *hopeth* all things, endureth all things.
>
> *Charity* never faileth: but whether *there be* prophecies, they shall fail; whether *there be* tongues, they shall cease; whether *there be* knowledge, it shall vanish away.
>
> For we know in part, and we prophesy in part.
>
> But when that which is perfect is come, then that which is in part shall be done away.

---

length of thy days: that thou mayest dwell in the land which the Lord sware unto thy fathers, to Abraham, to Isaac, and to Jacob, to give them" (Deuteronomy 30:16, 20).

"But take diligent heed to do the commandment and the law, which Moses the servant of the Lord charged you, to love the Lord your God, and to walk in all his ways, and to keep his commandments, and to cleave unto him, and to serve him with all your heart and with all your soul" (Joshua 22:5).

> When I was a child, I spake as a child, I understood as a child, I thought as a child: but when I became a man, I put away childish things.
>
> For now we see through a glass, darkly; but then face to face: now I know in part; but then shall I know even as also I am known.
>
> And now abideth *faith*, *hope*, *charity*, these three; but the greatest of these is charity. (1 Corinthians 13:1–13; emphasis added)

For most (if not all) Christians, a combination of the Sermon on the Mount, Jesus's teaching on the two great commandments, and the Apostle Paul's discourse of charity (or love) may be the most inspiring guideposts from the New Testament for living a true Christian life.

In the Book of Mormon
In the Book of Mormon, Mormon, Alma, and Moroni taught the subject of charity.

What Mormon Taught
Moroni recorded his father Mormon's sermon concerning faith, hope, meekness, and charity as follows:

> For no man can be saved, according to the words of Christ, save they shall have *faith* in his name; wherefore, if these things have ceased, then has *faith* ceased also; and awful is the state of man, for they are as though there had been no redemption made.
>
> But behold, my beloved brethren, I judge better things of you, for I judge that ye have *faith* in Christ because of your *meekness*; for if ye have not faith in him then ye are not fit to be numbered among the people of his church.

And again, my beloved brethren, I would speak unto you concerning *hope*. How is it that ye can attain unto *faith*, save ye shall have *hope*?

And what is it that ye shall *hope* for? Behold I say unto you that ye shall have *hope* through the atonement of Christ and the power of his resurrection, to be raised unto life eternal, and this because of your *faith* in him according to the promise.

Wherefore, if a man have *faith* he must needs have *hope*; for without *faith* there cannot be any *hope*.

And again, behold I say unto you that he cannot have *faith and hope*, save he shall be *meek, and lowly of heart*.

If so, his *faith* and *hope* is vain, for none is acceptable before God, save the *meek and lowly in heart*; and if a man be *meek and lowly in heart*, and confesses by the power of the Holy Ghost that Jesus is the Christ, he must needs have *charity*; for if he have not *charity* he is nothing; wherefore he must needs have *charity*.

And *charity* suffereth long, and is kind, and envieth not, and is not puffed up, seeketh not her own, is not easily provoked, thinketh no evil, and rejoiceth not in iniquity but rejoiceth in the truth, beareth all things, believeth all things, hopeth all things, endureth all things.

Wherefore, my beloved brethren, if ye have not *charity*, ye are nothing, for *charity* never faileth. Wherefore, cleave unto *charity*, which is the greatest of all, for all things must fail—

But *charity* is the *pure love of Christ*, and it endureth forever; and whoso is found possessed of it at the last day, it shall be well with him.

Wherefore, my beloved brethren, pray unto the Father with all the energy of heart, that ye may be filled with this *love*, which he hath bestowed upon all who are true followers of his Son, Jesus Christ; that ye may become the sons of God; that when he shall appear we shall be like him, for we shall see him as he is; that we

> may have this *hope*; that we may be purified even as he is
> pure. Amen. (Moroni 7:38–48; emphasis added)

Mormon added "meek and lowly of heart" to faith, hope, and charity. He also specified that hope is for the Atonement of Christ, the power of His Resurrection, and to be raised unto life eternal (see verse 41). With faith, hope, and meekness and lowliness of heart, one must have charity to confess by the power of the Holy Ghost that Jesus is the Christ (see verse 44). He defined charity the same as the Apostle Paul had done (see verse 45).

While the Apostle Paul taught the significance of faith, hope, and charity, Mormon tied faith, hope, meekness, and charity to Christ, the Resurrection and Atonement, and the power of the Holy Ghost. Thus, the Nephites were taught that charity (or love) requires faith in Christ, hope through Christ, and meekness of heart to work with the Holy Ghost. Mormon taught that charity is closely connected with Christ and the Holy Ghost. Their two discourses may be represented in the following graphic diagram:

What Alma Taught

Alma also taught faith, hope, and charity in conjunction with good works:

> And now I would that ye should be humble, and be submissive and gentle; easy to be entreated; full of patience and long-suffering; being temperate in all things; being diligent in keeping the commandments of God at all times; asking for whatsoever things ye stand in need, both spiritual and temporal; always returning thanks unto God for whatsoever things ye do receive.
>
> And see that ye have *faith, hope, and charity, and then ye will always abound in good works.* (Alma 7:23–24; emphasis added)

This may be the same sort of teaching as that by the Apostle James: "Even so faith, if it hath not works, is dead, being alone" (James 2:17). Thus, good works are essential along with faith, hope, and charity; we show our faith, hope, and charity through good works.

What Moroni Taught

Moroni also quoted the Lord: "Behold, I will show unto the Gentiles their weakness, and I will show unto them that faith, hope and charity bringeth unto me—the fountain of all righteousness" (Ether 12:28).

Combining all the referenced teachings on charity and love from both the Bible and the Book of Mormon, we can conclude that the two greatest commandments are love of God and love of our neighbors: *With hope for the Atonement and resurrection of Jesus Christ, and with love of God and neighbors manifested through good works, one will be able to confess Jesus Christ in faith and meekness by the power of the Holy Ghost and live of the fountain of all righteousness of the Lord.*

"Justification by Faith" versus "Judgment According to Works"

Jesus Christ taught the scribes and Pharisees that judgment, mercy, and faith are the weightier matters of the law (see Matthew 23:23). In teachings on these three weightier matters from both scriptures, the word *judgment* can be closely related to *justice* and/or *justify*; *mercy* can be closely related to *grace*; and *faith* can be closely related to *works* or *deeds*. In combining these words, it is noticeable that the terms *judged by faith* and *justified by works* are not taught, but there are many teachings on *justified by faith*, *judged according to works*, and *justice and mercy*.

In the Bible

In the New Testament, the Apostle Paul's fourteen epistles[81] constitute about 30 percent of the New Testament. If we include the writing on his proselyting (or evangelical) life from Acts 16 to its end (Acts 28) and combine overlapping stories in the four Gospels, about 40 percent of the New Testament contains records about or by the Apostle Paul. Consequently, Paul's teachings (in other word, the *Pauline doctrine*) can easily dominate the teachings of others. As an example, Paul taught the importance of faith with great emphasis; *faith* appears 245 times in the New Testament, and 70 percent of those (171 times) appears in Paul's epistles (mostly in Romans 3–4, Galatians 2–3, and Hebrews 11). Interestingly, *faith* appears only twenty-nine times in the four Gospels (none in the Gospel of John), but twenty-four times in Hebrews 11 alone.

Paul also taught the importance of being justified by faith and/or grace in conjunction with no need for circumcisions for Gentile converts. He taught the Hebrew (or Jewish) Christians, including Peter, that circumcision (in other words, work) was not necessary for the Gentiles to accept Jesus Christ.

Following are excerpts of some of Paul's addresses in Romans and Galatians.

Romans 3:27–31

> Where is boasting then? It is excluded. By what law? of works? Nay: but by the law of faith.
>
> Therefore we conclude that *a man is justified by faith* without the deeds of the law.
>
> *Is he* the God of the Jews only? is *he* not also of the Gentiles? Yes, of the Gentiles also:

---

[81] Some scholars do not think the book of Hebrews is Paul's epistle, and count only thirteen epistles by Paul in the New Testament.

Seeing it is one God, which shall *justify the circumcision by faith, and uncircumcision through faith.*

Do we then make void the law through faith? God forbid: yea, we *establish the law.* (Emphasis added)

Romans 4:5 and 5:1

"But *to him that worketh not, but believeth on him that justifieth the ungodly, his faith is counted for righteousness*" (emphasis added).

"Therefore *being justified by faith,* we have peace with God through our Lord Jesus Christ" (emphasis added).

Galatians 2:16

Knowing that a man is not justified by the works of the law, but by the faith of Jesus Christ, even we have believed in Jesus Christ, that we might be justified by the faith of Christ, and not by the works of the law: for by the works of the law shall no flesh be justified.

Galatians 3:8–24

And the scripture, foreseeing that *God would justify the heathen through faith,* preached before the gospel unto Abraham, saying, In thee shall all nations be blessed. . . .

But that *no man is justified by the law in the sight of God, it is evident: for, The just shall live by faith.*

And the law is not of faith: but, The man that doeth them shall live in them. . . .

Wherefore the law was our schoolmaster *to bring us* unto Christ, that we *might be justified by faith.* (Emphasis added)

Even if there is no doctrine that "one can be saved by faith alone" found in the New Testament,[82] the Apostle Paul strongly emphasized faith over works with comments like "dead works" (Hebrews 6:1; 9:14) and "justified by faith" (Romans 1:17; 3:28–30; Galatians 2:16). That emphasis might have led theologians like Martin Luther[83] to teach the so-called *sola fide* ("faith alone"). Contrary to this, the word *faith* cannot be found in the Gospel of John. Jesus Christ taught, "The Son of Man shall reward every man according to his works" (Matthew 16:27), the Apostle Peter taught "the Father judgeth according to everyman's work" (1 Peter 1:17), the Apostle John taught "being judged according to their works" (Revelation 20:12–13), and the Apostle James also taught "faith without works is dead":

> Even so *faith, if it hath not works, is dead, being alone.*
>
> Yea, a man may say, Thou hast faith, and I have works: shew me thy faith without thy works, and *I will shew thee my faith by my works.*
>
> Thou believest that there is one God; thou doest well: the devils also believe, and tremble.
>
> But wilt thou know, O vain man, that faith without works is dead?
>
> Was not Abraham our father justified by works, when he had offered Isaac his son upon the altar?
>
> Seest thou *how faith wrought with his works, and by works was faith made perfect?*
>
> And the scripture was fulfilled which saith, Abraham believed God, and it was imputed unto him for righteousness: and he was called the Friend of God.
>
> Ye see then *how that by works a man is justified, and not by faith only.* (James 2:17–24; emphasis added)

As shown above, even if Paul mostly seemed to refer to circumcision as work, what John and James taught appeared to contradict what Paul taught: being justified by works versus being justified by faith.

---

[82] The closest comment may be: "He even taught that the righteousness of God revealed from faith to faith: as it is written, The just shall live by faith" (Romans 1:17).
[83] See an example at http://www.iclnet.org/pub/resources/text/wittenberg/luther/luther-faith.txt

Interestingly, in the New Testament, the word *mercy* appears sixty-four times[84] (half of them were from Paul's epistles), but the word *justice* cannot be found. Thus, strong emphasis on faith and mercy over work and justice in the New Testament might have contributed to developing a theological concept like *sola fide*.

In the Book of Mormon

The term *justified by faith* is not found in the Book of Mormon. However, the term *judged according to works* was taught by many prophets as well as the resurrected Jesus.

Nephi

"Yea, they are grasped with death, and hell; and death, and hell, and the devil, and all that have been seized therewith must stand before the throne of God, and be *judged according to their works*" (2 Nephi 28:23; emphasis added).

"I will *judge the world, every man according to their works*, according to that which is written" (2 Nephi 29:11; emphasis added).

King Benjamin

" . . . whereof they shall *be judged, every man according to his works*, whether they be good, or whether they be evil" (Mosiah 3:24; emphasis added).

Abinadi

". . . to *be judged of him according to their works* whether they be good or whether they be evil" (Mosiah 16:10; emphasis added).

Alma and Amulek

". . . the day cometh that all shall rise from the dead and stand before God, and *be judged according to their works*" (Alma 11:41; emphasi added).

---

[84] In the Old Testament, the word mercy appears 258 times and justice appears twenty-eight times. Most references to mercy are related to the mercy seat on top of the ark (see Exodus 25 and 37; Leviticus 16). The Psalmist said that "mercy endureth forever" thirty different times. The word faith appears only two times (Deuteronomy 32:20, Habakkuk 2:4).

". . . before the bar of Christ the Son, and God the Father, and the Holy Spirit, which is one Eternal God, to *be judged according to their works*, whether they be good or whether they be evil" (Alma 11:44; emphasis added).

". . . raised from this mortality to a state of immortality, and being brought before the bar of God, to *be judged according to our works*" (Alma 12:12, emphasis added; see also Alma 12:8).

"Now of this thing ye must judge . . . it shall be unto *every man according to his work*" (Alma 32:20; emphasis added).

". . . that all men shall stand before him, *to be judged at the last and judgment day, according to their works*" (Alma 33:22; emphasis added).

". . . and be brought to stand before God, and *be judged according to their works*" (Alma 40:21; emphasis added).

"And it is requisite with the justice of God that men should *be judged according to their works*" (Alma 41:3; emphasis added).

". . . thus they are restored into his presence, to be *judged according to their works*, according to the law and justice" (Alma 42:23; emphasis added).

The Resurrected Jesus Christ

". . . according to the power of the Father I will draw all men unto me, that they may be *judged according to their works*" (3 Nephi 27:15; emphasis added).

Mormon

". . . twelve tribes of Israel, who shall *be judged according to your works* by the twelve whom Jesus chose to be his disciples in the land of Jerusalem" (Mormon 3:18; emphasis added).

". . . ye must stand before the judgment-seat of Christ, to *be judged according to your works*" (Mormon 6:21; emphasis added).

Moroni

"For behold, the same that j*udgeth rashly shall be judged rashly again; for according to his works* shall his wages be; therefore, he that smiteth shall be smitten again, of the Lord" (Mormon 8:19; emphasis added).

Thus, while Paul's teachings on faith overshadow teachings on work in the New Testament, the above quotes show that many taught a theology of "judged according to works" in the Book of Mormon.

Unlike in the New Testament, teachings on mercy and justice were more balanced in the Book of Mormon; *mercy* appears 102 times, and *justice* appears 70 times.[85] One notable discourse about the relationship between mercy and justice was given from Alma to his son Corianton:

> Therefore, according to justice, the plan of redemption could not be brought about, only on conditions of repentance of men in this probationary state, yea, this preparatory state; for except it were for these conditions, mercy could not take effect except it should destroy the work of justice. Now the work of justice could not be destroyed; if so, God would cease to be God.
>
> And thus we see that all mankind were fallen, and they were in the grasp of justice; yea, the justice of God, which consigned them forever to be cut off from his presence.
>
> And now, the plan of mercy could not be brought about except an atonement should be made; therefore God himself atoneth for the sins of the world, to bring about the plan of mercy, to appease the demands of justice, that God might be a perfect, just God, and a merciful God also. (Alma 42:13–15)

> But there is a law given, and a punishment affixed, and a repentance granted; which repentance, mercy claimeth; otherwise, justice claimeth the creature and executeth the law, and the law inflicteth the punishment; if not so, the works of justice would be destroyed, and God would cease to be God.
>
> But God ceaseth not to be God, and mercy claimeth the penitent, and mercy cometh because of the atonement; and the atonement bringeth to pass the resurrection of the dead; and the resurrection of the dead bringeth back men into the presence of God; and thus they are restored into his presence, to be judged according to their works, according to the law and justice.

---

85 In the Doctrine and Covenants, mercy outnumbers justice as well: mercy appears 102 times, justice 12 times.

For behold, justice exerciseth all his demands, and
also mercy claimeth all which is her own; and thus, none
but the truly penitent are saved.

What, do ye suppose that mercy can rob justice? I
say unto you, Nay; not one whit. If so, God would cease
to be God. (Alma 42:22–25)

In his discourse, Alma taught the doctrine of mercy and justice in
conjunction with repentance and the Atonement. He concluded that
mercy cannot rob justice, but there is a way for sinners to satisfy both the
needs of mercy and the demands from justice through repentance and
the Atonement of Christ.

The Parable of the Sower and the Analogy of Seeds

Jesus taught the Jews through the parable of the sower with four different
variations of the acceptance of the gospel. Out of the four, the prophet Alma
expanded on a good growth environment in which the Savior taught that the
gospel can bring forth a hundred-, or sixty-, or thirty-fold yield.

<u>In the Bible</u>

Jesus taught the Jews the parable of the sower:

And he spake many things unto them in parables,
saying, Behold, the sower went forth to sow;

And when he sowed, some seeds fell by the way side,
and the fowls came and devoured them up:

Some fell upon stony places, where they had not
much earth: and forthwith they sprung up, because they
had no deepness of earth:

And when the sun was up, they were scorched; and
because they had no root, they withered away.

And some fell among thorns; and the thorns sprung
up, and choked them:

*But other fell into good ground, and brought forth
fruit, some an hundredfold, some sixtyfold, some thirtyfold.*

Who hath ears to hear, let him hear. (Matthew 13:3–9,
emphasis added; see also Mark 4:14–20; Luke 8:4–8)

Jesus subsequently answered a question from His disciples by explaining the meaning of the four different kinds of environments in the
parable (see Luke 8:9–15).

In the Book of Mormon

In the following discourse, the prophet Alma taught how to develop
a good ground in the heart to bring the fruition of a hundred-, sixty-, or
thirty-fold yield that Jesus taught in the parable of the sower:

> Now, we will compare the word unto a seed. Now, if
> ye give place, that a seed may be planted in your heart,
> behold, if it be a true seed, or a good seed, if ye do not
> cast it out by your unbelief, that ye will resist the Spirit
> of the Lord, behold, it will begin to swell within your
> breasts; and when you feel these swelling motions, ye
> will begin to say within yourselves—*It must needs be that
> this is a good seed, or that the word is good, for it begin-
> neth to enlarge my soul; yea, it beginneth to enlighten my
> understanding, yea, it beginneth to be delicious to me. . . .*
>
> *But if ye will nourish the word, yea, nourish the tree as
> it beginneth to grow, by your faith with great diligence, and
> with patience, looking forward to the fruit thereof, it shall
> take root; and behold it shall be a tree springing up unto
> everlasting life.*
>
> *And because of your diligence and your faith and your
> patience with the word in nourishing it, that it may take
> root in you, behold, by and by ye shall pluck the fruit there-
> of, which is most precious, which is sweet above all that is
> sweet, and which is white above all that is white, yea, and
> pure above all that is pure; and ye shall feast upon this fruit
> even until ye are filled, that ye hunger not, neither shall ye
> thirst.*
>
> Then, my brethren, ye shall reap the rewards of your
> faith, and your diligence, and patience, and long-suffer-
> ing, waiting for the tree to bring forth fruit unto you.
> (Alma 32:28–43; emphasis added)

Connecting the parable of the sower and the analogy of seeds, the prophet Alma explained a process of bringing a hundred-, sixty-, or thirty-fold yield in the parable taught by Jesus Christ: nourishing the planted word of God (good seed) in one's heart (good ground).

Teachings on the Relationship between Adam and Jesus Christ

In the Bible (Teachings from the Apostle Paul)

In the four Gospels, Jesus never mentioned Adam. However, the Apostle Paul taught the relationship between Adam and Jesus Christ regarding death and resurrection:

Romans 5:12–17

> Wherefore, as by one man sin entered into the world, and death by sin; and so death passed upon all men, for that all have sinned. . . .
>
> Nevertheless death reigned from Adam to Moses, even over them that had not sinned after the similitude of Adam's transgression, who is the figure of him that was to come. . . .
>
> For if by one man's offence death reigned by one; much more they which receive abundance of grace and of the gift of righteousness shall reign in life by one, Jesus Christ.

1 Corinthians 15:21–22

> For since by man came death, by man came also the resurrection of the dead. For as in Adam all die, even so in Christ shall all be made alive.

With the above quotes, many Christians teach a concept of Adam's original sin, meaning that all mankind are born in sin because of Adam's Fall.

In the Book of Mormon (Teachings from the Prophet Lehi and King Benjamin)

The prophet Lehi taught his son Jacob the reason why Adam transgressed. He explained it with the principle of man's freedom to choose (agency) and the relationship of that freedom to the devil as well as to the Messiah. Lehi said that Adam's transgression was done by the great wisdom of the all-knowing God:

> But behold, all things have been done in the wisdom of him who knoweth all things.
>
> Adam fell that men might be; and men are, that they might have joy.
>
> And the Messiah cometh in the fulness of time, that he may redeem the children of men from the fall. And because that they are redeemed from the fall they have become free forever, knowing good from evil; to act for themselves and not to be acted upon, save it be by the punishment of the law at the great and last day, according to the commandments which God hath given. (2 Nephi 2:24–26)

Thus, the prophet Lehi taught the reason why Adam and Eve partook of the fruit by explaining that it was for their posterity (all mankind). Their purpose was to give all mankind opportunities to have joy through the great Mediator of all men. In exercising their agency, all mankind can achieve this by choosing liberty and eternal life through Christ over the captivity and death of the devil. This teaching by Lehi explains the principle taught by the Apostle Paul with a clear purpose of Adam's transgression in conjunction with the Messiah.

King Benjamin also taught ways to overcome the unrighteous nature of mankind (originating from Adam's transgression as Lehi and Paul taught) through the Atonement of Christ, and listening to the enticing of the Holy Ghost with a submissive attitude of a little child:

> For the natural man is an enemy to God, and has been from the fall of Adam, and will be, forever and ever, unless he yields to the enticings of the Holy Spirit, and putteth off the natural man and becometh a saint through the atonement of Christ the Lord, and becometh as a child, submissive, meek, humble, patient, full of love, willing to submit to all things which the Lord

seeth fit to inflict upon him, even as a child doth submit to his father. (Mosiah 3:19)

The process of overcoming the natural man is to:

1. Yield to the enticings of the Holy Ghost,
2. Put off the natural man,
3. Become a saint through the Atonement of Christ, and
4. Become as a child with attributes of absolute submissiveness to the Lord with humility and love.

One interesting note on the teachings of both Lehi and King Benjamin is that they taught the same principles long before the ministry of Jesus Christ: 588–570 BC in Lehi's case, and 121 BC in King Benjamin's case.

The records written in the Book of Mormon during the Old Testament period used the same terms that were used in the New Testament, such as Jesus Christ and His Atonement, the Holy Ghost, baptism, charity, and so on. In the Book of Mormon, there basically is no difference in teaching doctrines between the Old and New Testament periods.[86] This may demonstrate what Paul taught: "Jesus Christ the same yesterday, today and for ever" (Hebrews 13:8).

Dramatic Conversions by Direct Involvement of Jesus Christ from Heaven

A very dramatic conversion of the Apostle Paul is one of the most inspiring stories to most Christians; he was converted from being an anti-Christ Pharisee to being the most consecrated evangelical Apostle of Christ (see Acts 9). In the Book of Mormon, a similarly dramatic conversion experience from an anti-Christ to the consecrated missionaries of Christ was also recorded for Alma the Younger and the four sons of King Mosiah—Ammon, Aaron, Omner, and Himni (see Mosiah 27). Both cases involved divine interventions from Jesus or an angel.

---

[86] The Book of Mormon was edited and compiled by its last writers, Mormon and Moroni. Throughout the book except in the book of Moroni (the last book), the phrase it came to pass appears as many as 1,359 times, showing that it was narrated/edited afterward.

Both conversions are very similar, which may show that Jesus Christ worked with the same level of involvement for both tribes of Judah and Joseph. The Apostle Paul was the Apostle for the Gentiles who brought the gospel of Jesus Christ to the Gentiles (see Romans 11:13; 1 Timothy 2:7). Alma established the Church of Jesus Christ among the Nephites (see Alma 4–16), and the four sons of King Mosiah converted a large group of the Lamanites to Jesus Christ (see Alma 17–26).

In the Bible: Apostle Paul's Conversion Experience
The dramatic conversion story of the Apostle Paul is recorded in Acts:

> And as he journeyed, he came near Damascus: and suddenly there shined round about him a light from heaven:
> And he fell to the earth, and heard a voice saying unto him, Saul, Saul, why persecutest thou me?
> And he said, Who art thou, Lord? And the Lord said, I am Jesus whom thou persecutest: it is hard for thee to kick against the pricks.
> And he trembling and astonished said, Lord, what wilt thou have me to do? And the Lord said unto him, Arise, and go into the city, and it shall be told thee what thou must do.
> And the men which journeyed with him stood speechless, hearing a voice, but seeing no man.
> And Saul arose from the earth; and when his eyes were opened, he saw no man: but they led him by the hand, and brought him into Damascus.
> And he was three days without sight, and neither did eat nor drink. (Acts 9:3–9)

The Apostle Paul briefly recounted his conversion experience in Acts 22,[87] and in Acts 26 he also related to King Agrippa his whole life story,

---

[87] From both accounts of Paul's conversion, a major difference was whether men who were with him heard the voice from heaven (compare Acts 9:7 to Acts 22:9).

including his conversion experience. Overall, it is clear that Paul was a chosen vessel of Jesus Christ to be the Apostle for the Gentiles, and it may be reasonable to conclude that he indeed was the main instrument of the Lord who planted the seeds of (Hellenic) Christianity among the Gentiles.

In the Book of Mormon: Conversion Experience of Alma and the Four Sons of King Mosiah

These young men were born to good fathers, one a very righteous prophet and one a great king. But these young men were bad examples to the people, and they attempted to destroy the Church of Jesus Christ against their fathers' wishes. Their conversion experience is recorded in Mosiah:

> And as I said unto you, as they were going about rebelling against God, behold, the angel of the Lord appeared unto them; and he descended as it were in a cloud; and he spake as it were with a voice of thunder, which caused the earth to shake upon which they stood;
>
> And so great was their astonishment, that they fell to the earth, and understood not the words which he spake unto them.
>
> Nevertheless he cried again, saying: Alma, arise and stand forth, for why persecutest thou the church of God? For the Lord hath said: This is my church, and I will establish it; and nothing shall overthrow it, save it is the transgression of my people.
>
> And again, the angel said: Behold, the Lord hath heard the prayers of his people, and also the prayers of his servant, Alma, who is thy father; for he has prayed with much faith concerning thee that thou mightest be brought to the knowledge of the truth; therefore, for this purpose have I come to convince thee of the power and authority of God, that the prayers of his servants might be answered according to their faith.
>
> And now behold, can ye dispute the power of God? For behold, doth not my voice shake the earth? And can

ye not also behold me before you? And I am sent from God.

Now I say unto thee: Go, and remember the captivity of thy fathers in the land of Helam, and in the land of Nephi; and remember how great things he has done for them; for they were in bondage, and he has delivered them. And now I say unto thee, Alma, go thy way, and seek to destroy the church no more, that their prayers may be answered, and this even if thou wilt of thyself be cast off.

And now it came to pass that these were the last words which the angel spake unto Alma, and he departed.

And now Alma and those that were with him fell again to the earth, for great was their astonishment; for with their own eyes they had beheld an angel of the Lord; and his voice was as thunder, which shook the earth; and they knew that there was nothing save the power of God that could shake the earth and cause it to tremble as though it would part asunder.

And now the astonishment of Alma was so great that he became dumb, that he could not open his mouth; yea, and he became weak, even that he could not move his hands; therefore he was taken by those that were with him, and carried helpless, even until he was laid before his father. (Mosiah 27:11–19)

Alma also recounted their conversion experience to his son Helaman in Alma 36:7–20.

The four sons of King Mosiah served their mission for fourteen years in their enemy country of the Lamanites, and they converted many in the Lamanite kingdom, including its king and his family. With Alma's help, they were able to bring the converted Lamanites to Nephite country, and the converted Lamanites were settled in the land named Jershon. This caused a major change in the history of the remnants of Joseph, Lehi's posterity.

Through divine intervention, both conversions definitely changed the whole landscape as well as the history of Christianity—Paul for the

Judeo-Christian society, the others for the Nephite and Lamanite societies. After their conversions, they all consecrated the rest of their lives
to fulfilling their missions as commanded by Jesus Christ. The Apostle
Paul summarized his consecrated effort by saying, "I have fought a good
fight, I have finished my course, I have kept the faith" (2 Timothy 4:7).
Alma and Ammon left their records reviewing their mission experiences
for the Lord, and testifying of Jesus Christ with their joyful feelings of
missionary works and testimonies in detail (see Alma 26 and 29).

Teachings on "The Last Shall Be First, and the First Shall be Last"

In the Bible: For the Twelve Disciples
At one point, Peter asked Jesus, "we have forsaken all, and followed
thee; what shall we have therefore?" Jesus gave him the following answer:

> *But many that are first shall be last; and the last shall
> be first.*
> For the kingdom of heaven is like unto a man that is
> an householder, which went out early in the morning to
> hire labourers into his vineyard.
> And when he had agreed with the labourers for a
> penny a day, he sent them into his vineyard.
> And he went out about the third hour, and saw oth-
> ers standing idle in the marketplace,
> And said unto them; Go ye also into the vineyard, and
> whatsoever is right I will give you. And they went their way.
> Again he went out about the sixth and ninth hour,
> and did likewise.
> And about the eleventh hour he went out, and found
> others standing idle, and saith unto them, Why stand ye here
> all the day idle?
> They say unto him, Because no man hath hired us.
> He saith unto them, Go ye also into the vineyard; and
> whatsoever is right, that shall ye receive.
> So when even was come, the lord of the vineyard
> saith unto his steward, Call the labourers, and give them
> their hire, beginning from the last unto the first.

And when they came that were hired about the eleventh hour, they received every man a penny.

But when the first came, they supposed that they should have received more; and they likewise received every man a penny.

And when they had received it, they murmured against the goodman of the house,

Saying, These last have wrought but one hour, and thou hast made them equal unto us, which have borne the burden and heat of the day.

But he answered one of them, and said, Friend, I do thee no wrong: didst not thou agree with me for a penny?

Take that thine is, and go thy way: I will give unto this last, even as unto thee.

Is it not lawful for me to do what I will with mine own? Is thine eye evil, because I am good?

So the last shall be first, and the first last: for many be called, but few chosen.[88] (Matthew 19:30–20:16, emphasis added; see also Mark 10:28–31)

Answering the question from Peter, Jesus told him that the disciples will be the judges of the twelve tribes of Israel, and this is a case of "the first shall be last, and the last shall be first." He added that many will be called, but only few will be chosen.[89] Jesus also taught that those who sacrifice their personal lives for the Lord will receive an hundred fold, even everlasting life.

In Luke 13:24–30, Jesus also taught the same principle by saying, "there are last which shall be first, and there are first which shall be last."

In the Book of Mormon: Prophecies by the Prophet Nephi and Moroni

Regarding the Jews and the Gentiles being a case of the first being the last and vice versa, an angel taught Nephi the following:

---

[88] Some other versions of the Bibles, such as the New Revised Standard Version, do not have the phrase "for many be called, but few chosen" that appears in verse 16 of the King James Version.

[89] See Doctrine and Covenants 121:34–35 for the reason why many will not be chosen.

And the time cometh that he shall manifest himself unto all nations, both unto the Jews and also unto the Gentiles; and after he has manifested himself unto the Jews and also unto the Gentiles, then he shall manifest himself unto the Gentiles and also unto the Jews, and the last shall be first, and the first shall be last" (1 Nephi 13:42).

This message indicates that Jesus came to the Jews first in His mortal ministry, but He will come to the Gentiles first in His Second Coming. Thus, the last shall be first and the first shall be last.

Regarding the New and the Old Jerusalem, Moroni prophesied the following:

And then cometh the New Jerusalem; and blessed are they who dwell therein, for it is they whose garments are white through the blood of the Lamb; and they are they who are numbered among the remnant of the seed of Joseph, who were of the house of Israel.

And then also cometh the Jerusalem of old; and the inhabitants thereof, blessed are they, for they have been washed in the blood of the Lamb; and they are they who were scattered and gathered in from the four quarters of the earth, and from the north countries, and are partakers of the fulfilling of the covenant which God made with their father, Abraham.

And when these things come, bringeth to pass the scripture which saith, there are *they who were first, who shall be last; and there are they who were last, who shall be first.* (Ether 13:10–12; emphasis added)

Most of the members of The Church of Jesus Christ of Latter-day Saints are converts to Jesus Christ from Gentile origins, and they are numbered among the Israelites (all twelve tribes with a great portion of the Josephites) in this dispensation. According to the above prophecies, in the end of the world, the Josephites will be blessed to reside in the New Jerusalem, and the Jews will gather in the Old Jerusalem. The prophecies also teach that Jesus will come to the Josephites in the New

Jerusalem first before His visit to the Old Jerusalem. This is an example of the first being last and the last being first.

Comparing and Combining John 1:1–18 and 3 Nephi 9:15–22 (Verses from the Book of Mormon are in italics)

John 1:1 In the beginning was the Word, and the Word was with God, and the Word was God. 2 The same was in the beginning with God. 3 All things were made by him; and without him was not any thing made that was made.

3 Nephi 9:15 Behold, I am Jesus Christ the Son of God. I created the heavens and the earth, and all things that in them are. I was with the Father from the beginning. . . .

John 1:4 In him was life; and the life was the light of men. 5 And the light shineth in darkness; and the darkness comprehended it not.

3 Nephi 9:18 I am the light and the life of the world. I am Alpha and Omega, the beginning and the end.

Commenting about John the Baptist:

John 1:6 There was a man sent from God, whose name was John.

7 The same came for a witness, to bear witness of the Light, that all men through him might believe.

8 He was not that Light, but was sent to bear witness of that Light.

9 That was the true Light, which lighteth every man that cometh into the world.

10 He was in the world, and the world was made by him, and the world knew him not.

11 He came unto his own, and his own received him not.

3 Nephi 9:16 I came unto my own, and my own received me not. And the scriptures concerning my coming are fulfilled.

John 1:12 But as many as received him, to them gave he power to become the sons of God, even to them that believe on his name:

13 Which were born, not of blood, nor of the will of the flesh, nor of the will of man, but of God.

14 And the Word was made flesh, and dwelt among us, and we beheld his glory, the glory as of the only begotten of the Father, full of grace and truth.

3 Nephi 9:17 And as many as have received me, to them have I given to become the sons of God; and even so will I to as many as shall believe on my name, for behold, by me redemption cometh. . . .

John 1:15 John bare witness of him, and cried, saying, This was he of whom I spake, He that cometh after me is preferred before me: for he was before me.

16 And of his fulness have all we received, and grace for grace.

17 For the law was given by Moses, but grace and truth came by Jesus Christ.

3 Nephi 9:17 . . . and in me is the law of Moses fulfilled.

19 And ye shall offer up unto me no more the shedding of blood; yea, your sacrifices and your burnt offerings shall be done away, for I will accept none of your sacrifices and your burnt offerings.

John 1:18 No man hath seen God at any time; the only begotten Son, which is in the bosom of the Father, he hath declared him.

3 Nephi 9:15 . . . [Jesus's declaration] I am in the Father, and the Father in me; and in me hath the Father glorified his name.

20 And ye shall offer for a sacrifice unto me a broken heart and a contrite spirit. And whoso cometh unto me with a broken heart and a contrite spirit, him will I baptize with fire and with the Holy Ghost, [An example for the Nephites] even as the Lamanites, because of their faith in me at the time of their conversion, were baptized with fire and with the Holy Ghost, and they knew it not.

21 Behold, I have come unto the world to bring redemption unto the world, to save the world from sin.

22 Therefore, whoso repenteth and cometh unto me as a little child, him will I receive, for of such is the kingdom of God. Behold, for such I have laid down my life, and have taken it up again; therefore repent, and come unto me ye ends of the earth, and be saved.

These two scriptures are an example of a hand-in-glove-type fit. The Book of Mormon (the stick from the tribe of Joseph) testifies point by point the nearly identical message found in the Bible (the stick from the tribe of Judah), confirming the validity of the teachings of John 1:1–18 in the Bible

The teachings in John 1:1–18 are frequently quoted by theologians who profess the Trinity doctrine. At the same time, some New Testament critics argue that these verses seem to have been added later by some Trinitarian scribes. As evidence of that argument, they say a Trinitarian sentence—"there are three that bear record in heaven, the Father, the Word, and the Holy Ghost:" in 1 John 5:7—was added to the Greek text in the sixteenth century (compare 1 John 5:7 in KJV with NRSV or NIV). Nonetheless, having the same message taught point by point by the resurrected Jesus Christ in the Book of Mormon, it testifies of the truthfulness of the messages in John 1:1–18. At the same time, it also made clear that Jesus is not the Father, which refutes the Trinity doctrine. While the Gospel of John in the Bible was written in the third person, 3 Nephi in the Book of Mormon is a direct quote from the resurrected Jesus Christ and is written in the first person.

The Discipleship of Jesus Christ

In both the Bible and the Book of Mormon, there are many admonitions that true discipleship involves following Jesus Christ and keeping His commandments. Jesus Christ taught the nine "blessed" doctrines in both the Sermon on the Mount and the Sermon on the Temple. The Apostle Peter taught the nine things required to make election sure. The Apostle Paul taught the nine fruits of the Spirit, and the prophet Alma taught the nine ways to walk after the holy order of God.

Following are all nine attributes for Christian discipleship:

	Jesus Christ (Matthew 5:3–11, 3 Nephi 12:3–11) The Nine Blessed Doctrines	Apostle Peter (2 Peter 1:5–7)[90] The Nine Things to Make Election Sure	Apostle Paul (Galatians 5:22–23) The Nine Fruits of the Spirit	Prophet Alma (Alma 7:23–24) The Nine Ways to Walk after the Holy Order of God
1	Be poor in spirit	Diligence	Love	Humble
2	Be mournful for comfort	Faith	Joy	Submissive
3	Be meek	Virtue	Peace	Easy to be entreated
4	Be hungry and thirsty for righteousness	Knowledge	Longsuffering	Full of patience and longsuffering
5	Be merciful	Temperance	Gentleness	Temperate in all things
6	Be pure in heart	Patience	Goodness	Diligent in keeping commandments
7	Be a peacemaker	Godliness	Faith	Ask for whatever things are needed
8	Be persecuted for righteousness' sake	Brotherly kindness	Meekness	Return thanks to God
9	Be persecuted for Jesus's sake	Charity	Temperance	Filled with faith, hope, and charity

[90] D&C 4:6 has an almost identical list.

Periodically checking one's own discipleship with the above teachings from both the Bible and the Book of Mormon would be a good way to evaluate one's status of being salt, light, and a shepherd for the world as Jesus taught (see Matthew 5). This also is a good way to check and to follow the Apostle Peter's admonition, "Moreover I will endeavor that ye may be able after my decease to have these things always in remembrance" (2 Peter 1:15).

While it is not included in the above table, it would also be wise to answer the questions posed by Alma: "Have ye spiritually been born of God? Have ye received his image in your countenances? Have ye experienced this mighty change in your hearts?" (Alma 5:14).

An Example of Unique Teachings in the Book of Mormon

In some cases, the teachings in the Book of Mormon are rather similar to teachings in Oriental religious scriptures such as the Chinese I Ching and the Won Buddhism sutra (scripture).[91] For example, the basic principle in Chinese I Ching is that there is an opposition in everything. In the Book of Mormon, Lehi also said, "For it must needs be, that there is an opposition in all things" (2 Nephi 2:11).

As another example, the "O" (unfilled or void round circle) in Won Buddhism is a symbol of enlightenment of the truth through self-realization from nothingness. Similar descriptions can be found in the Book of Mormon:[92] "the course of the Lord is one eternal round" (1 Nephi 10:19); "All things must needs be a compound in one" (2 Nephi 2:11); "therefore, his course is one eternal round" (Alma 7:20); "his paths are straight, and his course is one eternal round" (Alma 37:12); and "For behold, if the knowledge of the goodness of God at this time has awakened you to a sense of your nothingness, and your worthless and fallen state" (Mosiah 4:5). These principles cannot be found in the Bible.

In summary, there can be many more examples of joint teachings between the Bible and the Book of Mormon than the ones discussed in this chapter. However, the above ten examples in the chapter demonstrate the following:

---

[91] Dr. Goo-Hwan Kim correlated the teachings of the Chinese I Ching and Won Buddhism with teachings in the Book of Mormon in his paper, "Structure of One Eternal Round: Comparing One Eternal Round between the Restored Gospel, I Ching, and Buddhism."

[92] The term eternal round cannot be found in the Bible. It also appears two times in the Doctrine and Covenants (see D&C 3:2, 35:1).

1. "The doctrine of Christ" example demonstrates that the Book of Mormon provided a definition of what was taught in the Bible.
2. The example of faith, hope, meekness, and charity along with the two greatest commandments demonstrates that the Book of Mormon provided ways to link the faith, hope, and charity taught in the Bible to good works centering on the Holy Ghost and the Resurrection and Atonement of Jesus Christ.
3. The example of being *justified by faith* versus being *judged according to works* demonstrates that the Book of Mormon clarifies teachings in the Bible.
4. The parable of the sower and the analogy of the seed demonstrates that the Book of Mormon extended and magnified teachings in the Bible.
5. The discussion of Adam's transgression and the Atonement of Jesus Christ demonstrates that the Book of Mormon is a second witness that helps avoid wresting of the teachings in the Bible.
6. The examples of dramatic conversions demonstrate that the Lord loves the tribe of Joseph as He does the tribe of Judah.
7. The teachings of *the last being first and the first being last* demonstrate that the Book of Mormon applies a message in the Bible to a specific prophecy of the Second Coming of Jesus Christ.
8. Comparing teachings in John 1:1–18 and 3 Nephi 9:15–22, they fit like a hand in a glove, confirming the messages together. However, the resurrected Jesus Christ made clear in the Book of Mormon that He is not the Father, as has been commonly interpreted in the verses of John.
9. The discussion about the discipleship of Jesus Christ demonstrates that both the Bible and the Book of Mormon teach and admonish Christians jointly how to live as true disciples of Jesus Christ.
10. The example of unique teachings demonstrates that teachings of the Book of Mormon correlate not only with teachings of the Bible, but also the teachings of non-Christian religions.

While the number of examples in this chapter is limited, they demonstrate that both scriptures from the tribes of Judah and Joseph can teach as one scripture (in other words, as one stick). As discussed in the Introduction, this may be an evidence of the fulfillment of teachings by Ezekiel (see Ezekiel 37:19), Lehi (see 2 Nephi 3:12), and Mormon (see Mormon 7:9).

Chapter 8
Last Words of Patriarchs and Prophets

YEA, COME UNTO CHRIST, AND be perfected in him, and deny yourselves of all ungodliness; and if ye shall deny yourselves of all ungodliness, and love God with all your might, mind and strength, then is his grace sufficient for you, that by his grace ye may be perfect in Christ; and if by the grace of God ye are perfect in Christ, ye can in nowise deny the power of God.

And again, if ye by the grace of God are perfect in Christ, and deny not his power, then are ye sanctified in Christ by the grace of God, through the shedding of the blood of Christ, which is in the covenant of the Father unto the remission of your sins, that ye become holy, without spot.

And now I bid unto all, farewell. I soon go to rest in the paradise of God, until my spirit and body shall again reunite, and I am brought forth triumphant through the air, to meet you before the pleasing bar of the great Jehovah, the Eternal Judge of both quick and dead. Amen. (Moroni 10:32–34)

The last words on one's deathbed are usually the most serious, genuine, and precious. In this chapter, we will review records of the last blessings or words given around the time of death of several prophets and patriarchs in both the Bible and the Book of Mormon.

Being a historical literature of many generations, the Old Testament contains patriarchal blessings given by the ancient patriarchs as well as the last words of some prophets. Since the New Testament is a record of a single generation, it virtually contains no last words; one exception is that of Jesus Christ giving His final charge or commandments to His disciples from the time of His last trip to Jerusalem to His ascension. In the Book of Mormon, the succession between prophets was well recorded, and it contains many records of the last words of the prophets in detail.

In the Bible

Starting in the book of Genesis, the first account close to a patriarchal blessing is from Noah to his sons:

> And he [Noah] said, Cursed be Canaan; a servant of servants shall he be unto his brethren.
> And he said, Blessed be the Lord God of Shem; and Canaan shall be his servant.
> God shall enlarge Japheth, and he shall dwell in the tents of Shem; and Canaan shall be his servant. (Genesis 9:25–27)

Before his death, Jacob gathered his twelve sons to bless them, saying, "Gather yourselves together, that I may tell you that which shall befall you in the last days. Gather yourselves together, and hear, ye sons of Jacob; and hearken unto Israel your father" (Genesis 49:1–2).

Jacob's Blessings

Followings are Jacob's blessings to all twelve of his sons.

Blessing upon Reuben, the First Son

> Reuben, thou art my firstborn, my might, and the beginning of my strength, the excellency of dignity, and the excellency of power: Unstable as water, thou shalt not excel; because thou wentest up to thy father's bed; then defiledst thou it: he went up to my couch. (Genesis 49:3)

Blessing upon Simeon, the Second Son, and Levi, the Third Son

Simeon and Levi are brethren; instruments of cruelty are in their habitations.

O my soul, come not thou into their secret; unto their assembly, mine honour, be not thou united: for in their anger they slew a man, and in their selfwill they digged down a wall.

Cursed be their anger, for it was fierce; and their wrath, for it was cruel: I will divide them in Jacob, and scatter them in Israel. (Genesis 49:5–7)

Blessing upon Judah, the Fourth Son

Judah, thou art he whom thy brethren shall praise: thy hand shall be in the neck of thine enemies; thy father's children shall bow down before thee.

Judah is a lion's whelp: from the prey, my son, thou art gone up: he stooped down, he couched as a lion, and as an old lion; who shall rouse him up?

The sceptre shall not depart from Judah, nor a lawgiver from between his feet, until Shiloh come; and unto him shall the gathering of the people be.

Binding his foal unto the vine, and his ass's colt unto the choice vine; he washed his garments in wine, and his clothes in the blood of grapes:

His eyes shall be red with wine, and his teeth white with milk. (Genesis 49:8–12)

Blessing upon Zebulun, the Fifth Son
"Zebulun shall dwell at the haven of the sea; and he shall be for an haven of ships; and his border shall be unto Zidon" (Genesis 49:13).

Blessing upon Issachar, the Sixth Son
"Issachar is a strong ass couching down between two burdens: And he saw that rest was good, and the land that it was pleasant; and bowed his shoulder to bear, and became a servant unto tribute" (Genesis 49:14–15).

Blessing upon Dan, the Seventh Son

> Dan shall judge his people, as one of the tribes of Israel.
>
> Dan shall be a serpent by the way, an adder in the path, that biteth the horse heels, so that his rider shall fall backward.
>
> I have waited for thy salvation, O Lord. (Genesis 49:16–18).

Blessing upon Gad, the Eighth Son

"Gad, a troop shall overcome him: but he shall overcome at the last" (Genesis 49:19).

Blessing upon Asher, the Ninth Son

"Out of Asher his bread shall be fat, and he shall yield royal dainties" (Genesis 49:20).

Blessing upon Naphtali, the Tenth Son

"Naphtali is a hind let loose: he giveth goodly words" (Genesis 49:21).

Blessing upon Joseph, the Eleventh Son

> Joseph is a fruitful bough, even a fruitful bough by a well; whose branches run over the wall:
>
> The archers have sorely grieved him, and shot at him, and hated him:
>
> But his bow abode in strength, and the arms of his hands were made strong by the hands of the mighty God of Jacob; (from thence is the shepherd, the stone of Israel:)
>
> Even by the God of thy father, who shall help thee; and by the Almighty, who shall bless thee with blessings of heaven above, blessings of the deep that lieth under, blessings of the breasts, and of the womb:
>
> The blessings of thy father have prevailed above the blessings of my progenitors unto the utmost bound of

the everlasting hills: they shall be on the head of Joseph, and on the crown of the head of him that was separate from his brethren. (Genesis 49:22–26)

Blessing upon Benjamin, the Twelfth Son
"Benjamin shall ravin as a wolf: in the morning he shall devour the prey, and at night he shall divide the spoil" (Genesis 49:27).

Jacob adopted Joseph's two sons, Manasseh and Ephraim (see Genesis 48:5), and he blessed them in a separate session prior to giving blessings to his twelve sons. Jacob confirmed that Ephraim,[93] the younger son, was before Manasseh, the older son (in other words, Ephraim received the birthright):

And when Joseph saw that his father laid his right hand upon the head of Ephraim, it displeased him: and he held up his father's hand, to remove it from Ephraim's head unto Manasseh's head.

And Joseph said unto his father, Not so, my father: for this is the firstborn; put thy right hand upon his head.

And his father refused, and said, I know it, my son, I know it: he also shall become a people, and he also shall be great: but truly his younger brother shall be greater than he, and his seed shall become a multitude of nations.

And he blessed them that day, saying, In thee shall Israel bless, saying, God make thee as Ephraim and as Manasseh: and he set Ephraim before Manasseh. (Genesis 48:17–20)

As shown above, it is clear that the blessings upon Judah and Joseph were uniquely special and that both tribes were blessed to be the leaders of all the tribes of Israel.

---

[93] 1 Chronicles 5:1–2 confirms that the birthright belongs to the sons of Joseph: "Now the sons of Reuben the firstborn of Israel, (for he was the firstborn; but, forasmuch as he defiled his father's bed, his birthright was given unto the sons of Joseph the son of Israel: and the genealogy is not to be reckoned after the birthright. For Judah prevailed above his brethren, and of him came the chief ruler; but the birthright was Joseph's:)."

For the tribe of Judah, the scepter and lawgiver would remain in his tribe until Shiloh (the Savior) came. Jesus was indeed born in the tribe of Judah in the lineage of King David (see Matthew 1:6; Luke 1:27; 3:31).

After the destruction of Jerusalem by the Romans in AD 70, their Jewish kingdom and temple disappeared. After a long dispersion, the Jewish nation was finally reestablished with help from the Gentile nations (in other words, the United Nations) in AD 1948. Christianity has become the largest religion, and billions of Christians have gathered around Jesus Christ and worshiped Him.

The tribe of Joseph was blessed to be prosperous, and some of them would run over the wall into a different area; they would be separated from the other tribes. The Josephites carried on the birthright from their progenitors (see 1 Chronicle 5:1–2). They would be hated by others but protected by the Lord. After Joseph Smith translated and published the Book of Mormon, it revealed that a small group of two Josephite families of Lehi and Ishmael migrated to the land of America from Jerusalem and were separated from the rest of the Israelites beginning in 600 BC.

Thus, Jacob's blessings to Judah and Joseph have been (or are in the process of being) fulfilled.

Joseph also left his last will to his brethren:[94]

> And Joseph said unto his brethren, I die: and God will surely visit you, and bring you out of this land unto the land which he sware to Abraham, to Isaac, and to Jacob.
>
> And Joseph took an oath of the children of Israel, saying, God will surely visit you, and ye shall carry up my bones from hence.
>
> So Joseph died, being an hundred and ten years old: and they embalmed him, and he was put in a coffin in Egypt. (Genesis 50:24–26)

---

[94] In addition to these words by Joseph recorded in Genesis 50:24–26, the Joseph Smith Translation has some additional prophecies by Joseph in Egypt; it has thirty-eight verses instead of twenty-six verses (KJV) in Genesis 50. These additional prophecies are very similar to Joseph's prophecies recorded in 2 Nephi 3:6–21.

To fulfill Joseph's will, the prophet Moses took the bones of Joseph when the Israelites left Egypt (see Exodus 13:19).

Moses's Last Blessings to the Tribe of Israel

Moses also gave his last blessings to all twelve tribes of Israel before his death.

Only three of those twelve blessings will be reviewed here—those given to Judah, Joseph, and Levi. While Moses's blessing upon the tribe of Judah is short, his blessing upon the tribe of Joseph (both the tribes of Ephraim and Manasseh) is long and special. The Levites were blessed with special assignments.

Moses's Last Blessing upon the Tribe of Judah

"And this is the blessing of Judah: and he said, Hear, Lord, the voice of Judah, and bring him unto his people: let his hands be sufficient for him; and be thou an help to him from his enemies" (Deuteronomy 33:7).

Moses's Last Blessing upon the Tribe of Joseph

> And of Joseph he said, Blessed of the Lord be his land, for the precious things of heaven, for the dew, and for the deep that coucheth beneath,
> And for the precious fruits brought forth by the sun, and for the precious things put forth by the moon,
> And for the chief things of the ancient mountains, and for the precious things of the lasting hills,
> And for the precious things of the earth and fulness thereof, and for the good will of him that dwelt in the bush: let the blessing come upon the head of Joseph, and upon the top of the head of him that was separated from his brethren.
> His glory is like the firstling of his bullock, and his horns are like the horns of unicorns: with them he shall push the people together to the ends of the earth: and they are the ten thousands of Ephraim, and they are the thousands of Manasseh. (Deuteronomy 33:13–17)

Moses's Last Blessing upon the Tribe of Levi (His Own Tribe)

> And of Levi he said, Let thy Thummim and thy Urim be with thy holy one, whom thou didst prove at Massah, and with whom thou didst strive at the waters of Meribah;
>
> Who said unto his father and to his mother, I have not seen him; neither did he acknowledge his brethren, nor knew his own children: for they have observed thy word, and kept thy covenant.
>
> They shall teach Jacob thy judgments, and Israel thy law: they shall put incense before thee, and whole burnt sacrifice upon thine altar.
>
> Bless, Lord, his substance, and accept the work of his hands: smite through the loins of them that rise against him, and of them that hate him, that they rise not again. (Deuteronomy 33:8–11)

From the blessings of Jacob, it is apparent that the tribes of Judah and Joseph are predestined to be the leading tribes; the Josephites will have the birthright of Israel and will be blessed and protected from their enemies. Moses confirmed many blessings upon the Josephites, and he revealed that there will be more posterity of Ephraim than Manasseh. Moses also blessed the Levites to be in charge of the sacred temple ordinances even after his death.

The Last Charge of Jesus Christ to His Disciples

Following are the last charges from Jesus Christ to His disciples recorded in the four Gospels and the book of Acts.

Matthew 28:18–20 (see also Mark 16:15–18; Luke 24:44–49)

> And Jesus came and spake unto them, saying, All power is given unto me in heaven and in earth.
>
> Go ye therefore, and teach all nations, baptizing them in the name of the Father, and of the Son, and of the Holy Ghost:

Teaching them to observe all things whatsoever I have commanded you: and, lo, I am with you alway, even unto the end of the world. Amen.

John 21:14–23

This is now the third time that Jesus shewed himself to his disciples, after that he was risen from the dead.

So when they had dined, Jesus saith to Simon Peter, Simon, son of Jonas, lovest thou me more than these? He saith unto him, Yea, Lord; thou knowest that I love thee. He saith unto him, Feed my lambs.

He saith to him again the second time, Simon, son of Jonas, lovest thou me? He saith unto him, Yea, Lord; thou knowest that I love thee. He saith unto him, Feed my sheep.

He saith unto him the third time, Simon, son of Jonas, lovest thou me? Peter was grieved because he said unto him the third time, Lovest thou me? And he said unto him, Lord, thou knowest all things; thou knowest that I love thee. Jesus saith unto him, Feed my sheep.

Verily, verily, I say unto thee, When thou wast young, thou girdedst thyself, and walkedst whither thou wouldest: but when thou shalt be old, thou shalt stretch forth thy hands, and another shall gird thee, and carry thee whither thou wouldest not.

This spake he, signifying by what death he should glorify God. And when he had spoken this, he saith unto him, Follow me.

Then Peter, turning about, seeth the disciple whom Jesus loved following; which also leaned on his breast at supper, and said, Lord, which is he that betrayeth thee?

Peter seeing him saith to Jesus, Lord, and what shall this man do?

Jesus saith unto him, If I will that he tarry till I come, what is that to thee? follow thou me.

Then went this saying abroad among the brethren, that that disciple should not die: yet Jesus said not unto

him, He shall not die; but, If I will that he tarry till I
come, what is that to thee?

Acts 1:4–8

> And, being assembled together with them, com-
> manded them that they should not depart from Jerusa-
> lem, but wait for the promise of the Father, which, saith
> he, ye have heard of me.
> For John truly baptized with water; but ye shall be
> baptized with the Holy Ghost not many days hence.
> When they therefore were come together, they asked
> of him, saying, Lord, wilt thou at this time restore again
> the kingdom to Israel?
> And he said unto them, It is not for you to know
> the times or the seasons, which the Father hath put in
> his own power.
> But ye shall receive power, after that the Holy Ghost
> is come upon you: and ye shall be witnesses unto me
> both in Jerusalem, and in all Judæa, and in Samaria, and
> unto the uttermost part of the earth.

Reviewing these charges, the synopsists and the writer of the book
of Acts recorded a common thread: Jesus asked His disciples to go out
into the world and baptize all by preaching His gospel until His return.
However, John's record is quite different from the others because it is
addressed only to Peter and John. Jesus told Peter to feed His sheep (or
lamb) three times, emphasizing His leadership role in ministering to followers of Jesus Christ, and answered his question indicating that John
would remain on the earth until Jesus's return.[95]
Based on the last charges Jesus gave His disciples, it is quite clear that
preaching and baptizing are very important to Jesus Christ. If baptism
is so important to the Savior, it should definitely be the top priority for
all Christians. This corrects a belief of some Christians who claim that

---

[95] Doctrine and Covenants 7 provides more detailed dialogs between Jesus and John
on this occasion. Jesus Christ also allowed three Nephite disciples to tarry on the
earth until His Second Coming (see 3 Nephi 28:4–9).

the baptism ordinance is not necessary as long as one lives righteously in faith and with charity.

In the Book of Mormon

In the Book of Mormon, multiple prophets recorded their final words.[96] For example, the prophet Lehi gave patriarchal blessings to his sons and others in his group with special doctrinal teachings and prophecies (see 2 Nephi 1–3). Nephi also left a record of his final teaching with testimonies, prophecies, and admonitions to his people (see 2 Nephi 25–33). King Benjamin left a profound sermon to his people of his kingdom in his last address as their king (Mosiah 2–4).[97] The last writer in the Book of Mormon, Moroni, left his final words to future readers of the Book of Mormon (see Mormon 8 and Moroni 10).

Lehi's Last Prophecies and Words (2 Nephi 1–4)

Lehi reviewed his vision and the family's journey to the promised land first, then he prophesied about the future of the promised land where he and his family had arrived and settled (the present land of America). He followed up with special discourses to his two younger sons Jacob and Joseph, who were born late in his life after they left Jerusalem. Afterwards, he left his last words to his sons' families and the families of Ishmael's sons separately. Unlike the brief blessings Jacob recorded, the blessings by Lehi were recorded in detail by his son, Nephi. Lehi's patriarchal blessings are summarized below.

Lehi's Address to His and Ishmael's Sons (2 Nephi 1)

Lehi reviewed their family's experience coming to the promised land under the Lord's direction and protection (see verses 1–3), reminded them of his vision of the destruction of Jerusalem[98] (see verse 5), prophesied the promised land being chosen to be an inheritance for his seed and being preserved for the righteous (see verses 5–9), pronounced curses upon the unrighteous being scattered by other nations (see verses

---

[96] Alma the younger also left his counsels to his three sons (see Alma 36–42). These cannot be considered as the last words before his death, so they are not included in this section.

[97] A part of King Benjamin's address is also discussed in Chapter 1 of this book.

[98] This prophecy of the destruction of Jerusalem was literally fulfilled in 587 BC.

10–12), and admonished them to wake up and remain righteous (see verses 13–23). He also defended Nephi and asked them to follow his leadership (see verses 24–27). He left his final words to his sons, the sons of Ishmael, and Zoram[99] (see verses 28–32).

Lehi's Last Words to Jacob (2 Nephi 2:1–13)

Lehi started out with his intimate feeling toward Jacob by calling him "my first born in the days of my tribulation in the wilderness" and counseling him to be faithful to Nephi (see verses 1–3). Lehi promised Jacob that God will consecrate his afflictions to his gain (see verse 4). He continued with teaching some profound doctrines of the Lord: the infinite Atonement and redemption in and through the merits, grace, and mercy of the Holy Messiah for those who believe Him with a broken heart and a contrite spirit; and that the way was prepared and "salvation is free" from the Fall of man (see verses 4–10). He taught, "there is an opposition in all things . . . and all things must needs be compounded in one" (2 Nephi 2:11). He also explained if there were no opposition, there would be no God, and concluded with the following words: "if there is no God we are not, neither the earth; for there could have been no creation of things, neither to act nor to be acted upon; wherefore, all things must have vanished away" (2 Nephi 2:12–13).

Lehi's Last Words to His Sons[100] (2 Nephi 2:14–30)

Lehi continued with his explanation of why it is necessary to have opposition in all things using an example of the forbidden fruit being opposite to the fruit of the tree of life[101]—the one being sweet and the other bitter (see verses 14–15), and that man acts by enticement from the one or the other (see verse 16). He taught that Adam's partaking of the forbidden fruit was an example of being enticed by Satan, who is a fallen angel from heaven and the father of all lies (see verses 17–18). He explained that Adam's fall caused the major changes of earth for his

---

[99] Zoram was a freed servant of Laban who joined Lehi's family when they fled from Jerusalem (see 1 Nephi 4:20–38).

[100] There must be another son (or sons) present along with Jacob by this time.

[101] The term *tree of life* can be found in Revelation 2:7, 22:2, 22:14 in the Bible; it is also found in the Book of Mormon in 1 Nephi 11:25, 15:22, 15:28, 15:36; 2 Nephi 2:15; Alma 5:34, 36; 12:21, 23, 36; 32:40; 42:2, 3, 5, 6.

new life and enabled Adam and Eve to have children for their joy (see verses 19–23). He pronounced that this was done in the wisdom of the all-knowing God (see verse 24): "Adam fell that men might be; and men are, that they might have joy" (verse 25).

Lehi prophesied that the Messiah would come to redeem and free the children of men from Adam's Fall, and that men have their own agency to choose liberty and eternal life through the great Mediator (Messiah) or captivity and death through the power of the devil (see verses 26–27). He concluded that he had chosen the good part, and he asked his sons to do the same for the everlasting welfare of their souls (see verses 28–30).

Lehi's Last Words to Joseph (2 Nephi 3)

Lehi left his last words to his youngest son, Joseph, who was born in the wilderness during their hardships. He blessed Joseph that the most precious land would be an inheritance for Joseph's seed and others of Lehi's seed (see verses 1–3). Lehi pronounced that he was from the tribe of Joseph, who truly saw Lehi's days, and he obtained a promise of the Lord that the Lord would raise up a righteous broken-off branch of the Josephites (see verses 4–5). Lehi taught that the Messiah will manifest Himself unto them (see verse 5).

Lehi also taught Joseph about the Restoration of the gospel in the latter days mostly by quoting the words of the ancient Joseph in Egypt. The following quotes from Joseph of Egypt cannot be found in the Bible and are found only in the Book of Mormon:

> Yea, Joseph truly said: A seer shall the Lord my God raise up, who shall be a choice seer unto the fruit of my loins. . . . Thus saith the Lord unto me: A choice seer will I raise up out of the fruit of thy loins; and he shall be esteemed highly among the fruit of thy loins. And unto him will I give commandment that he shall do a work for the fruit of thy loins, his brethren, which shall be of great worth unto them, even to the bringing of them to the knowledge of the covenants which I have made with thy fathers.
>
> And I will give unto him a commandment that he shall do none other work, save the work which I shall

command him. And I will make him great in mine eyes; for he shall do my work.

And he shall be great like unto Moses, whom I have said I would raise up unto you, to deliver my people, O house of Israel.

And Moses will I raise up, to deliver thy people out of the land of Egypt.

But a seer will I raise up out of the fruit of thy loins; and unto him will I give power to bring forth my word unto the seed of thy loins—and not to the bringing forth my word only, saith the Lord, but to the convincing them of my word, which shall have already gone forth among them.

Wherefore, the fruit of thy loins shall write; and the fruit of the loins of Judah shall write; and that which shall be written by the fruit of thy loins, and also that which shall be written by the fruit of the loins of Judah, shall grow together, unto the confounding of false doctrines and laying down of contentions, and establishing peace among the fruit of thy loins, and bringing them to the knowledge of their fathers in the latter days, and also to the knowledge of my covenants, saith the Lord.

And out of weakness he shall be made strong, in that day when my work shall commence among all my people, unto the restoring thee, O house of Israel, saith the Lord. . . .

Behold, that seer will the Lord bless; and they that seek to destroy him shall be confounded; for this promise, which I have obtained of the Lord, of the fruit of my loins, shall be fulfilled. Behold, I am sure of the fulfilling of this promise;

And his name shall be called after me; and it shall be after the name of his father. And he shall be like unto me; for the thing, which the Lord shall bring forth by his hand, by the power of the Lord shall bring my people unto salvation.

Yea, thus prophesied Joseph: I am sure of this thing, even as I am sure of the promise of Moses; for the Lord hath said unto me, I will preserve thy seed forever.

And the Lord hath said: I will raise up a Moses; and I will give power unto him in a rod; and I will give judgment unto him in writing. Yet I will not loose his tongue, that he shall speak much, for I will not make him mighty in speaking. But I will write unto him my law, by the finger of mine own hand; and I will make a spokesman for him.

And the Lord hath said unto me also: I will raise up unto the fruit of thy loins; and I will make for him a spokesman. And I, behold, I will give unto him that he shall write the writing of the fruit of thy loins, unto the fruit of thy loins; and the spokesman of thy loins shall declare it.

And the words which he shall write shall be the words which are expedient in my wisdom should go forth unto the fruit of thy loins. And it shall be as if the fruit of thy loins had cried unto them from the dust; for I know their faith.

And they shall cry from the dust; yea, even repentance unto their brethren, even after many generations have gone by them. And it shall come to pass that their cry shall go, even according to the simpleness of their words.

Because of their faith their words shall proceed forth out of my mouth unto their brethren who are the fruit of thy loins; and the weakness of their words will I make strong in their faith, unto the remembering of my covenant which I made unto thy fathers. (2 Nephi 3:7–21)

Through the above quotes of the ancient Joseph, Lehi taught that Joseph had shared what the Lord told him about Moses, who would bring the laws of the Lord to the Israelites. The Lord also told him about a latter-day seer named Joseph after his name and the name of his father. As he had saved the whole household of Jacob, Joseph also indicated that the seer would bring salvation to his seed. Nephi said in 2 Nephi 4:2 that these prophecies of Joseph were found on the plates of brass.

The Lord explained to Joseph the two records and their roles: the record from the tribe of Judah (the law of Moses) and the record out of the dust (from the ground) by the tribe of Joseph. These two records will grow together in strengthening the Lord's work. The Josephite record will provide simple messages to Lehi's posterity for their repentance. It will make them strong in their faith and will cause them to remember the covenants that the Lord made with their forefathers. Lehi continued with a confirmation of the ancient Joseph's prophecies that his posterity will not be destroyed, and they will hear about the Restoration through the seer. He closed with an admonition: "Remember the words of thy dying father" (2 Nephi 3:25).

Lehi's Blessing of His Grandchildren from Laman and Lemuel (2 Nephi 4:3–9)

Lehi gave the same blessings to the children of Laman and Lemuel separately. He taught them that if they are cursed, the cursing may be taken from them and be answered upon the heads of their parents. He also told them that God will not suffer that they and their seed will perish, but that they will instead be blessed.

Lehi's Blessing to Ishmael's Family and His Son Sam

Lehi blessed the household of Ishmael's family and admonished them to keep the commandments. He also blessed his son Sam separately, saying that his seed will be like unto the seeds of Nephi (see 2 Nephi 4:10–11).

After Lehi's last words, Nephi made an announcement of his father's death: "And it came to pass after my father, Lehi, had spoken unto all his household, according to the feelings of his heart and the Spirit of the Lord which was in him, he waxed old. And it came to pass that he died, and was buried" (2 Nephi 4:12).

Overall, the detailed records of Lehi's patriarchal blessings to his posterity may be summarized by saying that Lehi made it known to all that Nephi was their leader and that all should follow his leadership.[102] He admonished all to keep the commandments of the Lord. He taught Jacob and his other sons some profound doctrines: Adam's transgression

---

[102] At the time of Lehi's death, the total number of people can be estimated to be around thirty to forty (around ten from Lehi's family, around ten from Ishmael's family, Zoram, and an unknown number of children born after Lehi's children and Zoram married Ishmael's children).

being a win-win situation for the Lord and man through the Messiah, having opposites in everything but compounding in one, the importance of following the enticing voice from God in exercising their agency, and the eternal salvation in and through the Atonement of Christ.

To Joseph, Lehi revealed many prophecies about the Restoration by a chosen seer for the Josephites in bringing the Book of Mormon out of the ground, joint accomplishments between the Bible and the Book of Mormon, and their impacts on the Restoration in the latter days.

Nephi's Last Words of Admonition (2 Nephi 33)

Nephi recorded his family history and his personal experiences from the time his father saw a vision in Jerusalem (600 BC) to the time when his life was ending in the promised land (around 544 BC). Not long after his father died, his group separated themselves from his brothers' group, who tried to kill him.

Nephi had been leading his people in righteousness, and his tender love for his people was well expressed with his words, "For I pray continually for them [his people] by day, and mine eyes water my pillow by night, because of them" (2 Nephi 33:3). He taught his people by quoting the words of Isaiah several times.[103] Before his death, Nephi left his testimony of Jesus Christ, taught the doctrine of Christ, prophesied of the coming forth of the Book of Mormon and the Restoration of the gospel of Jesus Christ in the latter days, and left final admonishments (see 2 Nephi 25–33). This section reviews his last admonishments in 2 Nephi 33.

Nephi expressed his inadequacy of writing by saying that he was not mighty in writing as much as in speaking by the power of the Holy Ghost (see 2 Nephi 33:1–2), but he esteemed his words as of great worth, especially to his people (see 2 Nephi 33:3). Because his messages would persuade them to do good, to know their fathers, to speak of Jesus, to believe in Him, and to endure to the end for their eternal life, he knew that the Lord would consecrate his words for the gain of his people and that his weak writings would be made strong unto his people (see 2 Nephi 33:4). Nephi also said that he glories of Jesus in plainness and truth (see 2 Nephi 33:5–6).

---

[103] Nephi mostly quoted Isaiah 2–14, 29, 48–49.

Nephi expressed his charity for his people, the Jews and the Gentiles, and his hope that all will be reconciled unto Christ (see 2 Nephi 33:7–9). He invited all to hear his words and to believe in Christ. He promised that they will know at the judgment bar of the Lord at the last day that he was commanded to write his words (see 2 Nephi 33:10–11).

Nephi said that he prays to the Father in the name of Christ that many may be saved in the great and last day with the following final words:

> And now, my beloved brethren, all those who are of the house of Israel, and all ye ends of the earth, I speak unto you as the voice of one crying from the dust: Farewell until that great day shall come.
>
> And you that will not partake of the goodness of God, and respect the words of the Jews, and also my words, and the words which shall proceed forth out of the mouth of the Lamb of God, behold, I bid you an everlasting farewell, for these words shall condemn you at the last day.
>
> For what I seal on earth, shall be brought against you at the judgment bar; for thus hath the Lord commanded me, and I must obey. Amen. (2 Nephi 33:13–15)

Nephi's final words were so full of love of Christ and people that it is easy to feel his genuine desire for the eternal welfare of his seed, the Jews, and the Gentiles. He concluded that all he had done was to obey the Lord. Nephi may be one of the most perfect Christians to emulate.

The Last Address by King Benjamin (Mosiah 1–6)

According to Mormon, King Benjamin was a good protector of his people from their enemies (in a military way), a benevolent and righteous king, and a holy man (see Words of Mormon 1:17–18). Three years prior to his death, King Benjamin decided to step down from his throne and confer his kingdom to his eldest son, Mosiah. He gave the plates of brass, the plates of Nephi, and other sacred artifacts to Mosiah; reviewed the writings on the plates with his sons; and testified his personal witness of the truthfulness of the teachings of those records (see Mosiah 1:1–7).

King Benjamin gathered his people in the city of Zarahemla on the temple grounds, where he gave his last address (see Mosiah 2:1). He first offered the sacrifice and burnt offerings according to the law of Moses (see Mosiah 2:2–3). Because there were so many people there, they had to address some logistical issues, such as situating people by family unit toward the temple in an orderly manner, erecting a tower for him so that people could hear him better, writing down his address so that people could also read it, allowing the people to provide feedback, and so on.

King Benjamin began by teaching the importance of service by sharing an example of his own labor to lighten the burden on the people in his effort to be a fair and righteous judge. He also taught a profound principle: "when ye are in the service of your fellow beings, ye are only in the service of your God" (Mosiah 2:17). He admonished them, "I say, if ye should serve him with all your whole souls yet ye would be unprofitable servants" (Mosiah 2:21); he also taught that men are always in debt to the Lord considering that the Lord first created us and granted us our lives and that He immediately blesses us when we keep His commandments (see Mosiah 2:22–25).

King Benjamin shared the glad tidings of great joy that an angel of God declared unto him: the coming of the Lord Omnipotent (Jesus Christ) to the children of men in a not-far-distant time. King Benjamin explained that Jesus Christ would minister to people with many miracles and would suffer severe physical pains, hunger, thirst, and fatigue. His anguish because of the wickedness and abomination of people would be such that blood would come from every pore of His body. King Benjamin prophesied that:

- Jesus is the Creator of all things from the beginning.
- His mother's name would be Mary.
- He would be crucified but would rise from the dead on the third day.
- His blood would atone for the sins of those who have fallen by the transgression of Adam, those who died in sin without knowing the will of God, those who sin ignorantly, and those who rebelled but repented and have faith in Jesus (see Mosiah 3:1–13).

King Benjamin also taught that the law of Moses is a precursor to the Atonement of Jesus Christ for the stiffnecked people, and the law of Moses avails nothing except it were through the Atonement of Jesus's blood. The blood of Christ atones for the sins of children, and infants are not damned at their deaths. Unless man yields to the enticing of the Holy Spirit and puts off the natural man, becomes a saint through the Atonement of Christ, and becomes like a little child with total submissiveness, he cannot be saved, for "the natural man is an enemy to God" from the Fall of Adam (see Mosiah 3:14–19). He taught that the time will come when the knowledge of the Savior will spread to every nation, kindred, tongue, and people, and all men will be judged according to their works (see Mosiah 3:20–27).

After King Benjamin delivered what the angel taught him, the people cried aloud in one voice, "O have mercy, and apply the atoning blood of Christ that we may receive forgiveness of our sins, and our hearts may be purified; for we believe in Jesus Christ, the Son of God who created heaven and earth and all things; who shall come down among the children of men" (Mosiah 4:2). King Benjamin's teaching was so powerful that his people were filled with joy and exceeding faith in Jesus Christ (see Mosiah 4:3).

After an interim check with a very positive result of his address, King Benjamin continued his address on the impacts of the Atonement of Jesus Christ, the conditions for salvation with relation to the knowledge of the greatness of God, our own nothingness, the Lord's longsuffering toward each individual, deep humility, daily calling on the Lord, and standing steadfastly in the faith of Jesus Christ (see Mosiah 4:4–11). He taught that the blessings and love of God would follow the retaining of a remission of sins, gaining just and true knowledge, having no mind to injure one another but to live peacefully, raising children properly, succoring those who are in need of help, sharing substance with the poor, not running faster than one's own strength, and returning all borrowed items, and others (see Mosiah 4:12–29). He concluded with the following admonitions:

> . . . if ye do not watch yourselves, and your thoughts, and your words, and your deeds, and observe the commandment of God, and continue in the faith of what ye have heard concerning the coming our Lord, even unto the end of your lives, you must perish. And now, O man, remember, and perish not. (Mosiah 4:30)

> Therefore, I would that ye should be steadfast and immovable, always abounding in good works, that Christ, the Lord God Omnipotent, may seal you his, that you may be brought to heaven, that ye may have everlasting salvation and eternal life, through the wisdom, and power, and justice, and mercy of him who created all things, in heaven and in earth, who is God above all. Amen. (Mosiah 5:15)

After King Benjamin finished his address, people again cried with one voice that they believed all his words and desired to enter into covenants with God to do His will and be obedient to His commandments all the remainder of their days. Being spiritually begotten that day, they called themselves children of Christ (see Mosiah 6:1–2). Three years after giving his address, King Benjamin died in 124 BC (see Mosiah 6:5).

The Last Eight Exhortations by the Prophet Moroni (Moroni 10)

Unlike the Bible, which has little continuity between writers of the books or letters, the Book of Mormon has strong continuity from the first writer, Nephi, all the way to the last writer, Moroni. The last writer of the book, Moroni left his final words to future readers of the book and the descendants of Lamanites who survived. He finished the Book of Mormon with eight exhortations as his final words to those future readers then sealed the plates by burying them in the ground in AD 421 (see Moroni 10:1–2).

Exhortation 1: Read this book, and ponder how merciful the Lord has been.

> Behold, I would exhort you that when ye shall read these things, if it be wisdom in God that ye should read them, that ye would remember how merciful the Lord hath been unto the children of men, from the creation of Adam even down until the time that ye shall receive these things, and ponder it in your hearts. (Moroni 10:3)

Exhortation 2: Ask God in the name of Christ if this book is not true, and the Holy Ghost will manifest its truthfulness.

> And when ye shall receive these things, I would exhort you that ye would ask God, the Eternal Father, in the name of Christ, if these things are not true; and if ye shall ask with a sincere heart, with real intent, having faith in Christ, he will manifest the truth of it unto you, by the power of the Holy Ghost.
>
> And by the power of the Holy Ghost ye may know the truth of all things.
>
> And whatsoever thing is good is just and true; wherefore, nothing that is good denieth the Christ, but acknowledgeth that he is. (Moroni 10:4–6)

Exhortation 3: Deny not the power of God.

> And ye may know that he is, by the power of the Holy Ghost; wherefore I would exhort you that ye deny not the power of God; for he worketh by power, according to the faith of the children of men, the same today and tomorrow, and forever. (Moroni 10:7)

Exhortation 4: Deny not the gifts of God given to men by the manifestation of the Spirit of God.

> And again, I exhort you, my brethren, that ye deny not the gifts of God, for they are many; and they come from the same God. And there are different ways that these gifts are administered; but it is the same God who worketh all in all; and they are given by the manifestations of the Spirit of God unto men, to profit them.
>
> For behold, to one is given by the Spirit of God, that he may teach the word of wisdom;
>
> And to another, that he may teach the word of knowledge by the same Spirit;

And to another, exceedingly great faith; and to another, the gifts of healing by the same Spirit;

And again, to another, that he may work mighty miracles;

And again, to another, that he may prophesy concerning all things;

And again, to another, the beholding of angels and ministering spirits; And again, to another, all kinds of tongues;

And again, to another, the interpretation of languages and of divers kinds of tongues.

And all these gifts come by the Spirit of Christ; and they come unto every man severally, according as he will. (Moroni 10:8–17)

Exhortation 5: Remember every good gift comes of Christ.

"And I would exhort you, my beloved brethren, that ye remember that every good gift cometh of Christ" (Moroni 10:18).

Exhortation 6: Remember spiritual gifts and that salvation requires faith, hope, and charity.

And I would exhort you, my beloved brethren, that ye remember that he is the same yesterday, today, and forever, and that all these gifts of which I have spoken, which are spiritual, never will be done away, even as long as the world shall stand, only according to the unbelief of the children of men.

Wherefore, there must be faith; and if there must be faith there must also be hope; and if there must be hope there must also be charity.

And except ye have charity ye can in nowise be saved in the kingdom of God; neither can ye be saved in the kingdom of God if ye have not faith; neither can ye if ye have no hope.

And if ye have no hope ye must needs be in despair; and despair cometh because of iniquity.

And Christ truly said unto our fathers: If ye have faith ye can do all things which are expedient unto me.

And now I speak unto all the ends of the earth—that if the day cometh that the power and gifts of God shall be done away among you, it shall be because of unbelief.

And wo be unto the children of men if this be the case; for there shall be none that doeth good among you, no not one. For if there be one among you that doeth good, he shall work by the power and gifts of God.

And wo unto them who shall do these things away and die, for they die in their sins, and they cannot be saved in the kingdom of God; and I speak it according to the words of Christ; and I lie not. (Moroni 10:19–26)

Exhortation 7: Remember that the words of God will hiss forth from generation to generation.

And I exhort you to remember these things; for the time speedily cometh that ye shall know that I lie not, for ye shall see me at the bar of God; and the Lord God will say unto you: Did I not declare my words unto you, which were written by this man, like as one crying from the dead, yea, even as one speaking out of the dust?

I declare these things unto the fulfilling of the prophecies. And behold, they shall proceed forth out of the mouth of the everlasting God; and his word shall hiss forth from generation to generation.

And God shall show unto you, that that which I have written is true. (Moroni 10:27–29)

Exhortation 8: Come unto Christ and be perfected in Him.

And again I would exhort you that ye would come unto Christ, and lay hold upon every good gift, and touch not the evil gift, nor the unclean thing.

And awake, and arise from the dust, O Jerusalem; yea, and put on thy beautiful garments, O daughter of Zion; and strengthen thy stakes and enlarge thy borders forever, that thou mayest no more be confounded, that the covenants of the Eternal Father which he hath made unto thee, O house of Israel, may be fulfilled.

Yea, come unto Christ, and be perfected in him, and deny yourselves of all ungodliness; and if ye shall deny yourselves of all ungodliness, and love God with all your might, mind and strength, then is his grace sufficient for you, that by his grace ye may be perfect in Christ; and if by the grace of God ye are perfect in Christ, ye can in nowise deny the power of God.

And again, if ye by the grace of God are perfect in Christ, and deny not his power, then are ye sanctified in Christ by the grace of God, through the shedding of the blood of Christ, which is in the covenant of the Father unto the remission of your sins, that ye become holy, without spot. (Moroni 10:30–33)

After these eight exhortations, Moroni bids farewell, inviting readers to meet him before the pleasing bar of the great Jehovah, the Eternal Judge of both quick and dead: "And now I bid unto all, farewell. I soon go to rest in the paradise of God, until my spirit and body shall again reunite, and I am brought forth triumphant through the air, to meet you before the pleasing bar of the great Jehovah, the Eternal Judge of both quick and dead. Amen" (Moroni 10:34).

Of Moroni's eight exhortations, the first, second, and seventh are related to the truthfulness of the Book of Mormon; the third is related to faith and the power of God; the fourth, fifth, and sixth are related to gifts from God; and the eighth is an invitation to come unto Christ and be perfected and sanctified by His grace through His atoning blood. Thus, Moroni's final words in the Book of Mormon are an invitation to come unto Christ and be perfected and sanctified in Him through His merciful atoning blood.

After these eight sincere exhortations and admonitions to be perfected and sanctified in Christ, Moroni bid farewell to all readers of the Book of Mormon in the name of the great Jehovah, not Jesus Christ. This is the only place where the name of Jehovah is used in the Book of Mormon (one exception is Nephi's quote of Isaiah 12:2 in 2 Nephi 22:2). Being in the last sentence of the whole Book of Mormon, Moroni may be trying to teach that Jehovah is Jesus Christ of whom writers testified throughout the Book of Mormon. This may also be a symbolic dedication of the whole Book of Mormon to the God of Israel, Jehovah.

The last words of the first writer, Nephi, were to "believe in Christ and be obedient to the Lord." The last words of the last writer, Moroni, were to "come unto Christ and be perfected and sanctified in him." This strongly affirms that the Nephites from the tribe of Joseph were Christians and that the Book of Mormon truly is a Christian scripture.

Chapter 9

Unique Prophecies in the Book of Mormon

AND THEN COMETH THE NEW Jerusalem; and blessed are they who dwell therein, for it is they whose garments are white through the blood of the Lamb; and they are they who are numbered among the remnant of the seed of Joseph, who were of the house of Israel.

And then also cometh the Jerusalem of old; and the inhabitants thereof, blessed are they, for they have been washed in the blood of the Lamb; and they are they who were scattered and gathered in from the four quarters of the earth, and from the north countries, and are partakers of the fulfilling of the covenant which God made with their father, Abraham.

And when these things come, bringeth to pass the scripture which saith, there are they who were first, who shall be last; and there are they who were last, who shall be first. (Ether 13:10–12)

The Book of Mormon contains unique prophecies that cannot be found in the Bible; they are mostly found in 1 Nephi 10–15, 22; 2 Nephi 3, 25–33; Jacob 5; 3 Nephi 16, 20–21, 26–27, 29; Mormon 7–8; and Ether 3–5, 13. While each one of them contains specific prophecies, Jacob 5 is a prophecy that uniquely provides a whole spectrum of scattering and gathering of the Israelites. This chapter will first summarize the allegory of olive tree in Jacob 5. The remaining prophecies unique to the Book of Mormon will then be grouped and reviewed collectively in three categories: prophecies already fulfilled, prophecies being fulfilled, and prophecies yet to be fulfilled.

Zenos's Allegory of the Olive Tree quoted by Jacob (Jacob 5)

In 544 BC, Jacob provided a panoramic view of the scattering and gathering of the Israelites up until the end of the world by quoting the prophet Zenos. This allegory of the olive tree[104] can be closely related to the history of Judeo-Christianity and some prophecies in the Bible. If the book of Revelation by John is a book about the apocalypse at the end of the world, this allegory may be a chapter about scattering and gathering of the Israelites.

Overview of the Allegory of Olive Tree

This allegory can be divided into multiple phases with the following landmark points: the initial conditions and grafting (in other words, scattering); the good fruits and nourishment during the first visit; the evil fruits and corruption (in other words, apostasy) during the second visit; the re-grafting (in other words, gathering) and nourishment from the last to the first; and a final judgment and burning of the whole vineyard.

The Initial Conditions and Scattering

In verses 1–14, the allegory provides an initial condition of a tame olive tree that has a good root but whose top branches are decaying. The lord of the vineyard commands his servant to destroy the bad branches and nourish the tree, which then produces young and tender branches. The lord further commands his servant to graft those young and tender branches of the natural tree into wild trees in many different places and to graft some branches of the wild trees into the tame olive tree.

The First Return of the Lord and the Good Fruits

As described in verses 15–28, the lord returns to the vineyard with his servant after a long time, and he sees good overall results: both the tame trees with grafted wild branches and the wild trees with the grafted natural branches produce good fruits—even those on the poorest spot of soil. However,

---

[104] The Apostle Paul also used an analogy of grafting branches of an olive tree as a metaphor in Romans 11:16–21.

some of the trees on the good spot of ground produced good fruits, while some on the good soil produced bad fruits. The lord wants to burn the bad ones, but his servant convinces him to spare them, and the servant continues his work in the vineyard to produce good fruits.

The Second Return of the Lord and the Bad Fruits

After a long period of time near the end of the season, as described in verses 29–51, the lord and his servant return to the vineyard together a second time to discover that all the trees in the vineyard produce all sorts of fruits, most of them corrupt. The grafted wild branches overrun the good root of the tame tree and produce much evil fruit. All the natural branches grafted into the wild trees have also become corrupt, and the good branches have withered away and died. The lord laments and regrets not burning the bad branches on the good spot as he initially wanted. The servant explains that the problem is due to the loftiness of the branches that outgrew the roots. The lord and his servant decide to nourish the trees and spare them a little bit longer.

Gathering Near the End: The Last Becomes the First, the First Becomes the Last

In verses 52–76, the lord of the vineyard says that the end is nigh at hand, and he commands his servant to graft the original natural branches back to the mother tree, replacing the branches that have borne the bitterest fruits. He also asks his servant to call other servants to join in this last effort to bring good fruits, but their numbers are few.

After re-grafting the natural branches back into the mother tree, the lord's servants work hard to nourish and prune the trees. They balance the strength of the roots and the branches by cutting off and burning bad branches as needed. The lord commands the servants to begin nourishing from the last that they may be first, and that the first may be last. This is the last nourishment to the trees. This restoration work is successful, and the trees produce much good fruit. The lord says these fruits are precious from the beginning. The servants are rewarded for their efforts.

Final Judgment and Burning of the Whole Vineyard

When the evil fruits come again into the vineyard, the lord will cause the good and the bad to be gathered, as described in verse 77. He will preserve the good and cast away the bad into its own place. Afterwards, the end of the season will come, and the lord will cause the whole vineyard to be burned with fire.

There are diverse opinions on the interpretation of this allegory relating to Judeo-Christian history and prophecies of the events to occur in the last dispensation, but the following may be one way to correlate them:

After Abraham migrated from Haran to Canaan to worship the true God, and the Hebrews returned to the land of Canaan from Egypt under the direction of Jehovah through Moses, there were three major scatterings:

- First, the scattering of the Northern Kingdom by Assyrians in 721 BC (scattering the lost ten tribes)
- Second, the scattering of the Southern Kingdom by the Babylonians in 587 BC (they returned to Jerusalem around 520 BC)
- Third, the scattering of the Jews and massive destruction of Jerusalem by the Romans in AD 70.

A small group of the Josephites also migrated to a good spot (the promised land, or land of America) during 592–600 BC, and they were divided into two groups: the Nephites and the Lamanites. The Nephites were righteous (the good fruits), and the Lamanites were wicked (the bad fruits).

Representing the first return of the lord of the vineyard, Jesus Christ was born and resided among the Jews; He also visited the Nephites after His death and Resurrection. After the ministry of Jesus Christ and that of His Apostles, apostasy began with the Gentiles and has flourished for a long time. In the American continent, the Lamanites annihilated the Nephites around AD 400. Many of these historical events fit with the stories in this allegory by Zenos.

After the lord's second return to the vineyard near the end of the season, re-grafting (gathering) is done, more servants are called, and they work hard to make the trees produce good fruits by nourishing them, getting rid of bad branches and weeds along the way, balancing the strength of roots and branches, and so on. This fits with major Restoration events in the early nineteenth century:

- The visits of Jesus Christ to Joseph Smith through vision.
- The coming forth of the Book of Mormon, in which Jesus Christ taught that the gathering of the Israelites would commence when the book is published.
- The priesthood keys being delivered to Joseph Smith.
- Many being called to the work of the Restoration.

These events, among others, coincide with movements of other Jewish gatherings, such as the beginning of the Zionism movements in Europe by Theodor Herzl[105] in the late nineteenth century, the Balfour Declaration[106] in AD 1917, and the United Nations re-establishing a Jewish Nation in AD 1948. The true gospel of Jesus Christ was restored through the Josephites first in the nineteenth century, and the Jews were being gathered to their homeland during the twentieth century; some of them have come to know of the Restoration of the true gospel of Jesus Christ. These events may be fulfillment of the prophecy that the last would become first, and the first would be made last.

The end of the world is yet to come. Before the final judgment, the devil will be back to deceive people again. After the final judgment, the good and the bad will be rewarded or punished accordingly, and the whole earth will be burned with fire.

Book of Mormon Prophecies Already Fulfilled

The following list shows examples of fulfilled prophecies from the Book of Mormon.

---

[105] See details at https://www.jewishvirtuallibrary.org/quot-the-jewish-state-quot-theodor-herzl
[106] See details at https://www.history.com/topics/balfour-declaration

Destruction of Jerusalem and Scattering of the Jews

Subjects	Prophets and the Time of Prophecy	Scriptural References	Historical Fulfillments
Jerusalem will be destroyed.	Lehi (600–592 BC)	1 Nephi 1:4	The Kingdom of Judah was conquered by Babylonians, and Jerusalem was destroyed in 587 BC. Many were taken to Babylonia.
		1 Nephi 1:13	
		1 Nephi 10:3	
		2 Nephi 1:4	
Jews would be carried away captive to Babylon.	Nephi (559–545 BC)	2 Nephi 25:10	
Jews will return to Jerusalem.	Lehi (600–592 BC)	1 Nephi 10:3	Persia conquered Babylonia and allowed the Jews to return to Jerusalem from about 520 BC.
	Nephi (559–545 BC)	2 Nephi 25:11	
Jerusalem will be destroyed for the second time after Jesus's ministry.	Nephi (559–545 BC)	2 Nephi 25:14–15	Romans destroyed Jerusalem in AD 70, and the Jews were scattered abroad.

The Lamanites and the Nephites

Subjects	Prophets and the Time of Prophecy	Scriptural References	Historical Fulfillments
The Lamanites will not be destroyed, but the Nephites will be destroyed by the Lamanites in the end.	Nephi (600–592 BC)	1 Nephi 13:30–31	"After thousands of years, all were destroyed except the Lamanites" (Book of Mormon, Introduction).
The Gentiles will not destroy all the Lamanites.	Nephi (600–592 BC)	1 Nephi 10:30–31	

Restoration of the Gospel of Jesus Christ and the Book of Mormon

Subjects	Prophets and the Time of Prophecy	Scriptural References	Historical Fulfillments
In the latter days, a prophet of restoration will be named Joseph after his father's name, also having the same name as Joseph in Egypt.	Lehi (588–570 BC)	2 Nephi 3:7–8, 15	Joseph Smith was named after his father (he was the third son born to his parents).

The marvelous work of Restoration was to come forth among the Gentiles in the latter days.[107]	Nephi (588–545 BC)	1 Nephi 22:8	Joseph Smith saw the first vision (AD 1820), translated the Book of Mormon (AD 1829), received the priesthoods and their keys (AD 1829 and 1836), and organized a church (AD 1830).
		2 Nephi 27:26	
		2 Nephi 29:1	
	The resurrected Jesus Christ (AD 34)	3 Nephi 21:9	
Jesus will declare His Father's work through a man in the latter days.	The resurrected Jesus Christ (AD 34)	3 Nephi 21:9	Joseph Smith was called to be a prophet in the latter days.
The Bible and the Book of Mormon will grow together.	Lehi (588–570 BC)	2 Nephi 3:12	Both scriptures jointly testify of Jesus Christ.

---

[107] Isaiah 29:14 contains a similar prophecy.

There will be three witnesses and a few who will behold the book (the golden plates).	Nephi (559–545 BC)	2 Nephi 27:12–13	Three witnesses of the golden plates[108] were Oliver Cowdery, David Whitmer, Martin Harris.
The learned man will say, "Bring hither the book, and I will read them." The man will answer, "I cannot bring the book, for it is sealed." Then the learned man will say, "I cannot read it."	Nephi (559–545 BC)	2 Nephi 27:15–18	Martin Harris visited with Professor Anton in 1828, and these events transpired.

---

[108] The Testimony of the Three Witnesses, a statement made in AD 1829, is contained in the introductory pages of the Book of Mormon and specifies that they "have seen the plates which contain this record, which is a record of the people of Nephi, and also of the Lamanites, their brethren, and also of the people of Jared, who came from the tower of which hath been spoken."

The Book of Mormon was written to foster belief in the Bible. Believing the Bible also leads to a belief in the Book of Mormon.	Mormon (about 385)	Mormon 7:9	The Book of Mormon is another testament of Jesus Christ and helps us better understand the Bible.
After the Book of Mormon comes out, movements for the Jews to return to the Palestine area would commence.	The resurrected Jesus (AD 34)	3 Nephi 21:7, 26–28	Examples: Beginning of Zionism movements by Theodor Herzl in the late nineteenth century, the Balfour Declaration (AD 1917), United Nations reestablishment of a Jewish Nation (AD 1948).
	Mormon (AD 362)	Mormon 3:17	
	Moroni (AD 400–421)	Either 4:17	

The Establishment of Churches by the Gentiles and Coming Forth of the Bible

Subjects	Prophets and the Time of Prophecy	Scriptural References	Historical Fulfillments
Formation of a great church by the Gentiles that will bring much wickedness.	Nephi (600–592 BC)	1 Nephi 13:4–9	Birth of the organized Christian churches from the fourth century.
The record of the Jews (Bible) containing the fullness of the gospel of which the twelve Apostles bore record will go to the Gentiles in purity.	Nephi (600–592 BC)	1 Nephi 13:24	The original records of the New Testament have not survived, but multiple versions of copies are available.
Because the plain and precious parts and the covenants will be taken from the Bible by the Gentiles, many will stumble.	Nephi (600–592 BC)	1 Nephi 13:26–29	There are many different claims and interpretations of the Bible by different denominations.

Jesus will visit the Nephites and provide the plain and precious parts, but its record will be hid up. After the Gentiles stumble, the record will come forward unto the Gentiles.	Nephi (600–592 BC)	1 Nephi 13:34–35	Moroni hid the golden plates in AD 421. After the Book of Mormon was published in 1830 following a long period of apostasy, those missing parts can be found in it.
There will be only two churches: the church of the Lamb of God, and the church of the devil. The former will be globally present but small, but the latter will be huge and great in its presence around the world.	Nephi (600–592 BC)	1 Nephi 14:10–13	There are basically two branches of Christian churches: the Judeo-Christians and The Church of Jesus Christ of Latter-day Saints. In size, the latter is less than 1 percent of the former.
The church of the devil will start, and there will be wars and rumors of wars among all the nations.	Nephi (600–592 BC)	1 Nephi 14:15–17	There have been wars that were initiated and/or instigated by the Judeo-Christian churches.

| The Apostle John will write about the end of the world. The original writing will contain the plain and precious parts. | Nephi (600–592 BC) | 1 Nephi 14:22–27 | The book of Revelation by the Apostle John was included in the canonized Bible in 419, but its authenticity is not 100 percent certain. |
| | Moroni (AD 400–421) | Ether 4:17 | |

Jesus Christ's Mortal Ministry (see Chapters 1–3 for more detail)

Subjects	Prophets and the Time of Prophecy	Scriptural References	Historical Fulfillments
His birth 600 years after Lehi's departure out of Jerusalem.	Lehi (600–592 BC)	1 Nephi 10:4	The fulfillment of these prophecies is recorded in the four Gospels of the New Testament by Matthew, Mark, Luke, and John.
	Nephi (559-545 BC)	2 Nephi 25:19	
His name will be Jesus, and His mother's name will be Mary.	King Benjamin (124 BC)	Mosiah 3:8	
	Alma (83 BC)	Alma 7:10	
He will be baptized by John the Baptist.	Nephi (600–592 BC)	1 Nephi 10:9–10	
Ministry of Jesus Christ.	King Benjamin (124 BC)	Mosiah 3:2–9	
	Alma (83 BC)	Alma 7:9–13	
The Jews will crucify Jesus, but He will rise three days later.	Nephi (559–545 BC)	2 Nephi 25:12	

The Promised Land (the Land of America)

Subjects	Prophets and the Time of Prophecy	Scriptural References	Historical Fulfillments
A Gentile man will cross an ocean and reach the promised land where the Lamanites lived.	Nephi (600–592 BC)	1 Nephi 13:12	Columbus discovered the West Indies in AD 1492.
Many Gentiles who are white will come forward to the promised land and will scatter the Lamanites.	Nephi (600–592 BC)	1 Nephi 13:14–15	European pioneers migrated to the new land of America, won the wars against the American Indians in the seventeenth through nineteenth centuries, and scattered them.
The migrated white Gentiles will wage war against their mother countries and will win the wars through blessings of the Lord.	Nephi (600–592 BC)	1 Nephi 10:17–19	New colonizers won the war of independence against the European nations and established an independent nation (in the case of the United States: AD 1776).

| These Gentiles will bring a Jewish book with prophecies from the prophets and the records from the twelve Apostles. This book will be of great worth to them. | Nephi (600–592 BC) | 1 Nephi 10:20–25 | The Bible has been of great worth to the European pioneers for their religion and literacy. |
| The Lord will establish a free society in this land such that the remnant of Jacob can hear the gospel from the Gentiles. | The resurrected Jesus (AD 34) | 3 Nephi 21:4 | From Joseph Smith's days, the restored gospel has been preached to the American Indians both in North and South America. |

Book of Mormon Prophecies Still Being Fulfilled

Some prophecies are still in the process of being fulfilled.

Subjects	Prophets and the Time of Prophecy	Scriptural References	Fulfillment Status
The covenant people of the church of the Lamb of God will be armed with righteousness and the power of God.	Nephi (600–592 BC)	1 Nephi 14:14	There are many Saints in The Church of Jesus Christ of Latter-day Saints who have been faithful and righteous.

Many Gentiles will reject the Book of Mormon, saying, "A Bible, a Bible, we have got a Bible, and there cannot be any more Bible."	Nephi (559–545 BC)	2 Nephi 29:3, 6	Many Christians believe the canon is closed, and do not accept any additional scriptures.
In the last days, many false churches will be built up to get gain, they will deny the power of God, and they will teach their own precepts.	Nephi (559–545 BC)	1 Nephi 22:23	There are many honest and righteous people in all churches, but there are also churches and/or clergies who fit this description even in our present day.
		2 Nephi 28:3-6	
This land is a choice land that will be free from the bondage of other countries.	Moroni (AD 400–421)	Ether 2:12	America has been free from any occupation by foreign forces since its independence.

The covenant people will be gathered in Jerusalem, which is their inheritance.	The resurrected Jesus quoting His Father[109] (AD 34)	3 Nephi 20:29—34	Elder Orson Hyde dedicated the land of Israel for gathering of the Jews at Jerusalem in AD 1841. Since Israel was established in AD 1948, the Jews have been returning back to Israel. There are many Christian churches in Israel, but majority of Jews do not yet accept Jesus as the Christ.
		3 Nephi 21:26–28	
This will commence when the Book of Mormon comes to the Gentiles.	The resurrected Jesus Christ (AD 34)	3 Nephi 21:7	
		3 Nephi 21:26–28	
	Mormon (about 380)	3 Nephi 29:1	

---

[109] 3 Nephi 20:29–34: "And I will remember the covenant which I have made with my people; and I have covenanted with them that I would gather them together in mine own due time, that I would give unto them again the land of their fathers for their inheritance, which is the land of Jerusalem, which is the promised land unto them forever, saith the Father. And it shall come to pass that the time cometh, when the fulness of my gospel shall be preached unto them; And they shall believe in me, that I am Jesus Christ, the Son of God, and shall pray unto the Father in my name. Then shall their watchmen lift up their voice, and with the voice together shall they sing; for they shall see eye to eye. Then will the Father gather them together again, and give unto them Jerusalem for the land of their inheritance. Then shall they break forth into joy—Sing together, ye waste places of Jerusalem; for the Father hath comforted his people, he hath redeemed Jerusalem."

Moroni's Six Prophecies[110]

The prophet Moroni recorded the following six prophecies that virtually describe present social and religious situations. He started them by saying "it shall come in a day when . . ."

> And no one need say they shall not come, for they surely shall, for the Lord hath spoken it; for out of the earth shall they come, by the hand of the Lord, and none can stay it; and [1] *it shall come in a day* when it shall be said that miracles are done away; and it shall come even as if one should speak from the dead.
>
> And [2] *it shall come in a day* when the blood of saints shall cry unto the Lord, because of secret combinations and the works of darkness.
>
> Yea, [3] *it shall come in a day when* the power of God shall be denied, and churches become defiled and be lifted up in the pride of their hearts; yea, even in a day when leaders of churches and teachers shall rise in the pride of their hearts, even to the envying of them who belong to their churches.
>
> Yea, [4] *it shall come in a day when* there shall be heard of fires, and tempests, and vapors of smoke in foreign lands;
>
> And there shall also be heard of wars, rumors of wars, and earthquakes in divers places.
>
> Yea, [5] *it shall come in a day when* there shall be great pollutions upon the face of the earth; there shall be murders, and robbing, and lying, and deceivings, and whoredoms, and all manner of abominations; when there shall be many who will say, Do this, or do that, and it mattereth not, for the Lord will uphold such at the last day. But wo unto such, for they are in the gall of bitterness and in the bonds of iniquity.
>
> Yea, [6] *it shall come in a day when* there shall be churches built up that shall say: Come unto me, and for

---

110 Along with these six prophecies, Moroni also asks seven questions (see Mormon 8:33, 38, 39, 40).

your money you shall be forgiven of your sins. (Mormon 8:26–32; emphasis added)

All six of these prophecies are being fulfilled:

1. Not believing in miracles and denying the power of God,
2. Work of dark conspiracies in the world,
3. Corruption and pride among Christians and their churches,
4. Many natural disasters all over the world,
5. A rampant increase of moral pollutions, and
6. Monetary dealings within churches such as indulgences and/or obtaining church leadership positions with money (for example, paying for a position of elder or deacon).

Thus, it seems apparent that the prophet Moroni knew very well the status and practices of Christianity in the latter days.

Book of Mormon Prophecies to Be Fulfilled

Some of the prophecies by prophets in the Book of Mormon that are not yet fulfilled are reviewed here (some of the fulfilled prophecies will be included for clarification).

Prophecies by Nephi (the First Writer in the Book of Mormon)

1 Nephi 12:6–10 (600–592 BC)

An angel taught Nephi that the Twelve Apostles of Jesus Christ will judge all the twelve tribes of Israel at the final judgment. This confirms what Jesus taught the Twelve in Matthew 19:28 (see also Luke 22:30). The angel also taught him that the twelve Nephite disciples will judge Nephi's descendants. Mormon wrote in AD 363 that the Spirit told him the same messages (see Mormon 3:18–19).

1 Nephi 22:1–31 (588–570 BC)

After Nephi read some of the words of Isaiah from the plates of brass (see verse 1), he taught his brethren by answering their questions. His teaching was done in a chiasmus format[111] as he provided an overview

---

[111] There are many examples of chiasmus in the Book of Mormon (such as 1 Nephi 22,

of the scattering and gathering of the Israelites and the end of the world. The scattering and gathering was already fulfilled or is currently being fulfilled (see verses 2–12),[112] but the end of the world is yet to come (see verses 13–31).

- The great and abominable church, a whore of all the earth, will have internal fighting as well as fighting against Zion. But this church will tumble to the dust in great fashion (see verses 13–14).
- The time will soon come that the wrath of God will cause Satan to have no more power over the hearts of people; the wicked will perish but the righteous will not perish (see verses 15–19).
- The Holy One of Israel will come as prophesied by Moses: "A prophet shall the Lord your God raise up unto you, like unto me; him shall ye hear in all things whatsoever he shall say unto you" (1 Nephi 22:20). Nephi declared that the prophet whom Moses prophesied was the Holy One of Israel (see verse 21).
- The time will speedily come that all churches and people will be built up to get gain, to get power over people, to become popular in the world, to seek after lusts of the flesh and the things of the world, and to do all manner of iniquity. All who belong to the devil must be consumed as stubble (see verses 22–23).
- The righteous will help the Holy One of Israel reign in dominion, might, power, and great glory; He will gather all His children who will repent, and the Lord will feed them. Because of their righteousness, Satan will have no power and cannot be loosed for many years (see verses 24–28).

verses 1–3, 3–5, 7–8, 9–11, 13, 15–16, 20, 25, 26, 29–31). A list of chiasmus examples in the Book of Mormon is available at https://chiasmusresources.org/index-chiasm-book-mormon.

[112] After Nephi quoted Isaiah 48–49, he reviewed the scattering (see verses 2–12). His prophecies have been fulfilled: Some Israelites in Jerusalem were already scattered among all nations, and more will be scattered because they hardened their hearts against the Holy One of Israel (see verses 4–5). The scattered Israelites will be nursed by the Gentiles, and the Lord will raise up a mighty nation among the Gentiles who will scatter the Lamanites (see verses 6–7). The Lord will proceed to do a marvelous work among the Gentiles, through whom the Abrahamic covenant will be renewed to all people, including the Israelites (see verses 8–11). The Israelites will be brought out of captivity and darkness, will gather in the lands of their inheritance, and will know their Savior and Redeemer, the mighty one of Israel (see verse 12).

- Nephi testified that these things written on the plates of brass are true. To be saved at the last day, he concluded one must obey[113] the commandments of God and endure to the end (see verses 29–31).

2 Nephi 29:12–14 (559–545 BC)

Many tribes of Israel with the Abrahamic covenant will write their own records; records will be written by the Jews, the Josephites, and other tribes. All will have the records of the others. In the end, all records will be gathered into one. The Lord will remember His covenant people forever.

2 Nephi 30:7–18 (559–545 BC)

The Jews will gather, and many will believe in Christ. The Lord will globally commence His work of restoration for His people on the earth (see verses 7–8). The Lord will judge the world; while the wicked must be destroyed by fire, the righteous and faithful will be the girdle of his loins (see verses 9–11). Then the Millennium will start;[114] beasts will cohabitate peacefully, and a little child will lead them. All things of God will be revealed to the people fully, and there will be no secrets (as waters cover the sea).[115] There will be no works of darkness, and Satan will have no power over the hearts of people for a long time (see verses 12–18).

Prophecies by the Resurrected Jesus Christ

As discussed in Chapter 3, the resurrected Jesus Christ prophesied specifically about the relationships between the remnant of Joseph, the Gentiles, and the Jews in the latter days. Since most of these prophecies were introduced in Chapter 3, only those prophecies that are yet to be fulfilled will be summarized here.

---

[113] It is interesting that Nephi finished his first book (1 Nephi) with his testimony that "a man must be obedient to the commandments of God . . . if ye shall be obedient to the commandments and endure to the end, ye shall be saved at the last day" (1 Nephi 22:30–31), and he also finished his last book (see 2 Nephi 33) with his last words, "for thus hath the Lord commanded me, and I must obey" (2 Nephi 33:15). Nephi was very consistent in testifying and demonstrating the importance of obedience to God.

[114] Comparable messages can be found in Isaiah 11 and 2 Nephi 21.

[115] Similar prophecies can be found in Joel 2.

3 Nephi 20:12–22 (AD 34)

The Father's covenant with the house of Israel will be fulfilled; they will gather from all over the world, and the land of America will be inherited by the Josephites (see verses 12–14). If the Gentiles do not repent after they scatter the Lord's people, the remnant of Jacob will destroy them with the Lord's help.[116] The Lord's judgment will be upon them at that day unless they repent (see verses 15–20). The Lord will establish His people in a New Jerusalem on the land of America, fulfilling His covenant with Jacob (see verses 21–22).

3 Nephi 20:25–34, 46 (AD 34)

The Father sent the resurrected Jesus to the Nephites because they are the children of the covenant. The Gentiles will be blessed with the Holy Ghost. However, if they harden their hearts against Jesus after receiving the fullness of the gospel, the Father will return their iniquities upon their heads (see verses 25–28).

The Lord will remember His covenant with His people and will gather them in His own due time. He will give Jerusalem to them for their inheritance, and the fullness of the gospel of Jesus will be preached to them. They will believe in Jesus and will sing together with joy. Jesus assured that this will come to pass (see verses 29–34, 46).

3 Nephi 21:1–29 (AD 34)

Some of the prophecies of the relationship between the Israelites and the Gentiles have been fulfilled (see verses 1–10), and some are yet to be fulfilled (see verses 11–29). If the Gentiles will not believe the words of Jesus Christ delivered through His servant, the remnant of Jacob will be like a lion among the beasts of the forest to tread down and tear them into pieces. The unprecedented vengeance of the Lord will be upon the wicked Gentiles who will not repent (see verses 11–21).[117]

However, for the Gentiles who repent, hear the words of Jesus, and harden not their hearts, Jesus will establish His Church among them, and they will be numbered among the remnant of Jacob. Jesus will give them the land of America for their inheritance. They will assist the remnant of Jacob to gather and to build the New Jerusalem (see verses 22–25). At

---

[116] Micah gave similar warnings to the Jews (see Micah 4:13).
[117] Micah gave similar warnings to the Jews (see Micah 5:8–15).

that day when the work of the Father commences, this gospel will be preached even to the lost tribes of Israel as well as the surviving Lamanites so that they may come to the Father in the name of Jesus, and they will gather in the land of their inheritance[118] (see verses 26–29).

Prophecies by Ether (Written by Moroni)

Moroni wrote what the prophet Ether said concerning the gathering of the Jews in the Old Jerusalem and of the Josephites in the New Jerusalem (see Ether 13:2–13).

From the days of Noah (when the waters had receded), the land of America was chosen to be a choice land of the Lord above all other lands, and the New Jerusalem will come down out of heaven on this land as it is the holy sanctuary of the Lord (see verses 2–4). The Old Jerusalem in Israel will be destroyed but be built up again as a holy city unto the Lord, and the New Jerusalem will be built in the land of America with the remnant of the seed of Joseph (see verses 5–6).

The Father was merciful to bring out a remnant of Joseph from Jerusalem to the land of America. It will be a land of their inheritance until the end of the world. They will build up a holy city unto the Lord like the Old Jerusalem (see verses 7–8). There will be a new heaven and a new earth, and all things will become new.

The Josephites in the New Jerusalem whose garments are white through the blood of the Lamb will be blessed. The inhabitants in the Old Jerusalem will be washed in the blood of the Lamb and will be blessed with the fulfillment of the Abrahamic covenant (see verses 9–11). When these things happen, it will bring to pass the prophecy that the first will be last, and the last will be first (see verse 12).

What Moroni recorded here can basically be summarized: the Old Jerusalem in Israel is the inheritance of the Jews, and the New Jerusalem on the land of America is the inheritance of the Josephites. Both Jerusalems will be occupied by Israelites with the Abrahamic covenant.

---

[118] Other verses mentioning the land of America being the inheritance of the Josephites and/or being the site for the New Jerusalem include 3 Nephi 15:13, 16:16, 29:1; Mormon 3:17; Ether 2:15, 13:8.

Prophecies in the Book of Mormon: Key Points

About the Jews and Jesus Christ in the Future

The Jews would be carried away by a Gentile nation (the Babylonians) but would be able to return to Jerusalem. They would again be scattered after Jesus Christ's ministry. After a long period of their dispersion, they would gather again in Jerusalem aided by the Gentiles (the United Nations) under the influence of the Holy Ghost. They would then know Jesus is the Christ, their Messiah.

About the Josephites (the Remnant of Joseph or Jacob)

This is a small group branched off from the main Israelites. A part of their descendants would be righteous, and the other part would be wicked; one side would destroy the other side. They would be visited by Jesus Christ. They would be scattered by the Gentiles, but they would inherit this chosen land (the land of America) and establish the New Jerusalem with aid from a free and mighty Gentile nation.

About a Latter-day Prophet

The latter-day prophet's name would be Joseph after his father's name as well as after Joseph of Egypt. He would declare the true gospel of the Lord, bring forth the Book of Mormon, and establish the Church of the Lamb of God in the latter days. The devil would mar him, but the Lord would heal him.

About the Book of Mormon

A prophet would bring forth the Book of Mormon from the dust. This book and the Bible would establish the word of God by bringing truths, establishing peace among His people, and confounding false doctrines. It would provide many plain and precious parts and covenants that would be missing in the Bible. However, many would reject it because they already have the Bible. Those who accept it would be blessed, and those who reject it would be damned.

About the Land of America, and a Free and Mighty Gentile Nation

This land was a chosen land for the inheritance of the Josephites from the beginning. The white Gentiles would discover the land, colonize it, win wars against their mother countries, and establish a free and mighty nation in the land of America. All of these would be accomplished under the guidance of the Holy Ghost. These Gentiles would carry the remnant of Joseph, the Lamanites, upon their shoulders.

About Only Two Churches

There would be two churches only: the church of the Lamb of God and the church of the devil. The church of the Lamb of God would be throughout the world but would be relatively few in numbers. However, the church of the devil would be started by the Gentiles and would be huge globally. The church of the devil would have wars and rumors of wars among themselves and would persecute the Saints. It will tumble to the dust at the end, and great shall be the fall of it.

About the Bible

This Judeo-Christian scripture would originally be pure when it came from the Apostles of the Lord. However, in the process of transferring from the Jews to the Gentiles, many plain and precious parts and covenants would be left out under the influence of the devil. Because of this, many would stumble, not knowing the truth fully.

About Different Records from Different Tribes

Just as the Jews and the Josephites have their own records, other tribes would bring out their own records. All these records will be shared among all the tribes and collected into one at the end.

About Scattering and Gathering the Covenant People of the Lord

As mentioned previously, the Jews would be taken away to Babylon but would return to Jerusalem. They would crucify Jesus Christ, and they would be scattered around the world for a long time. After the Book of Mormon would be made available, their gathering would commence. Eventually, they would recognize Jesus as their God and would accept Him.

The remnant of Joseph, the Lamanites, would be scattered by the white Gentiles and would be carried on their shoulders. They would get to know their ancestry and the true gospel of Jesus Christ through the Book of Mormon. (For more prophecies about the scattering and gathering of the covenant people, see Orson Hyde's dedicatory prayer of Jerusalem in AD 1841 at the end of this chapter.)

About the Gentiles in the Latter Days

The Gentiles would scatter the covenant people of Abraham, but they would be instruments for gathering the covenant people under the influence of the Holy Ghost in the Lord's time. If they repent, accept Jesus Christ, are baptized, and keep the commandments, they would be adopted into the Abrahamic covenant. If they don't repent, the Josephites would rise and trample them to pieces.

About the Old and New Jerusalem

The Old Jerusalem would again be inhabited by the Jews, and they would accept Jesus Christ as their Messiah. The Lord will remember the lost ten tribes of Israel; they will be taught of Jesus Christ and His gospel, and will gather in the land of their inheritance. The Josephites and the converted Gentiles would establish the New Jerusalem on the land of America, and a city would come down from heaven to the New Jerusalem.

About the End of the World[119]

Prophecies about the end of the world are not very detailed in the Book of Mormon, but some general trends were taught. After the direct ministry of Jesus Christ on the earth with peace in righteousness, Satan will come back for a short period of time and spread wickedness again. Jesus will separate the righteous from the unrighteous at the final judgment with help from His angels and the Apostles. The world will be burned and be renewed. The earth will pass the sun, moon, and so on.

The above covers most of the prophecies from the Book of Mormon that are new to most Judeo-Christians. There are similar prophecies in the Bible in some cases, but most of these prophecies were not found in the canonized Bible.

---

[119] Since Nephi and others are very much influenced by the teachings of Isaiah through the plates of brass, this part of the prophecies is very similar to the ones that Isaiah prophesied (such as those in Isaiah 11, 24). The Doctrine and Covenants also reveals the general trends of the end of the world (see D&C 29, 133).

Orson Hyde's Dedicatory Prayer of Jerusalem on the Mount of Olives (November 22, 1841)

"O Thou! who art from everlasting to everlasting, eternally and unchangeably the same, even the God who rules in the heavens above, and controls the destinies of men on the earth, wilt Thou not condescend, through thine infinite goodness and royal favor, to listen to the prayer of Thy servant which he this day offers up unto Thee in the name of Thy holy child Jesus, upon this land, where the Son of Righteousness set in blood, and thine Anointed One expired.

"Be pleased, O Lord, to forgive all the follies, weaknesses, vanities, and sins of Thy servant, and strengthen him to resist all future temptations. Give him prudence and discernment that he may avoid the evil, and a heart to choose the good; give him fortitude to bear up under trying and adverse circumstances, and grace to endure all things for Thy name's sake, until the end shall come, when all the Saints shall rest in peace.

"Now, O Lord! Thy servant has been obedient to the heavenly vision which Thou gavest him in his native land; and under the shadow of Thine outstretched arm, he has safely arrived in this place to dedicate and consecrate this land unto Thee, for the gathering together of Judah's scattered remnants, according to the predictions of the holy Prophets -- for the building up of Jerusalem again after it has been trodden down by the Gentiles so long, and for rearing a Temple in honor of Thy name. Everlasting thanks be ascribed unto Thee, O Father, Lord of heaven and earth, that Thou hast preserved Thy servant from the dangers of the seas, and from the plague and pestilence which have caused the land to mourn. The violence of man has also been restrained, and Thy providential care by night and by day has been exercised over Thine unworthy servant. Accept, therefore, O Lord, the tribute of a grateful heart for all past favors, and be pleased to continue Thy kindness and mercy towards a needy worm of the dust.

"O Thou, Who didst covenant with Abraham, Thy friend, and who didst renew that covenant with Isaac, and confirm the same with Jacob with an oath, that Thou wouldst not only give them this land for an everlasting inheritance, but that Thou wouldst also remember their seed forever. Abraham, Isaac, and Jacob have long since closed their eyes in death, and made the grave their mansion. Their children are scattered and dispersed abroad among the nations of the Gentiles like sheep that have no shepherd, and are still looking forward for the fulfillment of those promises which Thou didst make concerning them; and even this land, which once poured forth nature's richest bounty, and flowed, as it were, with milk and honey, has, to a certain extent, been smitten with barrenness and sterility since it drank from murderous hands the blood of Him who never sinned.

"Grant, therefore, O Lord, in the name of Thy well-beloved Son, Jesus Christ, to remove the barrenness and sterility of this land, and let springs of living water break forth to water its thirsty soil. Let the vine and olive produce in their strength, and the fig-tree bloom and flourish. Let the land become abundantly fruitful when possessed by its rightful heirs; let it again flow with plenty to feed the returning prodigals who come home with a spirit of grace and supplication; upon it let the clouds distil virtue and richness, and let the fields smile with plenty. Let the flocks and the herds greatly increase and multiply upon the mountains and the hills; and let Thy great kindness conquer and subdue the unbelief of Thy people. Do Thou take from them their stony heart, and give them a heart of flesh; and may the Sun of Thy favor dispel the cold mists of darkness which have beclouded their atmosphere. Incline them to gather in upon this land according to Thy word. Let them come like clouds and like doves to their windows. Let the large ships of the nations bring them from the distant isles; and let kings become their nursing fathers, and queens with motherly fondness wipe the tear of sorrow from their eye.

"Thou, O Lord, did once move upon the heart of Cyrus to show favor unto Jerusalem and her children. Do Thou now also be pleased to inspire the hearts of kings and the powers of the earth to look with a friendly eye towards this place, and with a desire to see Thy righteous purposes executed in relation thereto. Let them know that it is Thy good pleasure to restore the kingdom unto Israel -- raise up Jerusalem as its capital, and constitute her people a distinct nation and government, with David Thy servant, even a descendant from the loins of ancient David to be their king.

"Let that nation or that people who shall take an active part in behalf of Abraham's children, and in the raising up of Jerusalem, find favor in Thy sight. Let not their enemies prevail against them, neither let pestilence or famine overcome them, but let the glory of Israel overshadow them, and the power of the Highest protect them; while that nation or kingdom that will not serve Thee in this glorious work must perish, according to Thy word—Yea, those nations shall be utterly wasted.

"Though Thy servant is now far from his home, and from the land bedewed with his earliest tear, yet he remembers, O Lord, his friend: who are there, and family, whom for Thy sake he has left. Though poverty and privation be our earthly lot, yet ah! do Thou richly endow us with an inheritance where moth and rust do not corrupt, and where thieves do not break through and steal.

"The hands that have fed, clothed, or shown favor unto the family of Thy servant in his absence, or that shall hereafter do so, let them not lose their reward, but let a special blessing rest upon them, and in Thy kingdom let them have an inheritance when Thou shalt come to be glorified in this society.

"Do Thou also look with favor upon all those through whose liberality I have been enabled to come to this land; and in the day when Thou shalt reward all people according to their works, let these also not be passed by or forgotten, but in time let them be in readiness to enjoy the glory of those mansions which Jesus has gone to prepare. Particularly do Thou bless the stranger in Philadelphia, whom I never saw, but who sent me gold, with a request that I should pray for him in Jerusalem. Now, O Lord, let blessings come upon him from an unexpected quarter, and let his basket be filled, and his storehouse abound with plenty, and let not the good things of the earth be his only portion, but let him be found among those to whom it shall be said, `Thou hast been faithful over a few things, and I will make thee ruler over many.'

"O my Father in heaven! I now ask Thee in the name of Jesus to remember Zion, with all her Stakes, and with all her assemblies. She has been grievously afflicted and smitten; she has mourned; she has wept; her enemies have triumphed, and have said, `Ah, where is thy God?' Her Priests and Prophets have groaned in chains and fetters within the gloomy walls of prisons, while many were slain, and now sleep in the arms of death. How long, O Lord, shall iniquity triumph, and sin go unpunished?

"Do Thou arise in the majesty of Thy strength, and make bare Thine arm in behalf of Thy people. Redress their wrongs, and turn their sorrow into joy. Pour the spirit of light and knowledge, grace and wisdom, into the hearts of her Prophets, and clothe her Priests with salvation. Let light and knowledge march forth through the empire of darkness, and may the honest in heart flow to their standard, and join in the march to go forth to meet the Bridegroom.

"Let a peculiar blessing rest upon the Presidency of Thy Church, for at them are the arrows of the enemy directed. Be Thou to them a sun and a shield, their strong tower and hiding place; and in the time of distress or danger be Thou near to deliver. Also the quorum of the Twelve, do Thou be pleased to stand by them for Thou knowest the obstacles which they have to encounter, the temptations to which they are exposed, and the privations which they must suffer. Give us, [the Twelve] therefore, strength according to our day, and help us to bear a faithful testimony of Jesus and His Gospel, to finish with fidelity and honor the work which Thou hast given us to do, and then give us a place in Thy glorious kingdom. And let this blessing rest upon every faithful officer and member in Thy Church. And all the glory and honor will we ascribe unto God and the Lamb forever and ever. Amen."

Chapter 10

The Plain and Precious Parts and Covenants, and Other Findings

WHEREFORE, THOU SEEST THAT AFTER the book hath gone forth through the hands of the great and abominable church, that there are many plain and precious things taken away from the book, which is the book of the Lamb of God.

And after these plain and precious things were taken away it goeth forth unto all the nations of the Gentiles; and after it goeth forth unto all the nations of the Gentiles, yea, even across the many waters which thou hast seen with the Gentiles which have gone forth out of captivity, thou seest—because of the many plain and precious things which have been taken out of the book, which were plain unto the understanding of the children of men, according to the plainness which is in the Lamb of God—because of these things which are taken away out of the gospel of the Lamb, an exceedingly great many do stumble, yea, insomuch that Satan hath great power over them. (1 Nephi 13:28–29)

So far, we have compared, analyzed, and reviewed differences in the teachings of two predestined scriptures of Israel (the Bible and the Book of Mormon) from various angles. In this chapter, all the findings in the previous chapters are categorized in a summary, and their main subjects are generated. These subjects may approximate what an angel showed Nephi regarding the plain and precious parts and covenants in the vision around 600–592 BC.

The following new discoveries have been made in the course of this research and writing this book, and each subject will be viewed from the perspectives of both the Bible and the Book of Mormon:

- Twenty-four plain and precious parts missing in the Bible, but provided by the Book of Mormon
- Five priesthood ordinances with the associated covenants and the exact manner of performing them as shown in the Book of Mormon, but not in the Bible.
- Twenty-five subjects relating to the infinite Atonement of Jesus Christ specifically taught in the Book of Mormon.
- Thirteen unique prophecies found only in the Book of Mormon.
- Nine inferences by quantitative word count comparisons of the Bible and the Book of Mormon.
- Twelve incorrect beliefs and practices of mainstream Christianity pointed out in the Book of Mormon.

In the course of summarizing all of the above discoveries in this chapter, some subjects will overlap in more than one category.

Twenty-Four of the Plain and Precious Parts

There are many plain and precious parts, but twenty-five of those identified in the previous chapters are listed in this section. Some provide new knowledge that is not found in the Bible, some clarify teachings in the Bible, and some even correct things found in the Bible.

Foreordained Two Sticks of Israel

The Bible from the tribe of Judah and the Book of Mormon from the tribe of Joseph are predestined to coexist in the latter days.

The Bible from the tribe of Judah was predestined to go forth to the Gentiles from the Apostles of the tribe of Judah, and many people are to gather around Jesus Christ. In fulfillment of that, Christianity has become the largest religion with billions of adherents worldwide.

The Book of Mormon from the tribe of Joseph was predestined to come out of the dust (from the ground) in the latter days when apostasy becomes prevalent (see Mormon 8:26–32). It would grow together with the Bible, confounding false doctrines and establishing peace and teaching the Josephites about their ancestors (see 2 Nephi 3:12). When it comes out, movements for the gathering of the Jews will be commencing (see 3 Nephi 21:26–28; Ether 4:17; see also Orson Hyde's dedicatory prayer in Chapter 9).

The Bible and the Book of Mormon Grow Together

The Bible and the Book of Mormon are closely connected in many ways. From the plates of brass taught in the Book of Mormon, there are many quotes from the Bible; 35 percent of the book of Isaiah with some additions and omissions and 42 percent of the book of Malachi with one correction are quoted in the Book of Mormon. The resurrected Jesus Christ retaught the Sermon on the Mount to the Nephites in the Book of Mormon with some variations. All of these constitute about 7 percent of the Book of Mormon.

Ten different examples that demonstrate joint teaching between the Bible and the Book of Mormon are discussed in chapter 7:

1. The doctrine of Christ;
2. Faith, hope, meekness, and charity;
3. Justification by faith versus judgment according to works;
4. The parable of the sower and the analogy of the seed;
5. Adam's original sin and the Atonement of Jesus Christ;
6. Examples of dramatic conversions;
7. The prophecy of "the first being last, and the last being first";
8. An example of hand-and-glove-fit-type point-by-point teaching (John 1:1–18 and 3 Nephi 9:15–22);
9. The discipleship of Jesus Christ; and
10. A unique teaching example from the Book of Mormon.

This may be a fulfillment of what the Lord told Joseph in Egypt that the record of the Josephites would convince readers of the words of the Lord that have already gone forth (see 2 Nephi 3:11). This may also be a fulfillment of Mormon's prophecy that the Book of Mormon was written for the intent that we may believe the Bible, and if we believe in the Bible, we will also believe the Book of Mormon (see Mormon 7:8).

The Other Sheep: The Josephites

Jesus Christ told the Jews, "And other sheep I have, which are not of this fold: them also I must bring, and they shall hear my voice; and there shall be one fold, and one shepherd" (John 10:16). Jesus explained to the Nephites in the Book of Mormon that they are the other sheep He mentioned to the Jews:

> And verily I say unto you, that ye are they of whom I said: Other sheep I have which are not of this fold; them also I must bring, and they shall hear my voice; and there shall be one fold, and one shepherd.
>
> And they understood me not, for they supposed it had been the Gentiles; for they understood not that the Gentiles should be converted through their preaching.
>
> And they understood me not that I said they shall hear my voice; and they understood me not that the Gentiles should not at any time hear my voice—that I should not manifest myself unto them save it were by the Holy Ghost.
>
> But behold, ye have both heard my voice, and seen me; and ye are my sheep, and ye are numbered among those whom the Father hath given me. (3 Nephi 15:21–24)

Thus, Jesus confirmed that the other sheep to which He was referring were the Nephites (the Josephites) in the land of America. The resurrected Jesus taught the Nephites that the Jews did not know of the Nephites because of their iniquity (see 3 Nephi 15:19).

The Reason for a Chasm between the Old and New Testament

One unfortunate situation of Judeo-Christianity is a broken connection between the Judeo side and the Christian side; the Jews have not recognized Jesus as their God, Jehovah. There are in the New Testament many quotes from the Old Testament about their Messiah, but the Old Testament does not provide plain enough teachings about Jesus of Nazareth being the Messiah. For example, there is no mention of Messiah's name being Jesus, resurrection was not mentioned in the Old Testament, and there is no mention of the law of Moses being fulfilled by Jesus. Consequently, the Jews have not accepted Jesus of Nazareth as their Messiah.[120] At the same time, some Christian leaders like Martin Luther publicly showed anti-Semitic feelings and despised the Jews for crucifying Jesus Christ.

In the Book of Mormon, Jacob explained (sometime during 544–421 BC) why this chasm exists by saying:

> But behold, the Jews were a stiff-necked people; and they despised the words of plainness, and killed the prophets, and sought for things that they could not understand. Wherefore, because of their blindness, which blindness came by looking beyond the mark, they must needs fall; for God hath taken away his plainness from them, and delivered unto them many things which they cannot understand, because they desired it. And because they desired it God hath done it, that they may stumble. (Jacob 4:14)

This statement explains the reasons why God took away His plainness from the Jews and why they have stumbled and have not known that Jesus is their Messiah.

The Jews Will Eventually Accept Jesus as Their Messiah

John's baptism was a significant departure from the contemporary and traditional religious practices and temple ordinances of the Jews under the law of Moses. During the ministry of Jesus, some Jews accepted Jesus of Nazareth as the Messiah, but most of them didn't. Their leadership even arrested Him with a charge of blasphemy for claiming to be the Son of God. However, the prophet Nephi prophesied there will be a time after their gathering when the Jews will believe in Jesus as their Christ (559–545 BC):

> And it shall come to pass that the Jews which are scattered also shall begin to believe in Christ; and they shall begin to gather in upon the face of the land; and as many as shall believe in Christ shall also become a delightsome people.

---

[120] These examples do not count the Jewish traditional belief of their Mashiach.

And it shall come to pass that the Lord God shall commence his work among all nations, kindreds, tongues, and people, to bring about the restoration of his people upon the earth. (2 Nephi 30:7–8)

Moroni also taught that Jehovah is Jesus Christ, the eternal judge of both quick and dead (see Moroni 10:34).

The Law of Moses Was Fulfilled in Jesus

The New Testament makes clear that the law of Moses was the most important tradition for the Jews in the days of Jesus's ministry. For example, even Joseph and Mary observed it by Mary's purification (for example, mikveh) and offering sacrifice in the temple (see Luke 2:22–24). Jesus did not talk about the law of Moses specifically, but He taught His disciples that all the things concerning Him in the law of Moses, the prophets, and the psalms must be fulfilled (see Luke 24:44).

In the Book of Mormon, multiple prophets taught that the law of Moses would be fulfilled in Jesus (see 2 Nephi 25:24; Mosiah 3:15, 13:27; Alma 25:15–16, 34:13). The resurrected Jesus personally proclaimed that the law of Moses was fulfilled in Him by saying, "And as many as have received me, to them have I given to become the sons of God; and even so will I to as many as shall believe on my name, for behold, by me redemption cometh, and in me is the law of Moses fulfilled" (3 Nephi 9:17). The Nephites kept the law of Moses until the resurrected Jesus taught them that it was fulfilled in Him (see 4 Nephi 1:12).

Christians in the Old Testament Days

It is hard to say that there were Christians in the Old Testament. However, the Nephites (the remnant of Joseph) in the Book of Mormon were Christians who taught the doctrine of Christ in detail around 550 BC (see 2 Nephi 31), which was certainly during the Old Testament time period.

Even around 550 BC, the prophet Nephi made at least two powerful declarations about Jesus Christ: that "there is none other name given under heaven save it be this Jesus Christ, of which I have spoken, whereby man can be saved" (2 Nephi 25:20); and, "And we talk of Christ, we rejoice in Christ, we preach of Christ, we prophesy of Christ, and we write according to our prophecies, that our children may know to what source they may look for a remission of their sins" (2 Nephi 25:26).

And unlike the Jews in the Old Testament period, the Nephites practiced baptismal ordinances even before the birth of Jesus Christ in 147 BC (see Mosiah 18), and they call themselves Christians in 73 BC (see Alma 46).

This is quite a contrast to the Bible, having no Christian doctrines taught among the Jews in the Old Testament period. Christian doctrines were taught in the Bible only from the time of the New Testament. However, the Book of Mormon shows that Christianity existed among the Josephites in the Old Testament period. This may coincide with what Jesus said: "Verily, verily, I say unto you, Before Abraham was, I am" (John 8:58).

The Book of Mormon is a Doctrinal Bridge between the Old and New Testament

In the Bible, the Old Testament ends with the book of Malachi. The New Testament begins about four hundred years later, leaving a gap of four centuries between the two books. The Apocrypha may fill the Jewish history of this period, but the doctrinal gap between the Old and New Testament is very wide—even contradictory in some cases—especially regarding the messiahship of Jesus of Nazareth.

In the Book of Mormon, this doctrinal gap does not exist. The Nephites in the Book of Mormon worshipped Jesus Christ the same way throughout their thousand-year history. The Nephite prophets' teaching of Christ was seamless and consistent before and after Christ's birth. This may prove the Apostle Paul's statement that "Jesus Christ the same yesterday, and to day, and for ever" (Hebrews 13:8).[121] Thus, it may be safe to say that if the Apocrypha is a historical bridge between the Old and New Testament period, the Book of Mormon is a doctrinal bridge between the two periods.

Converts to Jesus Christ through Baptism Become the Seeds of Abraham

In the Bible, the Apostle Paul taught a significant new doctrine: "And if ye be Christ's, then are ye Abraham's seed, and heirs according to the promise" (Galatians 3:29).

---

[121] Multiple prophets taught the same point in the Book of Mormon as well (see 1 Nephi 10:13; 2 Nephi 2:4, 27:23, 29:9; Alma 3:17; Mormon 9:9; Moroni 10:19).

In the Book of Mormon, this is explained in multiple ways. Nephi's first quoted verse, Isaiah 48:1, has a significant addition, as shown in 1 Nephi 20:1. The addition of the phrase "or out of the waters of baptism" to the phrase "out of the waters of Judah" signifies that those who make covenant through baptism have the same blessings as those covenanted by the blood line (in other words, the Jews). This teaches that those who are legitimately baptized and converted to Jesus Christ have the same privilege of the covenant as those of Abrahamic lineage (see 2 Nephi 30:2).

Moroni taught that "turning the heart of fathers to children" in Malachi 4:6 means planting the promise that was made to the fathers (the Abrahamic covenant) in the hearts of the children (converts to Christ through baptism) (see D&C 2:2; Joseph Smith—History 1:39). Thus, those who accept Jesus Christ and are baptized will be counted as the seed of Abraham.

Purpose of Faith, Hope, and Charity (or Love)

In the Bible, Jesus Christ taught that the greatest commandment is to love God with all our heart, with all our soul, and with all our mind, and to love our neighbor as ourselves (see Matthew 22:35–40; Mark 12:28–34; Luke 10:25–37). Moses taught the Hebrews the same commandments (see Deuteronomy 6:5–6; Leviticus 19:18). In the Apostle Paul's discourse on faith, hope, and charity (see 1 Corinthians 13), he taught that charity is greater than faith or hope, but he did not specify what to hope for, and did not connect charity to Jesus and the Holy Ghost. This was done by the prophet Mormon.

In the Book of Mormon, the prophet Mormon gave a more detailed discourse on faith, hope, and charity (see Moroni 7:38–48). He added "meekness and lowliness of heart" to these three. He also defined charity as "the pure love of Christ" (Moroni 7:47), and taught that one should hope for the Atonement of Jesus Christ and the power of His Resurrection (see Moroni 7:41). He also taught that to have charity, one needs to be able to confess by the power of the Holy Ghost that Jesus is the Christ (see Moroni 7:44). The prophet Alma taught that faith, hope, and charity must always abound in good works (see Alma 7:24). The prophet Moroni defined faith, hope, and charity as the fountain of all righteousness (see Ether 12:28).

By combining teachings of faith, hope, meekness, and charity from the Bible and the Book of Mormon, the following summary statement can be made; it represents all the points taught on the subject.

<u>Two Greatest Commandments: Love of God and Neighbors</u>

With hope for the Atonement and Resurrection of Jesus Christ, and with love of God and neighbors manifested through good works, one will be able to confess Jesus Christ in faith and meekness by the power of the Holy Ghost and live by the fountain of all righteousness of the Lord.

The above teaching from both the Bible and the Book of Mormon is a good example of a fulfillment of Mormon's prophecy: "For behold, this [Book of Mormon] is written for the intent that ye may believe that [Bible]; and if ye believe that [Bible], ye will believe this [Book of Mormon] also . . ." (Mormon 7:9).

Definition of the Doctrine of Christ

In the four Gospels, Jesus Christ never specified what His doctrine is other than saying, "My doctrine is not mine, but his that sent me" (John 7:16). In Hebrews 6:1–2, the Apostle Paul taught the way to perfection is not repentance from dead works but faith toward God, the doctrine of baptism, laying on of hands, resurrection of the dead, and eternal judgment. Thus, it is not clear what the Doctrine of Christ actually is.

In the Book of Mormon, unlike in the Bible, the doctrine of Christ is plainly and clearly defined. Nephi explained the doctrine of Christ in simple and plain terms: faith, repentance, baptism by water and the Holy Ghost, and enduring to the end (see 2 Nephi 31). The resurrected Jesus Christ taught it plainly as well (see 3 Nephi 11, 27).

Non-Consubstantial Godhead: The Father, the Son, and the Holy Ghost

The word *trinity* is not found in the Bible, but there are multiple passages indicating that the Father and the Son are one (for example, John 10:28–30; John 17:21; 1 John 5:7–8). Since the theology of the Trinity was officially pronounced with the Nicene Creed in AD 325 and the Constantinople Creed in AD 381, most Christians have believed and preached the consubstantial nature of the Father, the Son, and the Holy Ghost. Due to an incomprehensible nature of this consubstantial Godhead, many Christian leaders have resorted to a mysticism of this theology.

In the Book of Mormon, the prophet Abinadi taught that the Father and the Son are one God in the sense of being one team or family (see Mosiah 15:1–5), and he confirmed that the Son was conceived by the

Highest (see Luke 1:35) by explaining, "the Son was conceived by the power of God [not by the Holy Ghost]" (Mosiah 15:3). Jesus also clarified the reason why He is called both the Father and the Son by saying, "I am Jesus Christ. I am the Father and the Son. In me shall all mankind have life, and that eternally, even they who shall believe on my name; and they shall become my sons and my daughters" (Ether 3:14).

The resurrected Jesus Christ taught the Nephites His subordinate relationship with His Father through phrases such as "Father commanded me," "I go to the Father," "Father sent me," "Pray to the Father in my name," and so forth. Thus, the Book of Mormon clarifies the theology of the Godhead by teaching that the Father and the Son are not consubstantial but are two separate personages.

The Plan of Salvation

The plan of salvation—along with the other terms by which it is called, *the plan of redemption* or *the plan of happiness*—cannot be found in the Bible. However, these terms are uniquely found twenty-two times in the Book of Mormon.[122] Each one of these terms has a different nuance, but they seem to be similar and can be used interchangeably.

Alma taught this principle the most. He taught that this plan was prepared from the foundation of the world (see Ether 3:14; Alma 12:25, 30; 18:39; 34:16), and this is possible because the Father provided the merciful Atonement of the Savior for the redemption of mankind with a condition of repentance, not hardening their heart, and according to their works (see Alma 34:16, 31; 42:13, 16). For example, Alma taught that even our first parents needed their probationary state so they could repent of their transgression (see Alma 12:26; 42:5). He also taught that mercy meets the demands of justice through the infinite Atonement of Jesus Christ for the eternal salvation of the penitent (see Alma 42:22–23).

Body of Spirit and the Premortal Existence

In the Bible, this subject is not taught, but it is taught in the Book of Mormon. Jesus showed himself to the brother of Jared (around the time of the Tower of Babel in the Old Testament) and said, "Behold,

---

[122] None of these terms can be found in the Doctrine and Covenants, but the plan of salvation appears once in the book of Moses (see Moses 6:16). Thus, these terms are uniquely found in the Book of Mormon.

this body, which ye now behold, is the body of my spirit; and man have I created after the body of my spirit; and even as I appear unto thee to be in the spirit will I appear unto my people in the flesh" (Ether 3:16). Thus, Jesus taught that His spirit has a spiritual body that resembles his future physical body.

As Moroni tried to understand it, he qualified it by saying: "And now, as I, Moroni, said I could not make a full account of these things which are written, therefore it sufficeth me to say that Jesus showed himself unto this man in the spirit, even after the manner and in the likeness of the same body even as he showed himself unto the Nephites" (Ether 3:17). This teaches not only a doctrine of premortal existence, but also implies our spirits in the premortal existence have shapes and genders.[123] Thus, the Holy Ghost (the Holy Spirit) has a spiritual body.

The Land of America: Inheritance of the Josephites and the Site for the New Jerusalem

Moses and Joshua allocated an inheritance of land for each of the tribes of Israel, including two sons of Joseph: Ephraim and Manasseh (see Numbers 34:29; Joshua 11:23).

However, the resurrected Jesus Christ taught that the Father commanded him to give the Nephites (the remnant of Joseph) the land of America for their inheritance: "And the Father hath commanded me that I should give unto you [the remnant of Joseph] this land, for your inheritance" (3 Nephi 20:14; see also 3 Nephi 16:16). He also taught that they will establish the New Jerusalem on that land (see 3 Nephi 21:22–24; Ether 13:4, 6). Furthermore, He taught that the Father will gather the Jews to the Old Jerusalem in His due time when the fullness of the gospel of Jesus Christ will be preached (see 3 Nephi 20:46; Ether 13:5).

Searching the Words of Isaiah Is a Commandment

The resurrected Jesus Christ taught the Nephites the words of Isaiah from the present Isaiah 52 and 54 in the Old Testament, and said, "Yea,

---

[123] Joseph Smith received a revelation regarding the physical nature of the Father, the Son, and the Holy Ghost: "The Father has a body of flesh and bones as tangible as man's; the Son also; but the Holy Ghost has not a body of flesh and bones, but is a personage of Spirit. Were it not so, the Holy Ghost could not dwell in us" (D&C 130:22). He also received a revelation that spirit and element are inseparably connected (see D&C 93:33).

a commandment I give unto you that ye search these things diligently; for great are the words of Isaiah" (3 Nephi 23:1).

Nephi, Jacob, and Abinadi also taught and quoted the words of Isaiah. About 35 percent of the book of Isaiah[124] in the Old Testament is quoted in the Book of Mormon (Isaiah 2–14, 29, 48–54). Nephi quoted the words of Isaiah the most, and he said that his soul delights in the words of Isaiah (see 2 Nephi 11:2). However, the words of Isaiah that are quoted in the Book of Mormon contain some meaningful additions, omissions, and corrections when compared to the present book of Isaiah in the Bible.

Teaching of the Priesthood Ordinances with Exactness

In the Old Testament, there are many detailed instructions about sacrificial ordinances performed in the temple by the Levites (the holders of the Levitical Priesthood). In the New Testament, the Apostle Paul taught about the two priesthoods, the Levitical and the Melchizedek (see Hebrews 7). Jesus Christ and His Apostles performed priesthood ordinances such as baptism, conferring the Holy Ghost, the administration of the sacrament,[125] and other priesthood ordinances. However, there are no instructions in the New Testament on exactly how to perform these priesthood ordinances, including how to baptize (for example, see Matthew 3:13–17).

In the Book of Mormon, the resurrected Jesus Christ taught with exactness how to baptize (see 3 Nephi 11:23–26). The prophet Moroni taught with exactness how to confer the Holy Ghost, how to ordain teachers and priests, and how to bless and deliver the sacramental bread and wine (see Moroni 2–5). In the prayers of these ordinances, specific covenants are pronounced in association with each ordinance.

(Vicarious) Baptism for the Dead

In the Bible, the Apostle Paul briefly mentioned baptismal practices for the dead in conjunction with the Resurrection (see 1 Corinthians 15:29–30). Based on this simple statement, it is hard to know exactly what baptism for the dead means.

In the Book of Mormon, this subject was never mentioned. However, it was indirectly taught by the resurrected Jesus as He quoted Malachi 3–4

---

[124] The Dead Sea Scrolls contain the same book of Isaiah as the one in the Bible.
[125] As mentioned in Chapter 3, some Christians call these ordinances the Eucharist, Holy Communion, or Communion.

to the Nephites. The last two verses of the Old Testament Jesus quoted say, "Behold, I will send you Elijah the prophet before the coming of the great and dreadful day of the Lord: And he shall turn the heart of the fathers to the children, and the heart of the children to their fathers, lest I come and smite the earth with a curse" (Malachi 4:5–6; 3 Nephi 25:5–6). After He quoted these verses, the resurrected Jesus told the Nephites, "These scriptures which ye had not with you, the Father commanded that I should give unto you; for it was wisdom in him that they should be given unto future generations" (3 Nephi 26:2).

The book of Malachi was written more than a hundred years after Lehi left Jerusalem, and the Nephites could not have had the words of Malachi on their plates of brass. Since the Father commanded Jesus to teach these words about Elijah for future generations, it must be very important to the Father that future generations know these prophecies. This prophecy of the coming of Elijah was fulfilled in the Kirtland Temple on April 3, 1836 (see D&C 110:13–15). Since then, The Church of Jesus Christ of Latter-day Saints has been performing vicarious baptisms for the dead in its temples. Thus, this subject was addressed by the resurrected Jesus Christ in the Book of Mormon, and it is being fulfilled in our dispensation (to "future generations").

It is interesting to see the contrast between ordinances regarding the resurrection in the old temple of Herod and in the new modern-day temples. The Sadducees, who did not believe in resurrection, were in charge of the temple works during the time of the ministry of Jesus Christ. In contrast, members of The Church of Jesus Christ of Latter-day Saints perform all the priesthood ordinances vicariously for the dead in modern-day temples in preparation for the resurrection of the dead.

Prophecies of Joseph in Egypt and a Latter-day Seer

In the Book of Mormon, Lehi quoted the prophecies by Joseph in Egypt that are not found in the Bible (see 2 Nephi 3:7–21). Joseph was told by the Lord that the Lord will raise up a seer named Joseph after his name and the name of seer's father out of Joseph's loin. He was further told that this seer will be like Moses, whom the Lord will also raise up to deliver Joseph's people out of Egypt. The seer will have power to bring forth the Lord's words unto the Josephites and to convince them of the words that already preceded them. The words from both tribes of

Judah and Joseph will grow together, confounding false doctrines, laying down contentions, establishing peace among the Josephites, and bringing them to a knowledge of their fathers in the latter days. The words written by this seer will cry repentance from the dust.

Judging Roles of the Twelve Disciples of Both the Jews and the Josephites

Jesus taught His disciples that they will be judging the twelve tribes with Him when He said: "And Jesus said unto them, Verily I say unto you, That ye which have followed me, in the regeneration when the Son of man shall sit in the throne of his glory, ye also shall sit upon twelve thrones, judging the twelve tribes of Israel" (Matthew 19:28; see also Luke 22:30).

In the Book of Mormon, an angel taught Nephi the same teaching of Jesus Christ and added that the twelve Nephite disciples will be judging the Nephites (see 1 Nephi 12:9–10). Mormon confirmed what Nephi wrote, and added that the Nephite disciples will be judged by the twelve disciples from Jerusalem:

> Yea, behold, I write unto all the ends of the earth; yea, unto you, twelve tribes of Israel, who shall be judged according to your works by the twelve whom Jesus chose to be his disciples in the land of Jerusalem.
>
> And I write also unto the remnant of this people, who shall also be judged by the twelve whom Jesus chose in this land; and they shall be judged by the other twelve whom Jesus chose in the land of Jerusalem. (Mormon 3:18–19)

Example of Unknown Prophets of God in the Bible: Zenos and Zenock

The Book of Mormon reveals two prophets of God—Zenos and Zenock—who are not known in our current Bible. Zenos was mentioned twelve times and Zenock was mentioned five times in the Book of Mormon.

Zenos's allegory of the tame and wild olive tree quoted by Jacob shows that Zenos extensively prophesied the scattering and gathering of the Israelites (see Jacob 5). In addition to Jacob, others in the Book of Mormon quoted or mentioned Zenos and Zenock: they included two Nephis, Alma, Samuel the Lamanite, and the resurrected Jesus Christ.

As revealed in the Book of Mormon, Zenos and Zenock prophesied the coming of Jesus Christ and His ministry and the Restoration of His gospel in the latter days by the Josephites. Nephi taught (around 23–20 BC) that the prophet Zenos was slain because he boldly testified of the coming Christ and the destruction of Jerusalem (see Helaman 8:19).

The First Shall be Last, the Last Shall be First (the Second Coming of Jesus Christ)

Both the Bible and the Book of Mormon testify that Jesus Christ came to the Jews in His first coming, and the gospel of Jesus Christ came from the tribe of Judah. The Book of Mormon teaches that the restored gospel of Jesus Christ came first from the Josephites and the Gentiles, who will deliver it to the Jews. The Book of Mormon also prophesies that Jesus will come to the Josephites first in the New Jerusalem at His Second Coming. This will fulfill what Jesus taught the Jews: that the first will be last, and the last will be first (see Matthew 19:30, 20:16; Mark 10:31; Luke 13:30).

The Apostle John to Write about the End of the World

The last book added to the New Testament was the book of Revelation, which was included in the canonized New Testament as late as AD 419. The Council of Laodicea omitted it as a canonical book in AD 363, but it was canonized in the Synod of Hippo in AD 393; its canonization was finalized in the Council of Carthage in AD 419. There is still some controversy about the book among Judeo-Christians; for example, some Eastern Orthodox churches do not accept the book of Revelation as scripture.[126]

In the Book of Mormon, Jesus Christ and the prophet Nephi stated that the Apostle John was assigned to write about the end of the world (see Ether 4:16; 1 Nephi 14:27). It is not known how authentic the present book of Revelation is, but the Book of Mormon confirms that John was assigned to write it.

---

[126] Many Christian churches have researched the Bible in an attempt to figure out when the Second Coming of Jesus Christ will occur. Some have publicly announced what they believe to be the date (and places in some cases). To this day, none has been right. This proves what Jesus told of the calamities and signs that would precede His Second Coming and that no one knows the timing of His Second Coming except the Father (see Matthew 24:36; Mark 13:32; Acts 1:7).

Non-Christian Religions also Teach True Principles

There are some unique teachings in the Book of Mormon that are not found in the Bible but that are related to teachings of Confucianism and Buddhism. For example, the prophet Lehi taught "there is an opposition in all things" (2 Nephi 2:11), and he expounded this principle in depth. Having opposition in everything is the basic foundation of Chinese I Ching, which teaches the principle of "Um and Yang" (negative and positive) and explains everything in the universe based on this opposition principle.

The prophets Nephi and Alma taught that the Lord's course is "one eternal round" (1 Nephi 10:19; Alma 7:20, 37:12). This principle is the basic foundation of Won Buddhism, which teaches one can reach self-enlightenment through understanding principles that can be found through one void (totally unfilled) round circle, reaching a state of Nirvana by learning meanings from the infinite nothingness.

The Five Priesthood Ordinances and their Associated Covenants

Covenants are associated with priesthood ordinances. Even if it was recorded that Jesus Christ performed baptism and administered the sacramental bread and wine, there are no instructions on how to perform these ordinances in the New Testament. In contrast, the Book of Mormon provides specific instructions on how to perform the following five ordinances with their associated covenants:

- Baptism by water with a covenant to have faith and to repent (see 3 Nephi 11:23–27).
- Baptism by the Holy Ghost (or conferring the Holy Ghost) with a covenant to believe in Jesus Christ and be one in the Father and the Son (see Moroni 2; 3 Nephi 19:20–23).
- The ordinations of priests and teachers with a covenant to preach repentance and remission of sins through Jesus Christ and to endure to the end in His name (see Moroni 3).
- Administering the sacramental bread with a covenant to eat in remembrance of the body of Jesus Christ and witness to the Father by taking the name of the Son, remembering Him always, and keeping His commandments in order to have His Spirit (see Moroni 4).

- Administering the sacramental wine with a covenant to drink in remembrance of the blood of Jesus Christ and witness to the Father to always remember Him in order to have His Spirit (see Moroni 5).

With the inclusion of these in the Book of Mormon, the exact manner of how to perform the above five priesthood ordinances with their associated covenants are provided from the stick of Joseph (the Book of Mormon) to the stick of Judah (the Bible).

Twenty-Five Subjects Related to the Infinite Atonement of Christ

Unlike the Bible, the Book of Mormon expounds on the doctrine of the Atonement and Resurrection of Jesus Christ quite extensively. In the Bible, the word *atonement* appears eighty-one times in the Old Testament and once in the New Testament. In the Old Testament, virtually all mentions of *atonement* are related to sin-forgiving rituals involving animal sacrifice in the temple. In the New Testament, the Apostle Paul mentioned the Atonement once in Romans 5:11 in the King James Version (KJV), but it was translated as *reconciliation* in many other versions of the Bible. Even though there are some discourses by the Apostle Paul about the atoning or reconciliatory role of Jesus Christ, it is easy to see that the infinite and eternal Atonement of Jesus Christ was not taught plainly in the Bible.

The word *atonement* appears twenty-eight times in the Book of Mormon; the words *atoning*, *atone*, or *atoneth* also appear a total of eleven times. With an analysis of these thirty-nine descriptions about the Atonement, twenty-five different related explanations or subjects about the Atonement of Jesus Christ were discovered in the Book of Mormon. Following are those twenty-five subjects related to the Atonement of Jesus Christ:

1. Answering the end of the Atonement through opposition in all things.
2. The Jews to eventually believe in the Atonement of Christ.
3. The nature of the infinite Atonement.
4. Mercy meets the demand of justice through the Atonement.
5. Being raised from everlasting death through power of the Atonement.
6. Perfect knowledge of Christ through the Atonement.
7. All mankind being lost and perishing without the Atonement.

8. Salvation coming through the Atonement of Christ, not the law of Moses.
9. Overcoming of Adam's transgression through the atoning blood of Christ.
10. The Atonement covering those who die without a knowledge of Christ.
11. The law of Moses availing nothing without the Atonement of Christ.
12. The Atonement covering for little children.
13. Overcoming the natural man through the Atonement, allowing us to become like little children.
14. The Atonement was available from the foundation of the world.
15. The Atoning blood, suffering, and death of Christ for the sins of men.
16. The Atonement as a great plan of the eternal God.
17. The Atonement being the last and final sacrifice.
18. The infinite and eternal Atonement for all mankind.
19. Fulfilling the law of Moses through the Atonement of Christ.
20. The holy priesthood and the Atonement.
21. The atoning blood of Christ for forgiveness of sins and purifying of hearts.
22. The plan of mercy through the Atonement.
23. The Atonement brings the resurrection of the dead.
24. The role of the Atonement in being judged according to works.
25. Hope for the Atonement of Christ and power of the Resurrection.

In the Old Testament, the word *resurrection* is not found. Even though many disciples of Jesus Christ reported and testified of Jesus's Resurrection in the New Testament, there were diverse opinions about Jesus's Resurrection among the Jews. In the Book of Mormon, the resurrected Jesus came to visit the Nephites for three days after His death and Resurrection, and there was no doubt about His Resurrection among them.

Thirteen Unique Prophecies in the Book of Mormon

In the Book of Mormon, many prophecies are found in the allegory of the olive trees (see Jacob 5), Nephi's vision and visit by an angel (see 1 Nephi 10–15), Lehi's last words to Joseph (see 2 Nephi 3), Nephi's final words (see 1 Nephi 22; 2 Nephi 25–33), the teachings of the resurrected Jesus (see 3 Nephi 16, 20–22, 26–27, 29), the words of Mormon (see Mormon 7), and the words of Moroni (see Ether 4, 13). These prophecies are mostly about the following thirteen points:

1. The scattering and gathering of the Israelites with a commencing time of gathering.
2. The Restoration of the gospel of Jesus Christ in the latter days.
3. The land of America with a free and mighty nation being the inheritance for the Josephites.
4. The coming forth of the Book of Mormon as though a voice crying from the dust.
5. A latter-day prophet named Joseph and the Restoration of the gospel of Jesus Christ in the latter days.
6. The Bible and apostasy.
7. The existence of only two churches.
8. More records to come forward from other tribes.
9. The Jews' acceptance of Jesus Christ after the gathering.
10. The preparation and establishment of the New Jerusalem in the land of America.
11. The roles of the Josephites and the Gentiles in the latter days.
12. The gathering of Jews in the Old Jerusalem and of the Josephites in the New Jerusalem.
13. An example of the first being last and the last being first.

Many of these prophecies have been fulfilled, some are now being fulfilled, and some are yet to be fulfilled.

Quantitative Facts by Word Count Comparison: Nine Inferences and Theological Developments

Throughout this book, quantitative numbers are mentioned based on how many times a specific word or phrase appears in the Bible and the Book of Mormon. Based on these quantitative facts, nine inferences can be made, including development of some theologies such as *Trinity* and *faith* alone. These inferences support different findings in this book. The following table shows how many times some of the specific words or phrases appear in the King James Version of the Bible and the Book of Mormon.

	OLD TESTAMENT (KJV)	NEW TESTAMENT (KJV)		BOOK OF MORMON
JEHOVAH	4 TIMES (EXODUS 6:3, PSALMS 83:18, ISAIAH 12:2, 26:4)	NONE		2 TIMES (2 NEPHI 22:2 IN THE BC PERIOD, MORONI 10:34 IN THE AD PERIOD)
CRUCIFY, CRUCIFIED, CRUCIFIXION,	NONE	53 TIMES (38 TIMES FROM THE 4 GOSPELS, 11 TIMES BY PAUL)		9 TIMES (ALL FROM THE BC PERIOD)
RESURRECTED, RESURRECTION	NONE	41 TIMES (16 TIMES FROM THE 4 GOSPELS, 11 TIMES BY PAUL)		81 TIMES (75 TIMES IN THE BC PERIOD, 6 TIMES THE AD PERIOD)
ATONE, ATONETH, ATONING, ATONEMENT	81 TIMES (MOSTLY RELATED TO ANIMAL SACRIFICES)	1 TIME (ROMANS 5:11 IN KJV, OTHER VERSIONS COMMONLY TRANSLATED IT "RECONCILIATION")		39 TIMES (EXPLAINED THE ATONEMENT WITH THE 25 RELATED SUBJECTS)
FATHER AND THE SON (OR WORD) BEING ONE	NONE	4 TIMES (JOHN 1:1, 10:30, 17:21, 1 JOHN 5:7 (IN KJV)	MANY QUOTE THESE VERSES FOR THE TRINITY DOCTRINE	6 TIMES (MOSIAH 15:4; 3 NEPHI 11:27, 11:36, 19:23, 20:35, 28:10)
FAITH	2 TIMES	241 TIMES (171 TIMES (71%) FROM PAUL, NONE IN THE GOSPEL OF JOHN)	SOURCES OF THE "SOLA FIDE" DOCTRINE	263 TIMES (170 TIMES IN THE BC PERIOD, 93 TIMES IN THE AD PERIOD)
JUSTIFIED BY FAITH	NONE	3 TIMES (ONLY FROM PAUL, ROMANS 3:28, 5:1, GALATIANS 3:24)		NONE
JUDGED ACCORDING TO WORKS	NONE	3 TIMES (MATTHEW 16:27, 1 PETER 1:17, REVELATION 20:13)		17 TIMES BY MANY: THE RESURRECTED JESUS CHRIST, NEPHI, KING BENJAMIN, ABINADI, ALMA, AMULEK, MORMON, AND MORONI
MERCY	262 TIMES	64 TIMES		102 TIMES	A PART OF THE PLAN OF SALVATION EXPLAINED
JUSTICE	28 TIMES	NONE		70 TIMES	
BAPTISM, BAPTIZED	NONE	100 TIMES (55 IN THE 4 GOSPELS, 27 IN ACTS, 18 IN PAUL'S EPISTLE, NONE IN OTHER BOOKS)		145 TIMES (STARTING FROM THE 6TH CENTURY BC)
IT CAME TO PASS	396 TIMES (109 IN PENTATEUCH, 236 IN PROPHETS, 51 IN WRITINGS)	67 TIMES (52 IN THE 4 GOSPELS (6 BY MATTHEW, 4 BY MARK, 41 BY LUKE, 1 BY JOHN), 14 IN ACTS, 1 IN PAUL'S EPISTLE)		1359 TIMES (FOUND NONE IN THE BOOK OF MORONI, BUT FOUND ALL IN THE OTHER 14 BOOKS) (NONE IN 2 NEPHI 25-33)

Inferences and Some Theological Developments

1. The Old Testament says that Jehovah is their God, but there is no mention of Jehovah in the New Testament. This creates confusion among mainstream Christians as to whether Jesus of Nazareth is Jehovah. Moroni's calling Jesus Christ *Jehovah* at the end of the Book of Mormon confirms that Jesus Christ is Jehovah of the Old Testament (see Moroni 10:34).

2. The four Gospels in the New Testament addressed the Crucifixion of Jesus Christ the most (a total of fifty-three times). In the Book of Mormon, however, all the words about the Crucifixion (nine times) were mentioned in the BC period (years before the birth of Jesus Christ) (nine times). This indicates that the Nephites (the remnant of the tribe of Joseph) were taught of the Crucifixion of Jesus Christ before He was born.

3. Having no clear message about the Resurrection in the Old Testament, the Sadducees and Pharisees could justify their opposite beliefs on the Resurrection as shown in the New Testament (see Matthew 22:23; Mark 12:18; Luke 20:27; Acts 23:6–8). While the New Testament emphasizes the Crucifixion more than the Resurrection, the Book of Mormon seems to emphasize the Resurrection of Jesus Christ much more than His Crucifixion, while the New Testament emphasizes the Crucifixion more than the Resurrection. Emphasis on the Resurrection coincides with teachings by some of the Eastern Orthodox Christian branches. The Resurrection of Jesus Christ was prophesied in the Book of Mormon by many prophets before Christ was born. The Nephites anticipated the coming of Christ with a goodunderstanding of His Crucifixion and Resurrection.[127]

4. The Book of Mormon addresses the Atonement of Jesus Christ with much more detail than does the Bible. Nephi, Jacob, and Alma described it as "the infinite Atonement" (see 2 Nephi 9:7, 25:16; Alma 34:12), and it is not the atonement through animal sacrifices as taught in the Old Testament.

---

[127] If Essenes in Qumran is considered as an anticipating sect for their Messiah from the tribe of Judah, the Nephites can be considered as an anticipating Christian group from the tribe of Joseph.

5. In the New Testament, only the records of John mention the Trinitarian statement such as "the Father and the Son (or Word) being ONE." However, the Book of Mormon mentions the same principle more frequently than the Bible does. But the word Trinity is not mentioned in the Bible nor in the Book of Mormon. The Trinity doctrine is based on the writings of John and was developed after the days of the Apostles. In general, The King James Version has more statements friendly to the Trinitarian doctrine than other versions of the English Bibles (see 1 John 5:7).

6. *Sola fide* (meaning "faith alone") is a principle that stemmed from the Pauline doctrine in the New Testament by reformists like Martin Luther. The Book of Mormon teaches faith as much as—or maybe even more—than the New Testament without ever implying this principle. It is interesting that the word *faith* cannot be found in the Gospel of John. The doctrine of being judged according to works was taught by Jesus, Peter, and John in the New Testament, and James even declared that faith without work is dead (see James 2:17–18). However, for some Protestant denominations, the concept of being justified by faith as taught by the Apostle Paul diminished the importance of work. The Book of Mormon emphasizes not only faith, but it also teaches importance of being judged according to works.

7. The Old Testament, New Testament, and Book of Mormon all talk about *mercy* much more than justice. Interestingly, the word *justice* is not found in the New Testament. While it is quite evident that mercy was much more emphasized than *justice* in the Bible, it seems these two terms are mentioned in a more balanced way in the Book of Mormon. The Book of Mormon teaches that mercy cannot rob justice, but mercy meets the demands of justice through the Atonement of Jesus Christ, and this is an essential part of the plan of salvation (see Alma 42).

8. The Bible teaches that baptism was something new started by John the Baptist in the New Testament. The Book of Mormon teaches that the baptism by water and the Holy Ghost was taught and practiced among the Nephites in the Old Testament period as early as the sixth century BC (see 2 Nephi 31; Mosiah 18). The

exact manner of performing baptism is not taught in the New Testament (see Matthew 3:13–17), so there are many ways of performing baptism among Christian churches, such as total immersion, partial immersion, affusion, and aspersion. In the Book of Mormon, however, the resurrected Jesus taught how to perform the baptismal ordinance exactly by total immersion, and there is no confusion on this matter (see 3 Nephi 11:23–26).

9. Both the Old Testament and the Book of Mormon are written as the historical records of many generations. The phrase "it came to pass"[128] is used 369 times in the Old Testament but is overwhelmingly used more often in the Book of Mormon, 1,359 times (the Old Testament is more than two times longer than the Book of Mormon).[129] Being a historical record of just one generation, the New Testament has less of it; it appears 67 times. This phrase was used far more by Luke than the other writers of the Gospels. This phrase is used most in the books of Luke and Acts, and this may indicate that the same writer wrote these two records, as many New Testament scholars claim. Because this phrase is used so much in the Book of Mormon, it is obvious that the Book of Mormon is a document narrated afterward by historians. It is interesting to see that its last book, the book of Moroni, does not contain this phrase, indicating that the book of Moroni was written as a contemporary record by Moroni. It is also interesting to see that this phrase is not found in the last words of Nephi (see 2 Nephi 25–33), which also indicates that Nephi did not write his last words as a historical record.

Correcting the Christian Doctrines and Practices Traditionally Believed in, but Not Found in, the Bible

There are some traditional doctrines and practices of Judeo-Christian churches that have been widely accepted but cannot be found in the

---

[128] The phrase "it shall come to pass" appears 116 times in the Old Testament (twenty-five times in the Book of Isaiah), four times in the New Testament, and sixty times in the Book of Mormon.

[129] These numbers vary depending on which version it is, but there are about 800,000 words in the Old Testament, and about 234,000 words in the Book of Mormon.

Bible. There has been much dispute on whether these establishments of traditional doctrines have been from God or from theologians with good intentions (examples of man's philosophy mingled with scriptures). The Apostle Paul warned about such by saying, "For they being ignorant of God's righteousness, and going about to establish their own righteousness have not submitted themselves unto the righteousness of God" (Romans 10:3). The Book of Mormon agrees with the Apostle Paul that these traditional establishments are not from God but are established by men. Following are some examples of the Book of Mormon correcting some of the beliefs established by men.

Trinity

As already discussed, the word *trinity* is not found in the Bible. Even if this doctrine started as early as the second century, it was fully developed in the fourth and fifth century. Since then, it has become a household doctrine of the Judeo-Christian churches.

In the Book of Mormon, the prophet Abinadi taught the true nature of Deity in Mosiah 5:1–5. He taught that the Father and the Son are one God in the sense of a Godhead, and he confirmed what the angel Gabriel announced to Mary that her son, Jesus, is a Son of the Highest. In the Book of Mormon, beyond biblical teachings, the resurrected Jesus Christ made it clear about His subordinate relationship with the Father during His three-day visit to the Nephites (see 3 Nephi 18:27, 27:13).

Adam's Original Sin

This theology was developed around the same time as the Catholic Church started in the fifth century. It was based on teachings by the Apostle Paul, such as "as by one man sin entered into the world, and death by sin: and so death passed upon all men, for that all have sinned" (Romans 5:12) and "For as in Adam all die, even so in Christ shall all be made alive" (1 Corinthians 15:22). It was also influenced by the Psalmist's comment that "in sin did my mother conceive me" (Psalms 51:5).

In the Book of Mormon, the prophet Lehi expounded that Adam's partaking of the fruit of the tree of good and evil was not a sin but a transgression. He also confirmed that this was done in the wisdom of Him who knoweth all things, declaring, "Adam fell that men might be;

and men are, that they might have joy" (2 Nephi 2:25). He explained in detail the reason why Adam chose to partake of the fruit in conjunction with relationships between his transgression, Jesus Christ, and man's agency to choose (see 2 Nephi 2:19–27). Thus, the theology of Adam's original sin did not come from the God who knows all things.

The Essential Nature of Baptism

According to the New Testament, Jesus Christ began His ministry with His baptism by John the Baptist (see Matthew 3), and He and His disciples baptized people (see John 4:1–2). Right before His ascension to heaven, the resurrected Jesus commanded His disciples, "Go ye therefore, and teach all nations, baptizing them in the name of the Father, and of the Son, and of the Holy Ghost" (Matthew 28:19). Despite these teachings on baptism in the Bible, some faithful Christians of different denominations believe that faith is enough and that baptism is not essential for their salvation.

During his three-day visit to the Nephites, the first thing the resurrected Jesus Christ taught was a lesson on baptism, and He reinstituted the baptismal ordinance by teaching the Nephites exactly how to baptize (see 3 Nephi 11:21–28). The Nephites were baptized following the newly taught process with the authority given by Jesus Christ (see 3 Nephi 19:13). Toward the end of His visit, Jesus also commanded, "Now this is the commandment: Repent, all ye ends of the earth, and come unto me and be baptized in my name, that ye may be sanctified by the reception of the Holy Ghost, that ye may stand spotless before me at the last day" (3 Nephi 27:20).

In His ministries to both tribes of Israel, Jesus started with baptism and finished with His last charge to baptize or to be baptized. Thus, the Book of Mormon is the second witness of Jesus Christ's teaching that baptism is critically essential for one's salvation.

Baptism by Full Immersion (Submersion)

In the Bible, special purification by water was a common practice among the Jews beginning in Moses's day (see Numbers 8:6–7, 19:12–13; Ezekiel 36:25). In the first century BC, mikveh was commonly practiced for purification (see Luke 2:22). Thus, an ordinance for the remission of sins by submerging in water must have been familiar to the Jews, helping them accept John baptizing in the River Jordan.

As detailed in Matthew 3:13–17, John the Baptist baptized Jesus in the following way: John and Jesus discussed John's qualification to baptize Jesus, John baptized Jesus, Jesus came straight out of water, the Spirit of God descended from heaven in the form of a dove accompanied by a light that shined on Jesus from heaven, and the voice of Heavenly Father said, "This is my beloved Son, in whom I am well pleased."

These five verses did not specifically explain how Jesus was baptized—whether He was baptized by a full immersion, partial immersion, affusion, aspersion, or other method. Consequently, there are multiple baptismal methods among Judeo-Christian churches.

In the Book of Mormon, the resurrected Jesus taught the Nephites the specific baptismal process:

> Verily I say unto you, that whoso repenteth of his sins through your words, and desireth to be baptized in my name, on this wise shall ye baptize them—Behold, *ye shall go down and stand in the water, and in my name shall ye baptize them.*
>
> *And now behold, these are the words which ye shall say, calling them by name, saying:*
>
> *Having authority given me of Jesus Christ, I baptize you in the name of the Father, and of the Son, and of the Holy Ghost. Amen.*
>
> *And then shall ye immerse them in the water, and come forth again out of the water.*
>
> *And after this manner shall ye baptize in my name;* for behold, verily I say unto you, that the Father, and the Son, and the Holy Ghost are one; and I am in the Father, and the Father in me, and the Father and I are one. (3 Nephi 11:23–27; emphasis added)

Infant Baptism

With a belief in a combination of Adam's original sin and the essential nature of baptism, it is easy to form a belief that all, including infants, need to be baptized for their salvation. The practice of infant baptism started at a very early time in Christianity but has been controversial (for example, it was opposed by Anabaptists).

In the Book of Mormon, the prophet Mormon taught that the Holy Ghost manifested to him that "it is solemn mockery before God, that ye should baptize little children" (Moroni 8:9). He also said, "But little children are alive in Christ, even from the foundation of the world; if not so, God is a partial God, and also a changeable God, and a respecter to persons; for how many little children have died without baptism!" (Moroni 8:12). King Benjamin also confirmed that the blood of Christ atones for Adam's transgression and sins of children (see Mosiah 3:16).

Heaven Is Closed (Replaced with the Infallible Canonized Bible)

Belief that heaven is closed because we have the infallible canonized Bible has been prevalent among the reformed Christian churches since their reformation during the sixteenth century. In recent decades, many textual criticism scholars have discovered so many more copied texts of the New Testament with many variances that validity of infallibility of the Bible is very questionable. The Book of Mormon teaches that heaven has remained open, and the power of the Holy Ghost is continuously manifest among many faithful children of God (see Moroni 10:3–5). The Book of Mormon itself is proof of an "open canon."

In the Book of Mormon, the prophet Moroni prophesied in the early fifth century AD that the Book of Mormon would come in a day when men will say that miracles are done away and that they will deny the mercies of Christ and the power of His Holy Spirit (see Mormon 8:26). Moreover, the resurrected Jesus Christ taught that tribes other than the Jews and the Josephites will also write (see 3 Nephi 29:12), and more scriptures are to come.

Praying in the Name of People Other Than Jesus Christ

In the Bible, it is common to pray to the Father in the name of Jesus Christ, but there is no specific commandment to pray in the name of Jesus Christ. Some Christian churches teach their congregation to pray in the name of their church founders, holy Saints like Mary, or others.

In the Book of Mormon, the resurrected Jesus strictly instructed that we pray to the Father in His name: "Therefore, ye must always pray unto the Father in my name" (3 Nephi 18:19). He also said, "And they shall believe in me, that I am Jesus Christ, the Son of God, and shall pray unto the Father in my name" (3 Nephi 20:31).

Balanced Teaching between "Justified by Faith" and "Judged According to Works"

The doctrine of "justified by faith alone" is a good example of the Pauline doctrine: Jesus Christ did not teach it, but Paul did (see Romans 2–3; Galatians 3–4). The word *faith* appears 245 times in the New Testament, and 171 (70 percent) of them are found in Paul's fourteen epistles. It appears only twenty-nine times in the four Gospels (and is not found in the Gospel of John). The word *mercy* appears sixty-four times in the New Testament, but the word *justice* does not appear.

"Being saved by faith alone" has been a prevalent belief among many Christians based on the discourses of faith that the Apostle Paul taught in the epistles to the Romans, Corinthians, Galatians, Ephesians, Hebrews, and others, with comments like *dead works*[130] (Hebrews 6:1, 9:14). This belief has persisted despite:

- The fact that Jesus Christ taught that "he [Son of Man] shall reward every man according to his works" (Matthew 16:27)
- The fact that the Apostle Paul taught that "Who[God] will render to every man according to his deeds:" (Romans 2:6)
- The fact that the Apostle James taught that "faith without works is dead" (James 2:26)
- The fact that the doctrine of "being judged according to their works" is taught in Revelation 20:12–13

In the Book of Mormon, "justified by faith" cannot be found, but "judged according to works" is taught by many prophets: Nephi, King Benjamin, Abinadi, Alma, Amulek, Mormon, and Moroni. The word *mercy* appears 102 times, and the word *justice* appears 70 times in the Book of Mormon.

King Benjamin also taught that to be saved, we can overcome the natural man (who is an enemy to God) by applying the Atonement of Christ and being submissive to the enticing of the Holy Ghost (see Mosiah 3:19). Nephi summed it up well by saying that even if we are made alive in Christ because of our faith, the grace that comes from the Atonement of Jesus Christ is only applicable after all we can do (see 2 Nephi 25:23–25).

---

[130] Interestingly, in the Book of Mormon, Mormon called infant baptism a dead work (see Moroni 8:23).

Not Predestination, but Preordaining or Calling with Foreknowledge

Some protestant denominations such as the Calvinists believe in the doctrine of predestination, but this belief has been controversial. Among many versions of the English Bible, most of the versions use the term *predestinated* in Romans 8:30, and they seem to confirm the teaching by the Calvinists. However, some other versions translated the same term as *foreordained, chosen,* or *called,* among others.

In the Book of Mormon, Lehi and Jacob taught that we have freedom to choose (see 2 Nephi 2: 27; 2 Nephi 10:23), and Alma taught that God left His children free to choose with His foreknowledge (see Alma 13:3).[131] Thus, the Book of Mormon clarifies that it is more foreordaining or calling with foreknowledge with choices we make, not fixed predestination.

Name of Church Should Include "Jesus Christ"

In the Bible, there is no teaching on this subject. Consequently, countless names have been used by Christian churches since the Catholic Church started in AD 325.

In the Book of Mormon, the resurrected Jesus Christ specifically instructed that His name should be included in the name of His Church:

> And how be it my church save it be called in my name? For if a church be called in Moses' name then it be Moses' church; or if it be called in the name of a man then it be the church of a man; but if it be called in my name then it is my church, if it so be that they are built upon my gospel. (3 Nephi 27:8)

Jesus taught not only about the importance of the name of His Church, but also the consequences of being built upon the works of men or the devil instead of being built upon His gospel: "they have joy in their works for a season, and by and by the end cometh, and they are hewn down and cast into the fire, from whence there is no return" (3 Nephi 27:11).

---

[131] There seem to be some exceptions. For example, Jeremiah was ordained to be a prophet before his birth (see Jeremiah 1:5). Yet, he could exercise his agency to be a prophet of the Lord or run away from it as Jonah tried to flee (see Jonah 1:3).

Priestly Clergy System without the Melchizedek and Levitical Priesthood

In the Bible, the Apostle Paul taught about two priesthoods: the Levitical Priesthood and the Melchizedek Priesthood (see Hebrews 7). He taught that the leadership was based on the Levitical Priesthood in the days of Moses, but he explained that the Melchizedek Priesthood is higher than the Levitical Priesthood, and that Jesus Christ holds the Melchizedek Priesthood.

In the Book of Mormon, the prophet Alma taught the same about the Melchizedek Priesthood (see Alma 13). He added that the purpose of the higher priesthood is to lead people to the Savior.

However, the present leadership system of Judeo-Christian churches is not based on the priesthoods that the Apostle Paul and the prophet Alma taught, but is based on education in seminary and a diploma for priestly ministry in the denomination. This system is quite a departure from the leadership system based on the Levitical and Melchizedek priesthoods. The ecclesiastical leadership of The Church of Jesus Christ of Latter-day Saints operates by these two priesthood authorities (see D&C 20, 84, 88, 107, 110) as taught by Paul and Alma.

Money for Forgiving Sin (Indulgence)

Nowhere in the Bible does it teach that sins can be forgiven for money. However, even though it is not practiced anymore, *indulgence*—paying money to buy indulgence for forgiveness of sins—was practiced by the Catholic Church for many centuries. It may not be exactly the same practice, but it is not too unusual that big donors are invited to assume positions of leadership in many protestant churches.

In the Book of Mormon, the prophet Moroni prophesied in the early fifth century AD, "Yea, it [the Book of Mormon] shall come in a day when there shall be churches built up that shall say: Come unto me, and for your money you shall be forgiven of your sins" (Mormon 8:32). It seems that Moroni is referring to theological beliefs and practices like indulgence, or even appointing leadership positions based on the amount of donations.

The above corrections may be a fulfillment of what Joseph in Egypt quoted the Lord by saying, "[writings by fruit of loins of Judah and Joseph: the Bible and the Book of Mormon] shall grow together unto confounding of false doctrine" (2 Nephi 3:12).

Conclusion

The Bible contains a record of the tribe of Judah, which had ruled with the scepter until the coming of Jesus (Shiloh); since then, billions of people have flocked to Him. This fulfilled Jacob's patriarchal blessing on Judah. The Book of Mormon shows that a small group of the Josephites fulfilled Jacob's and Lehi's patriarchal blessings for the remnant of the tribe of Joseph in a promised land far away from Jerusalem.

Through my research on these two predestined scriptures, it is clear that the gospel of Jesus Christ is going through a cycle of Christianity that started with the Jews, and that it will return to the Jews at the end. The Jews had the gospel of Jesus Christ first; the gospel was delivered to the Gentiles through the Bible, which was missing some plain and precious parts and covenants; the converted Gentiles have brought the fullness of the gospel restored through the Book of Mormon, providing the missing plain and precious parts and covenants in the Bible to the Josephites and Gentiles; and the converted Josephites and Gentiles are going to bring the restored gospel back to the Jews. This full circle demonstrates that the first shall be last, and the last shall be first (see 1 Nephi 13:26–42).

This book demonstrates that the Book of Mormon helps us understand the Bible better in many ways by defining, linking, clarifying, extending, magnifying, correcting from wresting, demonstrating, applying, correlating, providing the plain and precious parts, teaching the priesthood ordinances with the associated covenants in exact manners, and so forth. Thus, this shows a fulfillment of two sticks of Israel becoming one stick in the hands of the Lord, as prophesied by Ezekiel, Lehi, Nephi, and Mormon. This also shows a fulfillment of blessings by Jacob, Moses, and Lehi and of prophecies by Joseph in Egypt. As the resurrected Jesus commanded His disciples to go into the world baptizing in the name of the Father, the Son, and the Holy Ghost as recorded in the Bible, the last writer of the Book of Mormon, Moroni, invited all to come unto Christ and be perfected and sanctified in Christ through His infinite and eternal Atonement and the grace of God.

As scriptures of Israel, both the Bible and the Book of Mormon jointly testify that God's love for all people is the same throughout all generations of time, regardless of whether those people are Jews, Josephites, or Gentiles. This book provides ample evidences that the stick of Judah and the stick of Joseph jointly testify of Jehovah, Jesus Christ, as one stick, and the prophecies by Ezekiel, Lehi, and others have literally been fulfilled in this last dispensation. As evidenced in this book, studying the Book of Mormon help us understand the Bible better.

Appendix: Questions and Answers

THROUGHOUT THIS BOOK, THE BIBLE and the Book of Mormon have been reviewed together from multiple angles regarding the ministry and teachings of Christ (Christology) and gospel principles. During this research, many questions have arisen. To increase clarity and understanding for readers, the following forty questions were selected and their answers provided in three categories: questions related to both the Bible and the Book of Mormon, questions related to the Bible, and questions related to the Book of Mormon.

Questions Related to both the Bible and the Book of Mormon

Question:

In his patriarchal blessings to his twelve sons, Jacob said that the tribe of Judah would keep the scepter until Shiloh would come; people would gather to Shiloh; and that the tribe of Joseph would run over the wall (be in different places) and would be hated by many but protected by the Lord. He also blessed Ephraim (the second son of Joseph) to carry the birthright of Israel and to be a father of many nations. Based on the historicity of Judeo-Christianity and The Church of Jesus Christ of Latter-day Saints, what correlations can be drawn regarding fulfillment of Jacob's blessings to the Jews and the Josephites?

Answer:

After Jesus was crucified, the Jews were scattered by the Romans around AD 70. Thus, the Jewish nation lasted until around the ministry of Shiloh (the Savior). However, billions of people have believed in Jesus as their Christ (Shiloh), and Christianity became the largest religion in the world. The Church of Jesus Christ of Latter-day Saints was organized in America in AD 1830 after Joseph Smith translated and published the Book of Mormon and received the Aaronic (Levitical) and Melchizedek priesthoods from angels (in other words, as if carrying on the birthright).

More than 100 million copies of the Book of Mormon, the Josephite record, have been distributed throughout the world as "Another Testament of Jesus Christ." Both the Judeo-Christian churches (large in size but diversified with many denominations) and The Church of Jesus Christ of Latter-day Saints (small in size and monolithic with little diversification) have coexisted in recent centuries. The former stems from the tribe of Judah, and the latter from the tribe of Joseph. Thus, Jacob's blessing on both tribes of Israel has been fulfilled.

Question:

The word *atonement* appears eighty-one times in the Old Testament. The Jews also celebrate a special Sabbath day of atonement (Yom Kippur), but their teachings on atonements are mostly about sin-forgiving ordinances (animal sacrifices) in the temple, not the infinite Atonement for all mankind through their Messiah. In the New Testament (KJV), the word *atonement* appears only once (see Romans 5:11–12), in which the Apostle Paul explained the infinite Atonement through Jesus Christ. At the same time, the infinite Atonement of Jesus Christ appears thirty-nine times in the Book of Mormon (*atonement* twenty-eight times; *atone, atoneth,* or *atoning* eleven times). What could we conclude from this major difference in emphasizing and teaching the infinite Atonement of Jesus Christ in the Bible and the Book of Mormon?

Answer:

It is clear that the Atonement of Jesus Christ was taught more frequently in the Book of Mormon than in the Bible. While teachings of the Resurrection and Atonement of Jesus Christ are virtually seamless between the BC and AD periods of the Book of Mormon, there is a big gap in teachings of Jesus Christ between the Old and New Testament of the Bible. Chapter 2 lists twenty-five related subjects with teachings about the Atonement from nine different prophets in the Book of Mormon.

Question:

For many Christians, *faith* may be one of the most important attributes, and they believe in a theology of "justification by faith." When He healed the afflicted, Jesus Christ often taught that they were healed because of their faith, and He even compared people's faith to a tiny mustard seed. Thus, Jesus taught the importance of faith. However, there is no record showing that Jesus taught "justification by faith," though Paul did (see Romans 3–4; Galatians 2–3).

While Paul taught this principle using Abraham's obedience to sacrifice his son, Isaac, as an example of "justification by faith," James interestingly taught the principle of "justification by works," also using the same story of Abraham (see James 2:21–25). Both Peter and John also taught "judgement according to works" (see 1 Peter 1:17; Revelation 20:12–13).

In the Book of Mormon, "justification by faith" cannot be found, but "judgment according to works" is taught by the resurrected Jesus Christ (see 3 Nephi 27:15) as well as by multiple prophets: Nephi (see 2 Nephi 28:23; 29:11), King Benjamin (see Mosiah 3:24), Abinadi (see Mosiah 16:10), Alma and/or Amulek (see Alma 11:41, 44; 12:8, 12; 32:20; 33:22; 40:21; 41:3; 42:23), Mormon (see Mormon 3:18; 6:21), and Moroni (see Mormon 8:19).

What are the reasons "faith" became so important for Christians, to the degree of believing in and preaching *sola fide* ("faith alone") as taught by reformists like Martin Luther? How should faithful Christians reconcile between being "justified by faith" as taught by Paul and "judged according to works" as taught by the others?

Answer:

Faith is the first principle of the doctrine of Christ, and its importance is very clear. The word *faith* appears 245 times in the entire New Testament—70 percent of them (171 times) in Paul's epistles (twenty-four times in Hebrews 11 alone), and only 12 percent of them (twenty-nine times) in the four Gospels. The word *faith* is not found in the Gospel of John.

It is obvious that the Pauline doctrine emphasizes faith such that it became a household word for most (Hellenic) Christians, especially for Protestants. Consequently, even though the Apostles Peter, James, and John taught "justification by works" in addition to faith, their teachings have been overshadowed by Paul's teachings for many Christians. Nonetheless, when the Apostle Paul mentioned works, he mostly referred to the law of Moses, such as circumcision and some rituals.

Concerning faith versus works, Nephi may have summed up this issue clearly in the following statements:

> For we labor diligently to write, to persuade our children, and also our brethren, to believe in Christ, and to be reconciled to God; for we know that it is by grace that we are saved, after all we can do.
>
> And, notwithstanding we believe in Christ, we keep the law of Moses, and look forward with steadfastness unto Christ, until the law shall be fulfilled.
>
> For, for this end was the law given; wherefore the law hath become dead unto us, and we are made alive in Christ because of our faith; yet we keep the law because of the commandments. (2 Nephi 25:23–25)

See Chapter 10 for more discussion on this subject.

Question:

In the Old Testament, the word *justice* appears twenty-eight times, and the word *mercy* appears 256 times, mostly in conjunction with the mercy seat placed on the Ark of the Covenant. In the New Testament, the word *mercy* appears sixty-four times, but the word *justice* never appears. Obviously, "justice" was not emphasized in the New Testament.

In the Book of Mormon, the word *mercy* appears 102 times, and *justice* appears seventy times. Thus, we can see that the use of *mercy* outnumbers the use of *justice* in both the Bible and the Book of Mormon, but it is more balanced in the Book of Mormon. Alma taught that mercy could satisfy the demands of justice, proclaiming, "If so, God would cease to be God" (Alma 42:25). According to Alma's teaching, in what conditions could mercy meet the demands of justice?

Answer:

Mercy and justice cover opposite sides in a court; mercy represents the defense side, and justice represents the prosecution side. To obtain a merciful judgment, the defense must counter or satisfy the demands of the prosecutor.

The prophet Alma answers this question by saying that the merciful Atonement of Jesus Christ will meet the demands of justice only for those who repent in their probationary state (on the earth):

> Therefore, according to justice, the plan of redemption could not be brought about, only on conditions of repentance of men in this probationary state, yea, this preparatory state; for except it were for these conditions, mercy could not take effect except it should destroy the work of justice. Now the work of justice could not be destroyed; if so, God would cease to be God.
>
> And thus we see that all mankind were fallen, and they were in the grasp of justice; yea, the justice of God, which consigned them forever to be cut off from his presence.
>
> And now, the plan of mercy could not be brought about except an atonement should be made; therefore God himself atoneth for the sins of the world, to bring about the plan of mercy, to appease the demands of justice, that God might be a perfect, just God, and a merciful God also. (Alma 42:13–15)

See Chapter 7 for more discussion on this subject.

Question:

The Lord's Prayer may be one of the most quoted and recited prayers throughout Christian history. In the New Testament, two versions are recorded: Matthew 6:9–13 and Luke 11:2–4. The version in Matthew 6, a part of the Sermon on the Mount, has been quoted most frequently. When the resurrected Jesus retaught the Sermon on the Mount to the Nephites, He taught another version of the Lord's Prayer (see 3 Nephi 13:9–13). What are the differences between these three versions, and what is the significance of those differences?

Answer:

In Luke's writing, the statement "For thine is the kingdom, and the power and the glory forever. Amen" is missing as it is found in Matthew.

This missing part is more of a statement honoring the Father, not something being prayed for. There are two phrases not mentioned in 3 Nephi compared to one in Matthew 6: "thy kingdom come" and "Give us this day our daily bread." This may indicate that God's kingdom had already come, since the resurrected Jesus was with them (the Atonement process had already taken place). Another indication may be that there was plenty of food available in the land of America, where the Nephites were living at the time. Interestingly in general, there are no mentions of the Nephites suffering from cold weather or a lack of food with the exception of the broken bow incident after Lehi's family arrived in the promised land. See Chapter 5 for more discussion on this subject.

Question:

Jesus taught His doctrine throughout His ministry (see Luke 7:22). He said that it was not His doctrine, but it was the doctrine of His Father who sent Him (see John 7:16). However, there are few records about the elements of His doctrine in the four Gospels of the New Testament. On the other hand, in the Book of Mormon, the resurrected Jesus explained to the Nephites what the elements of His doctrine are. Nephi also taught the five elements of the doctrine of Christ very plainly and succinctly. What are these five principles, and how well do they fit with teachings by different denominations of Judeo-Christianity?

Answer:

The first writer in the Book of Mormon, Nephi, succinctly outlined the five elements of the doctrine of Christ (see 2 Nephi 31). They are (1) faith in Jesus Christ, (2) repentance, (3) baptism by water, (4) baptism by the Holy Ghost, and (5) enduring to the end. Members of The Church of Jesus Christ of Latter-day Saints follow this exactly as taught by Nephi. In contrast, the teachings of Judeo-Christians seem to vary between the absolute necessity of baptism, to baptism being unnecessary because one can be saved by faith alone. See Chapter 7 for more discussion on this subject.

Question:

Moses, Jesus, Paul, Mormon, and Alma taught the importance of charity (or love). Thus, the importance of charity has been known from Moses's day. Jesus taught that love of God and neighbor were the greatest commandments, and He explained who "neighbors" are through the parable of the good Samaritan.

Paul taught that charity was greater than faith and hope. Mormon taught the same thing, but added one more attribute to faith, hope, and charity. Mormon also defined what to hope for and connected charity to Jesus Christ by the power of the Holy Ghost. Alma also taught that faith, hope, and charity should always abound in good works (see Alma 7:24), and Moroni taught that they bring forth "a fountain of all righteousness" unto God (Ether 12:28). What conclusion can be generated by combining all the teachings on faith, hope, and charity from the Bible and the Book of Mormon?

Answer:

The prophet Mormon added meekness and lowliness of heart to faith, hope, and charity (see Moroni 7:43–44). He taught to hope for our own salvation through the Atonement of Jesus Christ and the power of His Resurrection. He also taught that when one has charity, he or she should be able to confess by the power of the Holy Ghost that Jesus is the Christ. Combining all the teachings of charity (or love) from both the Bible and the Book of Mormon is somewhat difficult, but the purpose of charity can be summarized by saying that the two greatest commandments are love of God and love of neighbors. (With hope for the Atonement and resurrection of Jesus Christ, and with love of God and neighbors manifested through good works, one will be able to confess Jesus Christ in faith and meekness by the power of the Holy Ghost and live by the fountain of all righteousness of the Lord.) See Chapter 7 for more discussion on this subject.

Question:

The Apostle Paul briefly talked to the Corinthians about baptism for the dead (see 1 Corinthians 15:29). In the subsequent verses of the chapter, he continued with the subject of resurrection in conjunction with three types of glory and bodies (celestial, terrestrial, and telestial).[132] However, baptism for the dead was not mentioned in the Book of Mormon, which is known as the scripture with the fullness of the gospel. Who taught this subject indirectly in the Book of Mormon? What is the relationship between this teaching in the Book of Mormon and the present vicarious

---

[132] Paul did not use the term *telestial*, but he used the term *stars* (see 1 Corinthians 15:40–41). Joseph Smith did use the term *telestial* (see D&C 76:81).

ordinance works for the dead being performed in modern-day temples of The Church of Jesus Christ of Latter-day Saints?

Answer:

In his teachings to the Nephites, the resurrected Jesus Christ quoted Isaiah and Malachi. The book of Isaiah is a record from the seventh and eighth century BC, and those records could have been included on the plates of brass from which the Nephites quoted. However, the book of Malachi is a record from the fifth century BC—and since Lehi left Jerusalem in 600 BC, long before Malachi's days, that record could not have been included on the plates of brass. It was available to the Jews in Jerusalem during Jesus's ministry, but not to the Nephites in the land of America.

After the resurrected Jesus quoted Malachi 3 and 4 to the Nephites in 3 Nephi 24 and 25, he taught the Nephites, "These scriptures [Malachi 3 and 4] which ye [Nephites] had not with you, the Father commanded that I should give unto you; for it was wisdom in him that they should be given unto future generations [future generations who will have the Book of Mormon]" (3 Nephi 26:2).

The last two verses of the Old Testament say, "Behold, I will send you Elijah the prophet before the coming of the great and dreadful day of the Lord; And he shall turn the heart of the fathers to the children, and the hearts of the children to their fathers, lest I come and smite the earth with a curse" (Malachi 4:5–6). Thus, the resurrected Jesus taught that the prophet Elijah would come and turn the fathers and children's hearts to each other in the future.

This teaching was literally fulfilled in the Kirtland Temple on April 3, 1836, when Elijah came to visit Joseph Smith and Oliver Cowdery and restored the priesthood key to turn the hearts of the fathers to the children and vice versa (see D&C 110:13–15). Since then, about eighteen hundred years after the resurrected Jesus taught this to the Nephites, vicarious ordinances for the dead, including baptism, have been practiced in temples of The Church of Jesus Christ of Latter-day Saints. See Chapter 5 for more discussion on this subject.

Question:

Throughout their history, many Judeo-Christian churches have taught a theology of Adam's original sin based on Paul's teaching, "For as in Adam all die, even so in Christ shall all be made alive" (1 Corinthians 15:22), and a few other passages in the Bible. Thus, they believe that Adam's original sin caused mankind to be born as sinners, and that baptism is essential for salvation of all mankind, including infants. Thus, infant baptism has commonly been practiced in many Christian denominations, even in modern days. In the Book of Mormon, Mormon refuted this theology of infant baptism, even calling it "solemn mockery before God" (Moroni 8:9). What is the basis for denying this traditionally well-established theological belief?

Answer:

The prophet Lehi taught that Adam transgressed the law by partaking of the forbidden fruit for his posterity (the whole human race) with a full knowledge of the consequences when he said, "Adam fell that men might be; and men are that they might have joy. And the Messiah cometh in the fullness of time, that he may redeem the children of men from the fall" (2 Nephi 2:25–26). King Benjamin also taught:

> For the natural man is an enemy to God, and has been from the fall of Adam, and will be forever and ever, unless he yields to the enticings of the Holy Spirit, and putteth off the natural man and becometh a saint through the atonement of Christ the Lord, and become as a little child, submissive, meek, humble, patient, full of love, willing to submit to all things which the Lord seeth fit to inflict upon him, even as a child doth submit to his father. (Mosiah 3:19)

Thus, the Book of Mormon teaches that even if the natural man is an enemy to God because of Adam's transgression, the Lord has provided ways to overcome this natural man through the Atonement of Christ. However, He requires man to be innocent and submissive like little children, following the enticing of the Holy Spirit. Thus, it is not Adam's transgression that curses men; rather, it is their choices not to apply the Atonement of Christ and not to follow the enticing of the Holy Spirit in their lives. Mormon called infant baptism "solemn mockery before God" (Moroni 8:9). Thus, the Atonement of Jesus Christ took care of little children's needs for baptism for their salvation. See Chapter 10 for more discussion on this subject.

Question:

Even if there are some prophecies of their Messiah in the Old Testament, teachings of Christ—such as the doctrine of Christ—were not taught in the Old Testament period, but they were taught beginning in the New Testament period. Thus, Christianity started after the birth of Jesus Christ. In the Book of Mormon, the doctrine of Christ was taught by the first writer, Nephi, as early as 559–545 BC. Did Christians exist in the period before Christ's birth?

Answer:

Based on teachings in the Old Testament, it is hard to find traces of Christians who believed Jesus to be born in the future as their Christ and traces of His doctrine being taught in the BC period. However, in the Book of Mormon, Christians existed in the BC period. For example, the first writer, Nephi, revealed the name *Jesus Christ* and taught the doctrine of Christ as early as 559–545 BC (see 2 Nephi 25 and 31). A Nephite general named Moroni called his people "Christians" in 72 BC (see Alma 42).

Thus, there might not be Christians among the Jews according to the Old Testament, but Christians existed among the Josephites (Nephites) as early as the sixth century BC according to the Book of Mormon. Moreover, the Lord revealed to the brother of Jared His name, Jesus Christ, around the time of the Tower of Babel (see Ether 3:14) See the Introduction and Chapter 10 for more discussion on this subject.

Question:

About 7 percent of the Book of Mormon is comprised of quotations from the Bible. The book of Isaiah is quoted the most (mostly chapters 2–14, 29, 48–54), and the book of Malachi is also quoted (chapters 3–4). The resurrected Jesus Christ retaught the Sermon on the Mount from Matthew 5–7 with some variations in 3 Nephi 12–14, and some call it the Sermon on the Temple. What are the main points that were quoted from the books of Isaiah and Malachi? What are the major differences between the Sermon on the Temple and the Sermon on the Mount?

Answer:

In Nephi's quote from Isaiah 48–49 (see 1 Nephi 20–21), the main theme is that the Lord will eventually redeem Israel. He also quoted Isaiah 29 in a random fashion in his last words in 2 Nephi 25–28, the main themes of which are his prophecies on the coming forth of Christ, the establishment of a Gentile church and its apostasy, and the coming forth of a book from the dust. In a block of quotes from Isaiah 2–14 by Nephi (see 2 Nephi 12–24), the main themes are the birth of the Savior to a virgin, a gathering in the latter days, a punishment before the Second Coming of the Lord, happiness in the millennial reign of the Lord, and so forth. In Jacob's quote from Isaiah 49:24–52:2 (see 2 Nephi 6:16–8:25), the main themes are about the Savior's sufferings and the gathering of Israel in Zion. Abinadi quoted Isaiah 53 (see Mosiah 14), focusing on the Messiah's suffering and His Atonement. The resurrected Jesus quoted Isaiah 52 and 54 (see 3 Nephi 20 and 22), with a main theme that Israel in Zion will be triumphant at the end.

The resurrected Jesus Christ also quoted Malachi 3–4 (see 3 Nephi 24–25), the main themes of which are the importance of ordinances and tithes and Elijah coming to turn the hearts of the children to their fathers and vice versa.

The resurrected Jesus Christ retaught the Sermon on the Mount with some variations. The noticeable variations are to be perfect "*even as I [Jesus Christ]* or your Father who is in heaven" (emphasis added); variation in the Lord's Prayer; and addition of a message that the law of Moses was fulfilled. See page Chapter 5 for more discussion on this subject.

Question:

In 1 Nephi 20:1 of the Book of Mormon, Isaiah 48:1 is quoted: "Hearken and hear this, O house of Jacob, who are called by the name of Israel, and are come forth out of the waters of Judah, or *out of the waters of baptism*, who swear by the name of the Lord, and make mention of the God of Israel, yet they swear not in truth nor in righteousness" (emphasis added). In the Book of Mormon, the phrase "or out of the waters of baptism" is added to Isaiah 48:1. What is the significance of having this phrase added?

Answer:

This makes the covenant through baptism equal to the covenant through the bloodline. With the condition that they accept Jesus Christ and are baptized, all Gentiles are entitled to be covenant sons and daughters of God, the same as those who were born in the Abrahamic covenant. Since the book of Isaiah was written mostly for the Jews, it seems appropriate to mention the bloodline exclusively. However, the book of Nephi was written for the descendants of Joseph and the Gentiles in the latter days, and this added phrase was very pertinent for all, including the Gentiles. The Apostle Paul indicated the same line of thought in his letter to the Galatians: "That the blessing of Abraham might come on the Gentiles through Jesus Christ" (Galatians 3:14), and "And if ye be Christ's, then are ye Abraham's seed, and heirs according to the promise" (Galatians 3:29). See Chapter 5 for more discussion on this subject.

Question:

Dramatic conversions of anti-Christs are recorded in both the Bible and the Book of Mormon: Paul in the New Testament and Alma and the four sons of King Mosiah in the Book of Mormon. The Apostle Paul basically changed the landscape of Christianity among the Jews and the Gentiles, as did the others among the Nephites and the Lamanites. What were the main changes that they brought about for the future of Christianity?

Answer:

All these missionaries were anti-Christs at first. However, after their miraculous conversions, their past anti-Christ experiences were motivating factors not only for remorseful repentance but also for dedicating their lives to Jesus Christ. With unwavering love for Jesus, they could endure any hardship in bringing people to Jesus Christ (see 2 Corinthians 11; Alma 26, 29). They were mighty teachers and taught everyone without prejudice, regardless of their race, social status, or political status. When things were tough, they always relied on Jesus in overcoming their difficulties. They were very successful in their missionary endeavors, but they humbly credited all the glory to Jesus.

The Apostle Paul was the main instrument for the Lord in bringing the Gentiles into Christianity and establishing many branches of the Church of Jesus Christ among the Gentiles. The others were the main instruments for the Lord in bringing the Lamanites to join the Nephites and establishing the Church of Jesus Christ jointly, and they were unwavering pillars during tumultuous times in the Church. See Chapter 7 for more discussion on this subject.

Question:

When the angel Gabriel informed Zacharias of the birth of his son, John the Baptist, he said that John would turn the hearts of the fathers to the children in the spirit and power of Elias. Moroni retaught this when he visited with Joseph Smith. What did John do to turn the hearts of the fathers to the children?

Answer:

The Greek name of *Elias* in the New Testament is the same as the Hebrew name of *Elijah* in the Old Testament. Thus, John the Baptist was supposed to turn the hearts of the fathers to the children in the spirit and power of Elijah (see Luke 1:17), as was prophesied in Malachi 4:5–6. The angel Moroni taught Joseph Smith these same verses:

> And again, he [angel Moroni] quoted the fifth verse [Malachi 4:5] thus: *Behold, I will reveal unto you the Priesthood, by the hand of Elijah the prophet, before the coming of the great and dreadful day of the Lord.*

He also quoted the next verse differently [Malachi 4:6]:

> And <u>he shall plant in the hearts of the children the promises made to the fathers</u>, and the hearts of the children shall turn to their fathers. If it were not so, the whole earth would be utterly wasted at his coming. (Joseph Smith—History 1:38–39; emphasis added).

Thus, turning the hearts of the fathers to the children means planting the promises made to the fathers in the hearts of the children. When John the Baptist was born, his father, Zacharias, also prophesied that John's birth was partly to "perform the mercy *promised* to our fathers, and to remember his holy covenant; The oath which he sware to our father Abraham," (Luke 1:72–73). Jesus also confirmed that John the Baptist was Elias or Elijah (see Matthew 17:10–13).

One unique legacy of John the Baptist is baptism by water for repentance. Thus, baptism by water is a sacred ordinance that plants in the hearts of the children the promises made to the fathers. In other words, baptism by water is planting the Abrahamic covenants in the hearts of those who get baptized. Thus, those who are baptized by John's baptism become like the seed of Abraham and are entitled to the Abrahamic covenants just as the Hebrews are. As taught in 1 Nephi 20:1, the waters of baptism provide the same blessings as the waters of Judah (Abraham's covenant to his lineage). Thus, baptism by water plants the Abrahamic covenants in the hearts of those who are baptized. See Chapter 6 for more discussion on this subject.

Questions Related Only to the Bible

Question:

Jesus left His final charges or words to His disciples before His ascension to heaven. The synopsists recorded basically the same messages of what Jesus commanded His disciples. However, John's record is quite different from the other three; Jesus left some remarks to Peter and John only. In Acts 1, there is also a record of what Jesus told the disciples before His ascension. When we combine all the last words of Jesus Christ, what are the main commandments that Jesus left to His disciples?

Answer:

The main commandment that Jesus left to His disciples was to go into the world, baptizing people in the name of the Father, the Son, and the Holy Ghost (see Matthew 28:18–20; Mark 16:15–18; Luke 24:44–49) and to bear witness of Him throughout the world (see Acts 1:8). Jesus told Peter to feed His sheep and that John would tarry on the earth until His Second Coming (see John 21:15–23). See Chapter 8 for more discussion on this subject.

Question:

Despite the expertise of Jewish scripture like the Tanakh and Torah, the Sadducees and the Pharisees had opposing views on resurrection; Sadducees did not believe in it, but Pharisees did. For example, some Sadducees challenged Jesus about resurrection with a cynical story of a woman who hypothetically ended up marrying seven brothers (see Matthew 22; Mark 12; and Luke 20). As part of his defense strategies while being accused by the Jews, the Apostle Paul took advantage of their differences by bringing up the subject of resurrection, and these two groups argued among themselves, leaving him alone (see Acts 23:5–10). Even some of the disciples of Jesus Christ did not believe Jesus's Resurrection until they actually met the resurrected Jesus and could see physical evidence (see John 20). Why could these totally opposite beliefs about resurrection coexist among the pious Jewish leaders who had the same scriptures, and even among the disciples of Jesus?

Answer:

The word resurrection cannot be found in the Old Testament. However, some prophets like Isaiah and Ezekiel talked about rising after death (see Isaiah 25:8; Ezekiel 37:11–14). Thus, two different views can coexist. This might also be evidenced by the fact that when Jesus explained to His disciples that His death and Resurrection were imminent, the disciples did not understand His messages (see Matthew 16:21–23; Mark 8:31–33, 9:30–32). See Chapter 10 for more discussion on this subject.

Question:

Some Judeo-Christians have advocated the concept that heaven is closed to mankind because the canonized Bible has all the divine gospel messages for one's salvation. Thus, they believe there cannot be any more revelations, visions, and visits by angels, and they also believe that the Bible is infallible. In a way, it seems that the infallible Bible replaced the "windows of heaven," and this belief also leads to the closed canon of the Bible. Are they right or wrong? Are there evidences for continuous revelatory communications in our day between God in heaven and mankind on the earth?

Answer:

In attempts to replace the authority of the Pope with the Bible, some of the early Christian leaders of the reformation movements supported a *closed cannon*—the concept that the infallible Bible provides all the answers for one's salvation, and any additional revelations and visions from heaven are not necessary. Some Christians have experienced revelations and visions from heaven and believe in an *open cannon*—that heaven is open and divine revelations are still real. As one such example, The Church of Jesus Christ of Latter-day Saints continues to receive divine revelations and has selected and published the important revelations given to the modern-day prophets as a canonized scripture called the Doctrine and Covenants. See Chapter 10 for more discussion on this subject.

Question:

The Gospel of John is uniquely different from the Gospels of Matthew, Mark, and Luke in many aspects. For example, one of the most significant events recorded during the three-year ministry of Jesus Christ might be the Transfiguration, in which Moses and Elias came to visit Jesus Christ and His three head Apostles (Peter, James, and John) on Mount Hermon or Tabor. This event was recorded by all three of the synopsists (see Matthew 17; Mark 9; Luke 9), but John did not record it despite the fact that he was present at the Transfiguration—and as such, was the only one of the four Gospel writers who personally witnessed it. How should we take this major difference between the records from John and the other three synopsists?

Answer:

Since the four Gospels in the New Testament were presumably written with limited or nonexistent influence between them and there were no authors' explanations, it is hard to say why this was the case. The Transfiguration seems too special to be left out. A similar Transfiguration experience was reported in the Book of Mormon (see 3 Nephi 28:15–17). In a way, this type of similar experience in history may be an evidence for the Transfiguration. See Chapter 3 for more discussion on this subject.

Question:

In the Transfiguration, what was the purpose of Moses's and Elias's visit with Jesus and His three head disciples? Could it be just a social call, or did they come to carry out any special errands or assignments from the Father as the angel Gabriel did to Zacharias and Mary?

Answer:

The Transfiguration is recorded in Matthew 17:1–13, Mark 9:2–10, and Luke 9:28–36. The reported stories are about the same in all three, but Luke uniquely reported "and spake of *his decease* which he should accomplish at Jerusalem" (emphasis added in verse 31). Even if Matthew and Mark did not report this, Luke revealed that Moses and Elias came to visit Jesus Christ to discuss His impending Crucifixion in Jerusalem. Mark reported that Jesus told His three disciples not to share their Transfiguration experience until His Resurrection. This instruction puzzled them because they still did not understand that the Crucifixion and Resurrection would take place soon. See Chapter 3 for more discussion on this subject.

Question:

The most dramatic and significant miracle that Jesus performed was raising Lazarus from the dead four days after Lazarus's death, when his body already stank (see John 11:1–46). This could be considered the epoch of miracles performed by Jesus. While John provided much detail about this miracle, the other three Gospel writers did not record even a word about it. How should we take the fact that such a significant miracle performed by Jesus was reported only by John, but not the other three Gospel writers?

Answer:

This is an opposite example to that of the Transfiguration, which three of the Gospel writers reported but John did not. There is not a straight answer as to why this happened, and these issues raise a question on the comprehensiveness of the four Gospels. There is no clear answer for this in the Bible, but this may also indicate possibilities that either the writers of the four Gospels may have overlooked portions of their original writings, or scribes and/or translators might have left out portions at some points. The Gospel of John contains many unique stories that cannot be found in the other three Gospels. See Chapter 3 for more discussion on this subject.

Question:

Jesus prophesied of the future in Matthew 24, saying that the time would come when Herod's magnificent temple would be destroyed and that Jerusalem would be so desolate and devastated that people would rather die than live. In that chapter, He also said that the sun would be darkened, the moon would not give light, and the stars would fall like figs from a fig tree. On the way to Golgotha, suffering with great pain (even carrying His own cross), Jesus told the weeping women not to weep for Him, but to weep for their children (see Luke 23:27–30). Which of these prophecies spoken by Jesus Christ were already fulfilled during which time frames, and which ones are yet to be fulfilled?

Answer:

Reviewing the history of the Jews (as written, for example, by Josephus), most of the descriptive prophecies in Matthew 24 were about the destruction of Jerusalem in AD 70. The prophecies of the Second Coming of Jesus Christ and the end of the world in the chapter are yet to be fulfilled, but they are too general to know the details. In Mark 13:32, Jesus made it clear that only the Father knows the timing of His Second Coming. See Chapter 3 for more discussion on this subject.

Question:

In Matthew 1:20, it was recorded that the angel Gabriel announced to Joseph in his dream "for that which is conceived in her is of the Holy Ghost." In Luke 1:35, it was recorded that the same angel Gabriel told Mary, "The Holy Ghost shall come upon thee, and the power of the Highest shall overshadow thee: therefore also that holy thing which shall be born of thee shall be called the Son of God." Thus, whose baby is the Son of God: is He the baby of the Holy Ghost, or of the Highest? Or is the Holy Ghost the Highest?

Answer:

If the Trinitarian doctrine is correct, these questions may not be applicable because the Father, the Son, and the Holy Ghost are all one consubstantial being; the Trinitarian doctrine also teaches that the spiritual entity (God) could make a physical conception in flesh possible. If the Trinitarian doctrine is not correct, the Holy Ghost cannot be capable of conceiving a physical baby in the flesh because of being a spiritual entity without a physical body. This indicates that the Highest has a physical body (see D&C 130:22). Since the Bible does not provide answers to questions like this, it may be a source of confusion for students of the Bible. See Chapter 4 or more discussion on the subject.

Question:

The word *trinity* cannot be found in the Bible. Even before its official proclamation by the Catholic Church in the fourth century, there have been arguments for or against the doctrine of the Trinity. Both sides have tried to prove their arguments using different passages in the Bible. Due to difficulty in comprehending the consubstantiality of the Godhead that the Trinitarian doctrine proclaims, however, Catholic Church leaders have resorted to calling it a mysticism. Would this Trinity doctrine be a case of a truly divine revelation from God, or a case of Paul's teaching "going about to establish their own righteousness" (Romans 10:3), mingling man's philosophy with scripture?

Answer:

The concept of the Trinity is a doctrine that started after the days of the Apostles, most likely in the second century AD. Some passages in the New Testament make implications in favor of and some against this doctrine. Thus, it has caused much contention throughout the history of Christianity. However, the Book of Mormon shows that the Father, the Son, and the Holy Ghost are not consubstantial (see Mosiah 15:1–5). Having a confirmation from the Josephite record as another witness of Jesus Christ, it should be settled that the Trinitarian doctrine was not received through revelation from heaven. See Chapter 4 for more discussion on this subject.

Question:

The Levites were assigned to take care of the priesthood affairs in the tabernacle under the direction of Moses. In Solomon's temple, Zadok (a Levite) was in charge of managing the whole temple. In Herod's temple during the ministry of Jesus, the Sadducees (presumably Zadokites) were in charge of temple affairs. Since Herod's temple was burned down and the Jews were scattered in AD 70, there has been no succession of the Levites nor Sadducees. When the time comes for the Jews to build their temple and again offer sacrifices there, how will their priesthood be restored? Can rabbis fulfill the temple duty?

Answer:

There are no definite answers to this question, but there could be a couple of possibilities. One possibility may be that God will provide new prophets with the proper priesthood authority (such as the two prophets mentioned in Revelation 11:3–12). Another possibility may be that The Church of Jesus Christ of Latter-day Saints, which already has the Aaronic (or Levitical) and Melchizedek priesthoods, will ordain them. If this is the case, it stands as an example of how the first (tribe of Judah) will be last, and the last (tribe of Joseph) will be first. See Chapter 6 for more insight on this subject.

Question:

Contrary to the ordinance of animal sacrifice for sin forgiving by Sadducees in the temple, John's baptism was conducted for a remission of sins outside of the temple by one with new authority. There are both similar and opposite ramifications between these two priesthood ordinances: inside the temple by the Levites for sin forgiving versus outside the temple by one with new authority for remission of sin. What would the ramifications of John's baptism be in comparison to the sacrificial ordinances in the temple under the law of Moses that were the most critical religious practices for the Jews at the time?

Answer:

This new movement could imply that the ordinance of animal sacrifices under the law of Moses and the Levitical authority of the Sadducees could be replaced. It could also imply that there was someone who had a higher authority to supersede the traditional practices of the temple ordinances about which they were so dogmatic. See Chapter 6 for more discussion on this subject.

Question:

John the Baptist seemed to be popular among the Jews of his day, and his baptism seemed to be well accepted in his society. His baptism was a new ordinance but was somewhat similar to the mikveh that was commonly practiced for purification purposes (see Luke 2:22). When many Pharisees and Sadducees came to his baptism, John the Baptist accused them of being a generation of vipers, disclaimed the importance of Abraham's lineage, and introduced one with a higher authority who would baptize with the Holy Ghost (see Matthew 3:7–12). What might be reasons for the Jewish leadership not accepting John's baptism ordinance despite its popularity?

Answer:

If John could perform baptisms for the remission of sins using immersion that was similar to the mikveh, this could be viewed as a direct challenge to the Sadducees, who performed the ordinance of animal sacrifice for forgiveness of sin in the temple, following the law of Moses (remission of sins versus sin forgiving). By nullifying the importance of being the seed of Abraham and the sacrificial ordinances in the temple, this practice could be viewed by the contemporary Jewish leaders as the abominable activity of renegade liberals. See Chapter 6 for more discussion on this subject.

Question:

When John the Baptist baptized Jesus, the whole process was recorded in this sequence: Jesus came to John in the water; they discussed John's adequacy or qualifications to baptize Jesus; John baptized Jesus;

Jesus came straightway out of the water; the heavens opened and the Spirit of God descended as a dove; and a voice from heaven said, "This is my beloved Son in whom I am well pleased" (see Matthew 3:13–17). Later, the Apostles baptized people in the name of Jesus (see John 4:1–2). However, in the New Testament, nothing explains how John baptized Jesus nor how the Apostles baptized people. Consequently, the Christian churches of the Judeo-Christians use multiple baptismal methods, such as total immersion (submersion), partial immersion, affusion, or aspersion. What is the correct method of the sacred baptismal ordinance? Or does it matter? If so, why?

Answer:

Even if the exact method of baptism was not taught in the Bible, the resurrected Jesus taught the Nephites exactly how to perform baptism, which is contained in the Book of Mormon:

> And again the Lord called others, and said unto them likewise; and he gave unto them power to baptize. And he said unto them: On this wise shall ye baptize; and there shall be no disputations among you.
>
> Verily I say unto you, that whoso repenteth of his sins through your words, and desireth to be baptized in my name, on this wise shall ye baptize them—Behold, ye shall go down and stand in the water, and in my name shall ye baptize them.
>
> And now behold, these are the words which ye shall say, calling them by name, saying:
>
> Having authority given me of Jesus Christ, I baptize you in the name of the Father, and of the Son, and of the Holy Ghost. Amen.
>
> And then shall ye immerse them in the water, and come forth again out of the water. (3 Nephi 11:22–26)

Thus, the resurrected Jesus Christ specifically taught what should be said for the baptismal prayer, and He taught the method of total submersion in water. If this was recorded in the Bible, there could not be multiple baptismal methods. See Chapter 6 for more discussion on this subject.

Question:

In the Gospels of Matthew, Mark, and Luke, it specifies that no one would know the timing of the end of the world, including the angels; not even Jesus knows (see Matthew 24:36; Mark 13:32). However, some Judeo-Christian leaders have announced their calculated and/or speculative time (even including places in some cases) when the Second Coming of Jesus Christ would be. None of them have been right. Despite knowing what Jesus said about the timing of the end of the world, why would some Christians with in-depth knowledge of the Bible still prophesy the timing of the Second Coming of Jesus Christ?

Answer:

During the nineteenth century, there seemed to be a fad for predicting the timing of the Millennium, especially among Christian leaders of newer denominations. These leaders should be experts of the Bible, and should have known that the Gospel writers said that only Father knows the time. However, their research on this might have satisfied curiosities that (all) Christians have, and their announcements might have attracted more people to their denominations.

Joseph Smith also prayed about this, and got the following answer to his prayer:

> I was once praying very earnestly to know the time of the coming of the Son of Man, when I heard a voice repeat the following:
>
> Joseph, my son, if thou livest until thou art eighty-five years old, thou shalt see the face of the Son of Man; therefore let this suffice, and trouble me no more on this matter.
>
> I was left thus, without being able to decide whether this coming referred to the beginning of the millennium or to some previous appearing, or whether I should die and thus see his face.
>
> I believe the coming of the Son of Man will not be any sooner than that time [1890]. (D&C 130:14–17)

Since Joseph died at the age of thirty-eight in 1844, long before the age of eighty-five, this showed that the Lord did stick with His message of "trouble me no more on this matter." See Chapter 3 and Chapter 9 for more discussion on this subject.

Question:

A few centuries after the days of the Apostles, the Emperor Constantine organized the first unified Christian Church (Catholic Church) in the Council of Nicaea (AD 325). The Catholic Church announced that the Apostle Peter was the first Pope, and subsequent Popes have succeeded the priesthood authority from him (officially pronounced in the nineteenth century). Protestant Christian churches rejected this claim, and it has been very controversial. How would the priesthood succession have continued from the Church established by the Apostles to the Catholic Church established by the Emperor Constantine?

Answer:

The succession of Popes is not a biblical matter but a historical matter of the Catholic Church. There have been systematic and continuous successions of Popes after the Council of Nicaea throughout the history of the Catholic Church. However, there are no records showing how Peter and subsequent local leaders of the church in Rome systematically ordained their successors for ecclesiastic leadership during the period prior to the Council of Nicaea. Thus, it is a matter of opinion to call Roman bishops prior to the birth of the Catholic Church their Popes. For details on the papal successions, see http://www.historyworld.net/wrldhis/PlainTextHistories.asp?groupid=2851&HistoryID=ac65&gtrac k=pthc. See Chapter 6 for more discussion on this subject.

Question:

In the Judeo-Christian churches of the modern days, how do pastors, priests, and rabbis receive authority to minister to their congregations? Do they have the Levitical and Melchizedek priesthood authority like in the days of Moses and Jesus Christ, or are they just being priestly in administering and ministering their congregations?

Answer:

Spiritual leaders of Judeo-Christian churches—such as rabbis, priests, and pastors—are ordained leaders of their denominations through their education and training in academic seminary institutes. Thus, they are not the ordained priesthood holders of the Melchizedek and Levitical priesthoods. See Chapter 6 for more discussion on this subject.

Question:

According to the Apostle Paul, there are two priesthoods: the Levitical and the Melchizedek priesthoods (see Hebrews 5:5–8:2). Paul taught that Jesus Christ is a high priest forever after the order of Melchizedek (see Hebrews 6:20). Regarding priesthood authority, Jesus exercised His priesthood authority when He ordained His Apostles (see Mark 3:14) and the Seventy (see Luke 10:1). After His Resurrection, Jesus also gave them the Holy Ghost (see John 20:19–23). The Apostles had the authority to baptize and to represent Jesus. Among many Christian churches, which ones practice these two priesthood authorities in modern times?

Answer:

The Church of Jesus Christ of Latter-day Saints may be the only church in modern times that ordains its ecclesiastic leaders through the Levitical (or Aaronic) and Melchizedek priesthoods. See Chapter 6 for more discussion on this subject.

Questions Related Only to the Book of Mormon

Question:

The Nephites worshipped Jesus as the Christ from the start of their record around 600 BC. Even though there were some skeptics about the prophecies and some anti-Christ promoters among them, the Nephites in the Book of Mormon were quite opposite of the Jews in Israel. What would make the Nephites who originally came out of Jerusalem so different from the Jews in Jerusalem? Could they have different (or more) information or scriptures than the Jews had?

Answer:

The Old Testament is a Hebrew/Jewish record centered on their dealings with Jehovah, and the New Testament is a record of Jesus of Nazareth and His Apostles' testimony of Him being the Son of God and the Christ. Regarding Jesus of Nazareth being the Son of God, messages in the Old Testament are not perfectly harmonious with messages in the New Testament; there are not many synergetic similarities in the teachings of the gospel of Jesus between these two testaments of the Bible.

However, the Book of Mormon continually presents the same gospel message of Jesus Christ throughout its thousand-year history—600 years of the BC period, 421 years of the AD period—that Jesus of Nazareth is the Son of God and the Christ. Thus, there is a little difference in the messages about Jesus Christ in the Book of Mormon between the BC period and the AD period; all the messages are like the messages in the New Testament, testifying that Jesus is the Christ.

We know little about the contents of the plates of brass, but they were the Nephites' sole source for the teachings of Isaiah and others. Thus, there is a strong possibility that these plates might have some information about Jesus of Nazareth being the Son of God that are not available in the present Old Testament (example: prophets like Zenos and Zenock who are not known in the Bible). See Chapter 1 and Chapter 5 for more discussion on this subject.

Question:

In Mosiah 15:1–5, the prophet Abinadi taught that God Himself will come down and dwell in the flesh and will be called the Son of God, being subjected to the will of the Father. Being the Father and the Son (the Father because of conception by the power of God, and the Son because of the flesh), they become one God, the very Eternal Father of the heaven and of the earth. Did the Prophet Abinadi teach the Trinity doctrine?

Answer:

In-depth analysis shows that the prophet Abinadi did not teach the Trinitarian doctrine, but his key focus was the power of God. He taught that the Father and the Son are a team of Gods who govern the heaven and the earth. He confirmed what Luke quoted from the angel Gabriel in Luke 1:35 that Jesus is the Son of the Highest (God the Father). See Chapter 4 for the in-depth analyses of this subject.

Question:

Before his death, Lehi left his final parting words his son, Jacob, teaching him profound doctrine; among others, he taught some of the important doctrinal principles regarding the redemption from Adam's transgression and the principle of opposition in everything. What did Lehi teach about the reasons why Adam partook the fruit of the tree of knowledge of good and evil?

Answer:

One of the significant messages from Lehi to his son Jacob is that Adam's partaking of the fruit of the tree of good and evil was a deliberate transgression made through righteous judgment. He partook of the fruit for his posterity (the whole human race) and their joy. This was done with the wisdom of the all-knowing God. He also taught that if there was not opposition in everything, the Creation would have no purpose, and the wisdom of God would be destroyed. See Chapter 8 and Chapter 10 for more discussion on this subject.

Question:

Before his death, Lehi also left his final parting words to his youngest son, Joseph, prophesying about his posterity in the latter days by quoting the ancient Joseph in Egypt (see 2 Nephi 3:6–21). These quoted prophecies cannot be found in the canonized Bible. What could be the source for Lehi in quoting Joseph's prophecies? What are the main messages for the posterity of Joseph in his prophecy?

Answer:

As Nephi mentioned quoting from the plates of brass that Lehi's family possessed (see 1 Nephi 22:1; 2 Nephi 4:15), it is quite likely that this quote was from the plates of brass. The main messages include the future of Lehi's posterity, a latter-day seer named Joseph (Joseph Smith) who was named after his father, the coming forth of a Josephite record out of the dust (the Book of Mormon) in the latter days, the inheritance of the Josephites on the land of America, and so on. See Chapter 8 for more discussion on this subject.

Question:

From the first writer, Nephi, to the last writer, Moroni, many prophets in the Book of Mormon testified of Jesus Christ being the Son of God, their Savior and Redeemer. General Moroni in the Book of Mormon called the Nephites "Christians" four times (see Alma 46:13, 15, 16; 48:10). However, many Judeo-Christians do not consider the members of The Church of Jesus Christ of Latter-day Saints to be real Christians, partly because they believe in the Book of Mormon in addition to the Bible. What would be the main reasons for this irony?

Answer:

Answers to this question may vary, depending on what perceptions people have. Even if Judeo-Christians accept that The Church of Jesus Christ of Latter-day Saints believes in Jesus Christ, it is easy to see that the Church does not subscribe to many of the Christian traditions and beliefs, such as the Trinitarian doctrine, the paid professional clergy system, a symbolic usage of the cross, an afterlife limited to hell and heaven, infant baptism, and so forth. Moreover, the Church also has newly revealed beliefs and practices, such as more canonized scriptures in addition to the Bible (open canon), unpaid laymen leadership with priesthood authority (Aaronic and Melchizedek), sealing ordinances for eternal marriage, vicarious ordinances for the dead in their temples, belief in and sustaining of a living prophet, and so forth. The Articles of Faith, composed by Joseph Smith in AD 1842, succinctly show the thirteen main points of belief of The Church of Jesus Christ of Latter-day Saints. Some of these thirteen points differ from the traditional beliefs that stem from the creedal proclamations by the Catholic Church and some theologies developed by the reformists.

As Jesus taught, we are not to judge, but the fruits should tell the truth (see 3 Nephi 14:20). How consistently one believes and lives in discipleship to Jesus Christ is one such fruit. Regardless of people's perceptions, God may view those who keep His commandments and ordinances and maintain Christ-like discipleship as true Christians. See Chapter 8 for more discussion on this subject.

Question:

In the Book of Mormon, there are few prophecies about the Second Coming of Jesus Christ other than that there will be signs prior to the final burning at the end of the world. However, there are many prophecies about the scattering and gathering of the Israelites in both the Old and New Jerusalem, a seer in the latter days, a book crying from the dust, preparation of the American continent for the Restoration of the gospel of Jesus Christ by the Gentiles, and the roles of the tribe of Joseph and the Gentiles in the Restoration of the gospel of Jesus Christ in the latter days. Among these prophecies, which ones have been fulfilled so far, and which ones are yet to be fulfilled?

Answer:

Among those already fulfilled, here are some highlights: the discovery of the new land of America by Columbus, the migration of Europeans (the pilgrims) to America for religious freedom, the colonization of America by Europeans, the war for independence from the Europeans, the scattering of the American Indians by white Gentiles, the establishment of a mighty and free nation on the land of America, Joseph Smith, the Book of Mormon, the regathering of Jews in Israel, and so forth. Some of those yet to be fulfilled (or are in the process of being fulfilled) are the gospel of Jesus Christ being preached to the Jews by the Gentiles; the Jews recognizing Jesus Christ as their God; the restored gospel of Jesus Christ being preached to all nations, tongues, and people; the establishment of the New Jerusalem on the land of America; the Second Coming of Jesus Christ; the millennial reign of Jesus Christ; the burning of the whole earth; the formation of a new earth; and so on. See Chapter 9 for more discussion on this subject.

Question:

Moroni prophesied that the Book of Mormon would come forth at a time when there were six circumstances in the world. He prefaced each by saying that "it [the Book of Mormon] shall come in day when." What are these six circumstances?

Answer:

In Mormon 8:26–32, Moroni taught that Jesus Christ showed him that the Book of Mormon will come forth in a day as a voice speaking from the dust, at a time when (1) people shall say that miracles are done away; (2) the blood of Saints shall cry unto the Lord because of secret combinations and works of darkness; (3) the power of God shall be denied, churches will be defiled, and their leaders will be prideful; (4) there shall be many natural disasters, wars, and rumors of wars in diverse places; (5) there shall be widespread cultural pollutions, such as immorality and other abominations, and false teachings that wrongdoings will be eventually forgiven at the end; and (6) churches shall be built up to get monetary gain, with practices such as forgiving sins for money. See Chapter 9 for more discussion on this topic.

Question:

Throughout the one thousand years of their history in the Book of Mormon, the Nephites called their God *Jesus* or *Jesus Christ* (187 times). They called Him *Jehovah* in only two places; one is in a quote from the book of Isaiah (see Isaiah 12:2, quoted in 2 Nephi 22:2), and the other one is from Moroni. What ramifications can be implied when Moroni used the name *Jehovah* instead of *Jesus* or *Jesus Christ* in that particular time and situation?

Answer:

Throughout the entire Book of Mormon, none of the Nephite prophets called the Lord *Jehovah* except Moroni, and he did so only once. He completed his compilation of the whole Book of Mormon with this final sentence: "I am brought forth triumphant through the air, to meet you before the pleasing bar of the great *Jehovah*, the Eternal Judge of both quick and dead. Amen" (Moroni 10:34, emphasis added). In other words, he chose to call the Lord *Jehovah* in the last sentence of the Book of Mormon. By doing so, Moroni may show his confirmation that Jehovah, the Lord of the Old Testament mentioned by Isaiah, is Jesus Christ in the Book of Mormon. See Chapter 10 for more discussion on this subject.

Question:

In the Book of Mormon, there are records of people performing priesthood ordinances: baptism by Alma the Elder and the disciples of Jesus Christ, the ordaining of teachers and priests by Nephi and Alma the Younger, the conferring of the Holy Ghost, and administering the sacramental bread and wine by the resurrected Jesus Christ. In the Book of Mormon, who taught the exact manner how to perform each one of these priesthood ordinances?

Answer:

The resurrected Jesus Christ taught how to baptize in an exact manner (see 3 Nephi 11:23–26). Moroni recorded the exact manner of how the resurrected Jesus Christ conferred the Holy Ghost (see Moroni 2). Moroni also provided instructions on performing the other priesthood ordinances in their exact manners: how to ordain teachers and priests (see Moroni 3), how to administer the sacramental bread (see Moroni 4), and how to administer the sacramental wine (see Moroni 5). See Chapter 6 for more discussion on this subject.

References

Published Works

Berrett, LaMar C., and Van Dyke, Blair G. *Holy Lands* (American Fork, Utah: Covenant Communication, Inc., 2005).

Brown, S. Kent, and Holzapfel, Richard Nietzel. *Between the Testaments from Malachi to Matthew* (Salt Lake City: Deseret Book Company, 2002).

Bushman, Richard Lyman. *Joseph Smith: Rough Stone Rolling* (New York: Knopf, 2005).

"Epistle 337," in *Collected Works of Erasmus*, Vol. 3, 134.

Ehrman, Bart D. *Misquoting Jesus: The Story Behind Who Changed the Bible and Why* (Harper San Francisco, 2007)

Falconer, James E. *The New Testament Made It Harder: Scripture Study Questions* (Provo, Utah: Neal A. Maxwell Institute, Brigham Young University, 2015).

Galbraith, David B., Ogden, D. Kelly, and Skinner, Andrew C. *Jerusalem: The Eternal City* (Salt Lake City: Deseret Book Company, 1996).

Gaster, Theodore H. *The Dead Sea Scriptures: With Introduction and Notes by Theodore H. Gaster* (New York: Anchor Books, 1976).

Green, Steve, and Hillard, Todd. *The Bible in America* (DustJacket Press, 2013).

Green, Steven D. *The Tribe of Ephraim: Covenant and Bloodline* (Bountiful, Utah: Horizon Publishers and Distributors, 2007).

Harline, Craig. *A World Ablaze* (Oxford, England: Oxford, 2017).

Jenkins, Philip. *The Next Christendom: The Coming of Global Christianity* (Oxford, England: Oxford, 2002).

Josephus (Grand Rapids, Michigan: Kregel Publications, 1974).

Kimball, Spencer W. "Our Paths Have Met Again." *Ensign*, December 1975.

Largey, Dennis L. *Book of Mormon Reference Companion* (Salt Lake City: Deseret Book Company, 2003).

Madsen, Truman G., ed. *Reflections on Mormonism, Judaeo-Christian Parallels: Edited with an Introduction by Truman G. Madsen* (Provo, Utah: Religious Study Center, Brigham Young University, 1978).

McConkie, Bruce R. *Mormon Doctrine* (Salt Lake City: BookCraft, 1966).

Nelson, Russell M. "The Book of Mormon, the Gathering of Israel, and the Second Coming." *Ensign*, July 2014.

Nibley, Hugh. *Teachings of the Book of Mormon, Transcripts of Lectures Presented to an Honors Book of Mormon Class at Brigham Young University, 1988–1990*, Vols. 1–4 (Provo, Utah: FARMS, 2004).

_____. *The Approach of the Book of Mormon* (Provo, Utah: FARMS, 1988).

_____. *The Prophetic Book of Mormon* (Provo, Utah: FARMS, 1957).

Nibley, Hugh, and Welch, John W. *Since Cumorah* (Provo, Utah: FARMS, 1967).

Robinson, James M., ed. *The Nag Hammadi Library* (New York: Harper & Row Publishers, 1981).

Robinson, O. Preston, and Robinson, Christine H. *Christ's Eternal Gospel* (Salt Lake City: Deseret Book Company, 1976).

Schiffman, Lawrence H., and Patterngale, Jerry. *The World's Greatest Book* (Nashville, Tennessee: Worthy, 2017).

Shin, Yong-In S. *A Gift to My Missionaries* (Korea Daejeon Mission, 2016).

Skinner, Andrew, and Strathearn, Gaye. *Third Nephi: An Incredible Incomparable Scripture* (Salt Lake City: Deseret Book Company, 2012).

Smith, Morton. *The Secret Gospel* (Lower Lake, California: The Dawn Horse Press, 1973).

The Articles of Religion of the Methodist Church V–VIII. (The United Methodist Church., 2004).

Thomas, David. *Hebrew Roots of Mormonism* (Springville, Utah: Cedar Fort, 2013).

Top, Brent. *A Peculiar Treasure: Old Testament Messages for Our Days* (Salt Lake City: Deseret Book Company, 1997).

Websites

http://www.sacred-texts.com/bib/vul/jo1005.htm#007

https://bible.org/seriespage/3-christology-jesus-christ

https://bible.org/article/gospel-according-bart

https://www.biblegateway.com/verse/en/Romans%208:30

http://www.icr.org/article/resurrection-old-testament/

http://www.josephsmithpapers.org/paper-summary/printers-manu-script-of-the-book-of-mormon-circa-august-1829-circa-january-1830/1#full-transcript

https://www.lds.org/study/ensign/1990/12/i-have-a-question/i-have-a-question?lang=eng

http://www.jewfaq.org/qorbanot.htm

http://www.jewfaq.org/holiday4.htm

http://www.jewfaq.org/calendar.htm#Links

https://carm.org/verses-showing-justification-by-faith

http://www.newadvent.org/cathen/15006b.htm

http://www.newadvent.org/cathen/07790a.htm#IIIB

http://www.newadvent.org/cathen/12260a.htm

http://www.newadvent.org/cathen/02035a.htm

http://www.newadvent.org/cathen/11049a.htm

http://www.setapartpeople.com/mikvah-part-1-spiritual-cleansing

http://pemptousia.com/2017/10/emperor-constantine-and-the-theolo-gy-of-christianity-1/

https://plato.stanford.edu/entries/trinity/trinity-history.html#OneGod

https://www.britannica.com/biography/Theodor-Herzl

https://www.ucg.org/studienhilfen/broschuren/is-god-a-trinity/the-sur-prising-origins-of-the-trinity-doctrine

https://www.gotquestions.org/Peter-first-pope.html

https://www.biblword.net/what-is-the-trinity/?gclid=EAIaIQobChMIg vCunL3X1wIVl4l-Ch2SKwgsEAAYAyAAEgKjd_D_BwE

https://www.biblestudytools.com/lxx/

https://www.theopedia.com/irenaeus
https://www.ccel.org/creeds/nicene.creed.html
https://www.goarch.org/en/-/the-orthodox-church-an-introduction
https://www.biblestudytools.com/dictionary/essenes/
http://www.biblearchaeology.org/post/2012/02/17/The-Role-of-the-Septuagint-in-the-Transmission-of-the-Scriptures.aspx?gclid=EAIaIQobChMI4LPMzbbX1wIVB25-Ch3KlQb2EAAYASAAEgKbz_D_BwE#Article
http://www.dictionary.com/browse/apocalypse
http://www.differencebetween.net/miscellaneous/difference-between-lutheranism-and-calvinism/
http://www.christianitytoday.com/history/people/theologians/john-calvin.html
http://www.christianitytoday.com/history/people/theologians/john-calvin.html
https://www.ccel.org/ccel/wesley
https://www.biography.com/people/erasmus-21291705
https://www.gotquestions.org/Wesleyans.html
https://www.gotquestions.org/Trinity-Bible.html
http://www.Britannica.com/topic/arianism
https://www.history.com/this-day-in-history/the-balfour-declaration
https://chiasmusresources.org/index-chiasm-book-mormon
http://textusreceptusbibles.com/Desiderius_Erasmus
http://www.newadvent.org/cathen/11049a.htm
http://www.vatican.va/archive/ENG0015/__P3B.HTM
http://www.history.com/this-day-in-history/council-of-nicaea-concludes
http://www.christianitytoday.com/history/issues/issue-28/325-first-council-of-nicea.html
https://bible.org/seriespage/3-sadducees
https://bible.org/seriespage/6-preparing-day-lord-malachi-313-46
http://www.christianitytoday.com/ct/2008/april/heaven-is-not-our-home.html
https://www.lds.org/study/ensign/2017/11/saturday-afternoon-session/the-book-of-mormon-what-would-your-life-be-like-without-it?lang=eng
https://carm.org/verses-showing-justification-by-faith

https://en.wikipedia.org/wiki/Christianity
https://en.wikipedia.org/wiki/Papal_primacy
https://en.wikipedia.org/wiki/Essenes
http://www.luther.de/en/95thesen.html
https://en.wikipedia.org/wiki/Martin_Luther
https://en.wikipedia.org/wiki/Zadok
https://en.wikipedia.org/wiki/John_Calvin
https://en.wikipedia.org/wiki/John_Wesley
https://en.wikipedia.org/wiki/Josephus
https://en.wikipedia.org/wiki/Erasmus
https://en.wikipedia.org/wiki/Jehovah%27s_Witnesses
https://en.wikipedia.org/wiki/Presbyterianism
https://en.wikipedia.org/wiki/Methodism
https://en.wikipedia.org/wiki/Seventh-day_Adventist_Church
https://en.wikipedia.org/wiki/Ellen_G._White_bibliography
https://en.wikipedia.org/wiki/Anglicanism#.22Catholic_and_Re-
    formed.22
https://en.wikipedia.org/wiki/Charles_Taze_Russell
https://en.wikipedia.org/wiki/Reformation
https://en.wikipedia.org/wiki/Orthodoxy
https://en.wikipedia.org/wiki/Trinity
https://en.wikipedia.org/wiki/Biblical_inerrancy#Textual_tradition_
    of_the_New_Testament

About the Author

DR. YONG-IN S. SHIN HAS worked as a business executive, manager, and engineer for Samsung Electronics Corporation in Korea, Intel Corporation in the USA, and Philips Corporation in the Netherlands. He has also worked as an international business consultant for high-tech companies around the world. He has taught business and engineering management classes at the University of Utah, Seoul National University, Hanbat National University, Oregon Health and Science University, and Portland State University.

He has published and presented many articles related to business and engineering around the world. His publications include *Past Success, Present Dilemma, Future Growth Strategy: Samsung vs. Intel* (2009). He has been a keynote speaker at multiple conferences and owns a number of patents.

He has a doctorate degree in economics and business management from Erasmus University Rotterdam, and he holds master's and bachelor's degrees in electrical engineering from Brigham Young University.

He served as president of the Korea Daejeon Mission from 2013 to 2016 and has served in other priesthood capacities in The Church of Jesus Christ of Latter-day Saints. After completing his term as mission president, he retired and has been writing books. He and his wife, Hyosun Camilla Shin, are parents of six children and twelve grandchildren.